江苏高校优势学科建设工程三期项目
苏州大学外国语言文学学科资助出版

王雯 编著

莎士比亚经典撷英

英汉对照

苏州大学出版社
Soochow University Press

图书在版编目(CIP)数据

莎士比亚经典撷英：英汉对照 / 王雯编著. -- 苏州：苏州大学出版社，2023.6
ISBN 978-7-5672-4386-6

Ⅰ.①莎… Ⅱ.①王… Ⅲ.①英语-汉语-对照读物 ②莎士比亚(Shakespeare，William 1564-1616)-文学欣赏 Ⅳ.①H319.4:I

中国国家版本馆 CIP 数据核字(2023)第 107190 号

书　　名：莎士比亚经典撷英
Shashibiya Jingdian Xieying
编 著 者：王　雯
责任编辑：杨　华
装帧设计：刘　俊
出版发行：苏州大学出版社(Soochow University Press)
社　　址：苏州市十梓街1号　邮编：215006
印　　装：苏州工业园区美柯乐制版印务有限责任公司
网　　址：http://www.sudapress.com
邮购热线：0512-67480030
销售热线：0512-67481020
开　　本：787 mm×1 092 mm　1/16　印张：14.5　字数：268 千
版　　次：2023 年 6 月第 1 版
印　　次：2023 年 6 月第 1 次印刷
书　　号：ISBN 978-7-5672-4386-6
定　　价：55.00 元

若发现印装错误，请与本社联系调换。
服务热线：0512-67481020
苏州大学出版社邮箱　sdcbs@suda.edu.cn

前 言
Preface

　　莎士比亚赫赫有名，即便时隔400多年，其地位也依然高不可攀。在1999年英国广播公司（BBC）举办的英国"千禧伟人"（Man of the Millennium）的听众投票中，莎士比亚击败了丘吉尔，一举夺得头筹，可见其依然颇具影响力。

　　莎士比亚的影响力并非仅仅囿于英国，也不只是在欧洲广受欢迎，其剧作在北美也妇孺皆知，是英语国家不可或缺的一种文化底蕴。例如，被誉为"美国现代文学之父"的小说家马克·吐温（Mark Twain），其名著《哈克贝利·费恩历险记》（*Adventures of Huckleberry Finn*）中有一对冒充伦敦演艺明星的骗子，他们在密西西比河沿岸的小镇上演《罗密欧与朱丽叶》（*Romeo and Juliet*）、《哈姆雷特》（*Hamlet*）、《麦克白》（*Macbeth*）、《理查三世》（*Richard III*）等经典场景片段——实为拙劣的戏仿或混杂体。

　　这两个骗子为什么偏偏要挑战颇有难度的莎士比亚戏剧？那位自称公爵的骗子这样高度赞扬哈姆莱特的"生存还是毁灭"（To be or not to be）一段："哈姆莱特的独白，你知道的，莎士比亚最有名的一段。啊，太了不起，太了不起了！总是全场倾倒。"（Hamlet's soliloquy, you know; the most celebrated thing in Shakespeare. Ah, it's sublime, sublime! Always fetches the house.）这骗子的文化修养不高，并不真正理解那段独白，却不乏商业嗅觉，深知莎士比亚戏剧能招徕客源。

　　即便《哈克贝利·费恩历险记》是虚构作品，但也遵循现实主义原则，在很大程度上能反映莎士比亚戏剧在马克·吐温的时代颇为叫座，哪怕是在19世纪中叶文化相对落后的美国中部地区。有趣的是，那些小镇居民并没有像骗子所料想的那么好骗，那场破绽百出的表演很快就遭到观众们的报复，可见当时的小镇居民对莎

士比亚戏剧并非一无所知。

莎士比亚的戏剧与诗歌作为英国乃至西方文学的一大标杆，一直都是欧美中小学的教学内容。对于中国读者而言，阅读莎士比亚有利于增进对西方文化与思想传统的了解，也有助于熏陶人文主义精神。

不过，莎士比亚不易读，仅就语言而言，就障碍不少。不少人会抱怨莎士比亚佶屈聱牙的"古英语"——笔者已经不止一次碰到这种说法，特此郑重申明：莎士比亚使用的不是古英语（Old English），而是早期现代英语（Early Modern English）——莎士比亚所用的英语远远比真正的"古英语"好懂。即便如此，400年前的早期现代英语与现代英语也差异不小，无论词汇还是句法。因此，当今读者阅读莎士比亚作品原文，通常需要结合注释或借助于词典。

文化差异也会导致阅读莎士比亚的障碍，不仅有古今文化差异，而且还有中西文化差异，包括思想理念、内容结构、修辞意象等诸多方面。不过，不同文明或文化之间的差异能够拓宽我们的视野，让我们看到人类社会多种多样的可能性，以及丰富多彩的精神世界。不同或差异，不仅有利于避免认知固化、突破思维定式，而且能够激发人们的想象力与创造力。读者可以通过莎士比亚这个万花筒穿越时空，从而知晓另一个社会的思想观念，了解另一个时代的精神文化。

那么，中国读者应该如何理解、欣赏莎士比亚？目前国内市面上提供了如下几种选择。

第一，译本。国内读者通常读的是中文译本，试图完全绕开语言障碍来欣赏莎士比亚作品。不过，正如塞万提斯笔下的堂吉诃德所称，翻译如翻了面的壁毯，尽管不乏花纹，但是背面毕竟不同于正面。即便是名家名译，也只能在"信、达、雅"之间维持平衡，译本不可避免地存在一定程度的内容损耗与形式扭曲；从措辞到风格，从语义到表达，译本不可能百分之百地呈现原作。因此，译本可以当作开胃菜，英语良好的读者还是尽可能地阅读原汁原味的英语原文。

第二，简写本。对莎士比亚戏剧的简写、缩写或改编，蔚为大观，尤其是作为儿童读物与影视脚本，比如19世纪兰姆姐弟（Charles Lamb & Mary Lamb）编写的《莎士比亚戏剧故事》（*Tales from Shakespeare*），读者可以从中了解基本剧情与主要角色。不过，无论简写者的水平有多么高超，比起原作，简写本多少会黯然失色，甚至面目全非，如同提纯的蒸馏水一般寡淡无味，难以涵盖莎士比亚作品的真正精华——莎士比亚戏剧的精华并不只在于剧情而在于思想寓意与语言表达。因此，莎士比亚英文简写本只能作为英语启蒙与莎士比亚戏剧入门读物。

第三，选段集锦或语句摘录。目前国内现有的莎士比亚教材或美文欣赏多采用这种形式，选段之前可能提供或英文或中文的剧情介绍，之后可能附有思考题或资源补充。这是一种很好的入门途径。对于初学者而言，整本原著肯定难以下咽，不如先精选其中的经典名段，切片品尝。即便只吃到碎米，也能或多或少领略莎剧的风采。

相比国内现有的同类莎士比亚教材而言，这本《莎士比亚经典撷英》也采用片段节选的编纂体例，却不求大、求全——除了若干首十四行诗之外，本书仅介绍六部颇具代表性的剧目（按剧本创作年份排序）。之所以收录较少的剧目，就是为了在有限的篇幅内尽可能让读者深入而全面地理解这六个剧本，而不是在两三个孤立的零星选段的基础上，让众多剧本浮光掠影地一闪而过。

本书从每一部剧中节选了十几个脍炙人口的场景片段，并辅以导读与评点，尽可能让前后选段之间保持剧情的关联性、连贯性与整体性。这种编著工作犹如串联一堆散落的珍珠，尽可能避免让读者产生一鳞半爪、支离破碎之感。同一部剧的各个选段既具有相对的独立性与可读性，又不失剧情线索与逻辑关联，前后情境相互呼应，便于读者对每部剧进行整体把握。在主题思考或话题讨论中，既可以就某一个片段进行文本细读，也可以联系同一部剧中的多个选段进行解读。

对于每部剧的每个选段，编著者都独具匠心地赋予了双语标题：中文标题选用四字成语或短语，对选段的思想内容进行标记或概括；英文标题即为该选段中的点睛之句或关键语句。这种双语标题的拟定不仅能提纲挈领地概括该段的思想主题，而且便于读者识别、查找、记忆相应选段。何况，行走在中西语言文化之间，不同表达方式与思维模式相互碰撞，趣味横生。

英文选段出自阿登版莎士比亚（The Arden Shakespeare）的第二版或第三版，其中的注释主要参考阿登版莎士比亚单行本及亚历山大·施密德（Alexander Schmidt）编写的两卷本《莎士比亚词典》（*Shakespeare-Lexicon: A Complete Dictionary*）。

同时,为了便于读者的理解与赏析,本书为每一个剧本选段都额外增加了朱生豪先生的译文,将莎士比亚的英语原文与中译本进行对照,采用左页英文、右页中译文的排版模式,便于阅读理解与比较鉴赏。需要说明的是,虽然朱译精良,但是也并非尽善尽美。读者在名家名译之中,取其精华,弃其糟粕,有助于提高自身的理解能力与文学翻译水平。

本书期待引领读者心怀向往地登上莎士比亚殿堂,而不希望读者因其名望,望而却步。莎士比亚赫赫有名,却并非不可企及。毕竟,无论古今中外,人性不变,情感相通,中国读者在尽可能多地了解西方文化的同时,也不妨在中西文化差异中寻找共性,在相似中发现区别。

本书从编纂体例上看,具有较好的可读性,既可供读者自主阅读,又可作为课堂教材(迄今为止,编著者已为苏州大学英语系本科生讲授了四年"莎士比亚作品欣赏"课)。当然,此书只是一道开胃菜,任何导读或选本都无法替代原汁原味的原文作品。学有余力的读者不妨尝试一下莎士比亚戏剧的英文原作。

此书的问世离不开师友的帮助:首先感谢苏州大学外国语学院朱新福院长对我编写及出版此书的支持与鼓励;其次感谢苏州大学出版社的高效合作。此外,我不能忘记引领我进入中世纪与文艺复兴殿堂的北京大学英语系与历史系的诸位教授,还有一位在本书编纂过程中、通过微信聊天的方式给予我宝贵建议的教授朋友。为避免攀附之嫌,恕不在此罗列大名。此书若有任何疏漏之处,均由本人承担责任。特别感谢恩师托马斯·伦德尔(Thomas Rendall)教授为本书撰写后记。

王　雯
2023 年春于姑苏城内

目 录
Contents

一、《仲夏夜之梦》 001
　　"什么天使使我从百花的卧榻上醒来呢？"

二、《罗密欧与朱丽叶》 029
　　"罗密欧啊，罗密欧！为什么你偏偏是罗密欧呢？"

三、《裘力斯·凯撒》 063
　　"并不是我不爱凯撒，可是我更爱罗马。"

四、《皆大欢喜》 099
　　"逆运也有它的好处。"

五、《哈姆莱特》 135
　　"我所看见的幽灵也许是魔鬼的化身。"

六、《麦克白》 175
　　"大洋里所有的水，能够洗净我手上的血迹吗？"

七、莎士比亚十四行诗 205
　　"如果音乐与甜美的诗歌相合……"

后记 218

1. *A Midsummer Night's Dream* (1595) 001

   "What angel wakes me from my flowery bed?"

2. *Romeo and Juliet* (1596) 029

   "O Romeo, Romeo, wherefore art thou Romeo?"

3. *Julius Caesar* (1599) 063

   "Not that I loved Caesar less, but that I loved Rome more."

4. *As You Like It* (1599) 099

   "Sweet are the uses of adversity."

5. *Hamlet* (1600) 135

   "The spirit that I have seen may be a devil."

6. *Macbeth* (1606) 175

   "Will all great Neptune's ocean wash this blood clean from my hand?"

7. Shakespearean Sonnets 205

   "If music and sweet poetry agree ..."

Afterword 218

William Shakespeare

一、《仲夏夜之梦》

(*A Midsummer Night's Dream*)
(1595)

"什么天使使我从百花的卧榻上醒来呢？"

("What angel wakes me from my flowery bed?")

故事发生在古希腊时期的雅典。全剧四条线索,时而并行,时而交织,令人目不暇接。

第一条线索是雅典公爵大婚,一开场即宣布婚讯,次日一早去森林打猎,之后回城举行婚礼庆典。第二条也是该剧最重要的线索,是两对青年男女之间的爱情纠葛,当晚深夜,或逃或追,陆续潜入雅典城外的森林。第三条线索也有不少戏份,充满喜剧色彩——一帮雅典工匠为庆祝公爵的婚礼而在森林里偷偷排练戏剧,剧终即上演这台滑稽的"戏中戏"。第四条线索是森林里的仙王、仙后及其随员,他们自有争执与不快,却有意无意地掺和到人间的悲欢离合,产生了一系列阴差阳错的误会……

最终,皆大欢喜。仙王与仙后和好如初,而且见证了雅典城里三对新人的盛大婚礼……

《仲夏夜之梦》（*A Midsummer Night's Dream*）

场景 1：对簿公堂（"Full of vexation come I, with complaint ..."）1.1

场景 2：痴男怨女（"So quick bright things come to confusion."）1.1

场景 3：争风吃醋（"O that your frowns would teach my smiles such skill!"）1.1

场景 4：爱之盲目（"Love looks not with the eyes, but with the mind."）1.1

场景 5：捣蛋精灵（"I am that merry wanderer of the night."）2.1

场景 6：神仙吵架（"These are the forgeries of jealousy."）2.1

场景 7：顾影自怜（"The more my prayer, the lesser is my grace."）2.2

场景 8：连环误会（"Wherefore was I to this keen mockery born?"）2.2

场景 9：驴头艳遇（"What angel wakes me from my flowery bed?"）3.1

场景 10：匪夷所思（"Man is but an ass if he go about to expound this dream."）4.1

场景 11：爱之疯狂（"Lovers and madmen have such seething brains ..."）5.1

场景 12：滑稽悲剧（"Merry and tragical? Tedious and brief?"）5.1

场景1：对簿公堂

（"Full of vexation come I, with complaint ..."）

> 《仲夏夜之梦》开场伊始就是一场官司：伊吉斯（Egeus）非要把女儿赫米娅（Hermia）嫁给狄米特律斯（Demetrius），然而，赫米娅的芳心另有所属——拉山德（Lysander）。因此，伊吉斯在公爵面前控诉女儿与拉山德。

Egeus Full of vexation come I, with complaint
Against my child, my daughter Hermia,
Stand forth Demetrius. My noble lord,
This man hath my consent to marry her.
Stand forth Lysander. And, my gracious Duke,
This hath bewitch'd the bosom of my child.
Thou, thou, Lysander, thou hast given her rhymes,
And interchang'd love-tokens with my child:
Thou hast by moonlight at her window sung
With faining voice verses of feigning love,
And stol'n the impression of her fantasy
With bracelets of thy hair, rings, gauds[1], conceits[2],
Knacks[3], trifles, nosegays, sweetmeats (messengers
Of strong prevailment[4] in unharden'd youth):
With cunning hast thou filch'd my daughter's heart,
Turn'd her obedience (which is due to me)
To stubborn harshness. And, my gracious duke,
Be it so[5] she will not here, before your grace,
Consent to marry with Demetrius,

---

[1] gauds: showy toys.
[2] conceits: fancy articles.
[3] knacks: knick-knacks.
[4] prevailment: power to gain decisive influence.
[5] Be it so: Supposing.

I beg the ancient privilege of Athens:
As she is mine, I may dispose of her;
Which shall be either to this gentleman,
Or to her death, according to our law
Immediately provided in that case.

(*A Midsummer Night's Dream* 1.1)

伊吉斯 我怀着满心的气恼,来控诉我的孩子,我的女儿赫米娅。走上前来,狄米特律斯。殿下,这个人,是我答应把我女儿嫁给他的。走上前来,拉山德。殿下,这个人引诱坏了我的孩子。你,你,拉山德,你写诗句给我的孩子,和她交换着爱情的纪念物;你在月夜到她的窗前用做作的声调歌唱着假作多情的诗篇;你用头发编成的腕环、戒指、虚华的饰物、琐碎的玩具、花束、糖果——这些可以强烈地骗诱一个稚嫩的少女之心的"信使"来偷得她的痴情;你用诡计盗取了她的心,煽惑她使她对我的顺从变成倔强的顽抗。殿下,假如她现在当着您的面仍旧不肯嫁给狄米特律斯,我就要要求雅典自古相传的权利,因为她是我的女儿,我可以随意处置她;按照我们的法律,逢到这样的情况,她要是不嫁给这位绅士,便应当立时处死。

(朱生豪译《仲夏夜之梦》第 1 幕第 1 场)

评点

莎士比亚戏剧中不乏敢于违抗父命、藐视传统法律、不惜一切代价追求自身幸福的姑娘:《仲夏夜之梦》中的男女主人公最终修成了正果;《威尼斯商人》里的那位犹太姑娘也义无反顾地追随其基督教情郎;《奥赛罗》中的女主人公亦然,不顾父亲阻拦,执意嫁给异族人奥赛罗。

值得注意的是,在这几部剧中,母亲角色缺位,只是父亲控诉女儿叛逆,干涉其婚恋自由;女儿则宁可私奔也要追求个人幸福。此外,《罗密欧与朱丽叶》也是一个私奔未遂的悲剧故事,与我国的《梁祝》《孔雀东南飞》等作品中的女主人公有所不同。

违命不从,确实不乏风险,甚至可能走向毁灭,《奥赛罗》《罗密欧与朱丽叶》都是悲剧。《仲夏夜之梦》以一个类似的悲剧开场,却在仙王的干预下翻转为喜剧,重重矛盾得以在魔法森林里神奇化解。

场景 2：痴男怨女

（"So quick bright things come to confusion."）

> 家长与法律一道，棒打鸳鸯，赫米娅与拉山德进退两难，哀叹爱情的不顺与世道的不公……站在人生道路的十字路口，究竟如何选择：是屈从于命运，还是坚持自己的追求？

Lysander　Ay me! For aught that I could ever read,
　　　　　Could ever hear by tale or history,
　　　　　The course of true love never did run smooth;
　　　　　But either it was different in blood—
Hermia　O cross! too high to be enthrall'd to low.
Lysander　Or else misgraffed[1] in respect of years—
Hermia　O spite! too old to be engaged to young.
Lysander　Or else it stood upon[2] the choice of friends—
Hermia　O hell! to choose love by another's eyes.
Lysander　Or, if there were a sympathy[3] in choice,
　　　　　War, death, or sickness did lay siege to it,
　　　　　Making it momentany[4] as a sound,
　　　　　Swift as a shadow, short as any dream,
　　　　　Brief as the lightning in the collied[5] night,
　　　　　That, in a spleen[6], unfolds both heaven and earth,
　　　　　And, ere a man hath power to say 'Behold!',
　　　　　The jaws of darkness do devour it up:
　　　　　So quick bright things come to confusion.

(*A Midsummer Night's Dream* 1.1)

---

[1] misgraffed: ill-matched.
[2] stood upon: was dependent upon.
[3] a sympathy: a natural agreement.
[4] momentany = momentary (common in the 16th and 17th centuries).
[5] collied: blackened.
[6] spleen: fit of anger.

拉山德　　唉！我在书上读到的，在传说或历史中听到的，真正的爱情，所走的道路永远是崎岖多阻；不是因为血统的差异——

赫米娅　　不幸啊，尊贵的要向微贱者屈节臣服！

拉山德　　便是因为年龄上的悬殊——

赫米娅　　可憎啊，年老的要和年轻人发生关系！[1]

拉山德　　或者因为信从了亲友们的选择——

赫米娅　　倒霉啊，选择爱人要依赖他人的眼光！

拉山德　　或者，即使彼此两情悦服，但战争、死亡或疾病却侵害着它，使它像一个声音、一片影子、一段梦、黑夜中的一道闪电那样短促，在一刹那间展现了天堂和地狱，但还来不及说一声"瞧啊！"黑暗早已张开口把它吞噬了。光明的事物，总是那样很快地变成了混沌。

（朱生豪译《仲夏夜之梦》第1幕第1场）

评点

　　该选段看似两人对话，其实拉山德从头到尾只说了一句话（either ... or ... or ... or ...），感叹有情人难成眷属；赫米娅则与他同心同德，一唱一和，即便是哀叹，也带上了几分喜剧色彩。其中，"真正的爱情，所走的道路永远是崎岖多阻"（The course of true love never did run smooth）一句脍炙人口，近乎我国成语"好事多磨"。

　　面对社会习俗传统的强大势力，二人深知他们势单力薄，为了能与爱人长相厮守，只能一走了之。

---

[1] 参考梁实秋对此句的译文："啊呸！年纪太大不能匹配青春！"

场景 3：争风吃醋

（"O that your frowns would teach my smiles such skill!"）

> 赫米娅的闺蜜海丽娜（Helena）见自己的心上人狄米特律斯要娶赫米娅而不是自己，因此醋意大发。于是，赫米娅把自己即将与拉山德远走高飞的秘密透露给了海丽娜，以此说明自己不会与狄米特律斯有任何瓜葛。

Helena　Were the world mine, Demetrius being bated[1],
　　　　The rest I'd give to be to you translated.
　　　　O, teach me how you look, and with what art
　　　　You sway the motion of Demetrius' heart.
Hermia　I frown upon him; yet he loves me still.
Helena　O that your frowns would teach my smiles such skill!
Hermia　I give him curses; yet he gives me love.
Helena　O that my prayers could such affection move!
Hermia　The more I hate, the more he follows me.
Helena　The more I love, the more he hateth me.
Hermia　His folly, Helena, is no fault of mine.
Helena　None but your beauty; would that fault were mine!
Hermia　Take comfort: he no more shall see my face;
　　　　Lysander and myself will fly this place.
　　　　Before the time I did Lysander see,
　　　　Seem'd Athens as a paradise to me.
　　　　O then what graces in my love do dwell,
　　　　That he hath turn'd a heaven unto a hell!

(*A Midsummer Night's Dream* 1.1)

---

[1] bated: excepted.

海丽娜	要是除了狄米特律斯之外，整个世界都是属于我所有，我愿意把一切捐弃，但求化身为你。啊！教给我怎样流转眼波，用怎么一种魔力操纵着狄米特律斯的心？
赫米娅	我向他皱着眉头，但是他仍旧爱我。
海丽娜	唉，要是你的颦蹙能把那种本领传授给我的微笑就好了！
赫米娅	我给他咒骂，但他给我爱情。
海丽娜	唉，要是我的祈祷也能这样引动他的爱情就好了！
赫米娅	我越是恨他，他越是跟随着我。
海丽娜	我越是爱他，他越是讨厌我。
赫米娅	海丽娜，他的傻并不是我的错。
海丽娜	但那是你的美貌的错处；要是那错处是我的就好了！
赫米娅	宽心吧，他不会再见我的脸了；拉山德和我将要逃开此地。在我不曾遇见拉山德之前，雅典对于我就像是一座天堂；啊，我的爱人身上，存在着一种多么神奇的力量，竟能把天堂变成一座地狱！

（朱生豪译《仲夏夜之梦》第1幕第1场）

评点

在此前呈现的父女矛盾叠加"三角恋"的基础上，海丽娜的加入更增添一重矛盾，形成了错综复杂的"四角恋"。

就文体特色而言，之前赫米娅与拉山德商量私奔的那段台词使用的是素体诗（blank verse），真诚而自然；此时上场的海丽娜则咄咄逼人，与赫米娅针锋相对，二人对话则采用英雄双韵体（heroic couplet）——两两押韵，铿锵有力。由此可见台词文风随着场景内容与人物口吻的变化而变化。

场景 4：爱之盲目

（"Love looks not with the eyes, but with the mind."）

> 赫米娅在向海丽娜吐露秘密之时，恐怕万万没有料到海丽娜会泄露秘密——海丽娜为了博得狄米特律斯的青睐而将赫米娅的秘密出逃计划告诉了狄米特律斯。海丽娜深感爱情中的盲目。

Helena How happy some o'er other some can be!
　　　　Through Athens I am thought as fair as she.
　　　　But what of that? Demetrius thinks not so;
　　　　He will not know what all but he do know;
　　　　And as he errs, doting on Hermia's eyes,
　　　　So I, admiring of his qualities[1].
　　　　Things base and vile, holding no quantity[2],
　　　　Love can transpose to form and dignity:
　　　　Love looks not with the eyes, but with the mind,
　　　　And therefore is wing'd Cupid painted blind;
　　　　Nor hath Love's mind of any judgement taste:
　　　　Wings, and no eyes, figure[3] unheedy haste:
　　　　And therefore is Love said to be a child,
　　　　Because in choice he is so oft beguil'd.
　　　　As waggish[4] boys, in game, themselves forswear[5],
　　　　So the boy Love is perjur'd[6] everywhere;
　　　　For, ere Demetrius look'd on Hermia's eyne[7],
　　　　He hail'd down oaths that he was only mine;

---

[1] quality: virtue, power; accomplishment.
[2] holding no quantity: bearing no proportion (to what they are estimated at by love).
[3] figure: symbolize.
[4] waggish: roguish.
[5] foreswear: swear falsely; renounce upon oath.
[6] perjur'd: having sworn falsely, forsworn.
[7] eyne=eyes.

And when this hail some heat from Hermia felt,
So he dissolv'd and show'rs of oaths did melt.

(*A Midsummer Night's Dream* 1.1)

海丽娜 有些人比起其他的人来是多么幸福！在全雅典大家都认为我跟她一样美；但那有什么相干呢？狄米特律斯是不这么认为的；除了他一个人之外大家都知道的事情，他不会知道。正如他那样错误地迷恋着赫米娅的秋波一样，我也是只知道爱慕他的才智[1]；一切卑劣的弱点，在恋爱中都成为无足轻重，而变成美满和庄严。爱情是不用眼睛而用心灵看着的，因此生着翅膀的丘匹德常被描成盲目；而且爱情的判断全然没有理性，光有翅膀，不生眼睛，一味表示出卤莽的急躁，因此爱神便据说是一个孩儿，因为在选择方面他常会弄错。正如顽皮的孩子惯爱发假誓一样，司爱情的小儿也到处赌着口不应心的咒。狄米特律斯在没有看见赫米娅之前，也曾像下雹一样发着誓，说他是完全属于我的，但这阵冰雹一感到身上的一丝热力，便立刻溶解了，无数的盟言都化为乌有。

（朱生豪译《仲夏夜之梦》第1幕第1场）

评点

在西方传统绘画及文学意象中，小爱神丘比特的形象往往是一个蒙着眼睛、搭弓射箭的少年，象征着爱情的盲目；我国传统上也有"情人眼里出西施"的说法。不过，海丽娜只是觉得狄米特律斯迷恋赫米娅是盲目的、错误的，而自己对狄米特律斯的爱则可以包容他的一切。

爱情（love）、眼睛（eyes）与心灵（mind / heart）之间究竟是怎样的关系？海丽娜声称"爱情是不用眼睛而用心灵看着的"（Love looks not with the eyes, but with the mind）；《罗密欧与朱丽叶》中的劳伦斯神父则认为"年轻人的爱情并不真的藏在心里，而在眼里"[2]（Young men's love then lies / Not truly in their hearts, but in their eyes）。不妨联系具体语境，进行比较分析。

---

[1] 对于原文中的 qualities 一词，朱生豪译为"才智"，而梁实秋译为"优点"。
[2] 编者直译。朱生豪的译文为："年轻人的爱情，都是见异思迁，不是发于真心的。"

场景 5：捣蛋精灵

("I am that merry wanderer of the night.")

第一幕展现了雅典城里的人类社会图景，第二幕则切换到城外森林里的精灵世界。仙王的小跟班迫克（Puck）偶遇仙后麾下的小仙（Fairy），进行自我介绍。

Fairy Either I mistake your shape and making[1] quite,
Or else you are that shrewd[2] and knavish sprite
Call'd Robin Goodfellow. Are not you he
That frights the maidens of the villagery[3],
Skim milk, and sometimes labour in the quern,
And bootless[4] make the breathless housewife churn,
And sometime make the drink to bear no barm,
Mislead night-wanderers, laughing at their harm?
Those that Hobgoblin call you, and sweet Puck,
You do their work, and they shall have good luck.
Are not you he?

Puck   Thou speak'st aright;
I am that merry wanderer of the night.
I jest to Oberon, and make him smile
When I a fat and bean-fed horse beguile,
Neighing in likeness of a filly foal[5];
And sometime lurk I in a gossip's bowl
In very likeness of a roasted crab[6],
And when she drinks, against her lips I bob[7],

---

[1] making: building.
[2] shrewd: mischievous, malign.
[3] villagery: village population.
[4] bootless: all in vain.
[5] a filly foal: a young female horse.
[6] crab: crab apple.
[7] bob: knock.

And on her wither'd dewlap[1] pour the ale.
The wisest aunt, telling the saddest tale,
Sometime for three-foot stool mistaketh me;
Then slip I from her bum[2], down topples she,
And 'tailor'[3] cries, and falls into a cough;
And then the whole quire[4] hold their hips and loffe[5],
And waxen[6] in their mirth, and neeze[7], and swear
A merrier hour was never wasted there.

(*A Midsummer Night's Dream* 2.1)

小仙　要是我没有把你认错,你大概便是名叫罗宾好人儿的狡狯的、淘气的精灵了。你就是惯爱吓唬乡村的女郎,在人家的牛乳上撮去了乳脂,使那气喘吁吁的主妇整天也搅不出奶油来;有时你暗中替人家磨谷,有时弄坏了酒使它不能发酵;夜里走路的人,你把他们引入了迷路,自己却躲在一旁窃笑;谁叫你"大仙"或是"好迫克"的,你就给他幸运,帮他作工:那就是你吗?

迫克　仙人,你说得正是;我就是那个快活的夜游者。我在奥布朗跟前想出种种笑话来逗他发笑,看见一头肥胖精壮的马儿,我就学着雌马的嘶声把它迷昏了头;有时我化作一颗焙熟的野苹果,躲在老太婆的酒碗里,等她举起碗想喝的时候,我就拍的弹到她嘴唇上,把一碗麦酒都倒在她那皱瘪的喉皮上;有时我化作三脚的凳子,满肚皮人情世故的婶婶刚要坐下来一本正经讲她的故事,我便从她的屁股底下滑走,把她翻了一个大元宝,一头喊"好家伙!"一头咳呛个不住,于是周围的人大家笑得前仰后合,他们越想越好笑,鼻涕眼泪都笑了出来,发誓说从来不曾逢到过比这更有趣的事。

(朱生豪译《仲夏夜之梦》第2幕第1场)

评点

这个爱捣蛋的小精灵根源于英国民间文化传统。二者对话均采用英雄双韵体,在一长串生动活泼、令人目不暇接的社会风俗画中呈现人物形象。

---

[1] dewlap:(牛等)喉部的垂肉。
[2] bum: 屁股。
[3] tailor: There was a custom of crying "tailor" at a sudden fall backwards.
[4] quire: company.
[5] loffe=laugh.
[6] waxen=wax.
[7] neeze=sneeze.

场景 6：神仙吵架

("These are the forgeries of jealousy.")

> 仙王奥布朗（Oberon）与仙后提泰妮娅（Titania）在剧中的初次亮相就是在争风吃醋地争吵！即便贵为仙人，他们也人性十足，不能免除人性的弱点。精灵世界如人间社会一样，也是一地鸡毛。

Oberon Ill met by moonlight, proud Titania.

Titania What, jealous Oberon! Fairies, skip hence;
I have forsworn his bed and company.

Oberon Tarry, rash wanton[1]; am not I thy lord?

Titania Then I must be thy lady; but I know
When thou hast stol'n away from fairy land,
And in the shape of Corin, sat all day
Playing on pipes of corn, and versing love
To amorous Phillida. Why art thou here,
Come from the farthest step of India?
But that, forsooth, the bouncing Amazon,
Your buskin'd[2] mistress and your warrior love,
To Theseus must be wedded, and you come
To give their bed joy and prosperity?

Oberon How canst thou thus, for shame, Titania,
Glance at[3] my credit with Hippolyta,
Knowing I know thy love to Theseus?
Didst not thou lead him through the glimmering night
From Perigenia, whom he ravished;
And make him with fair Aegles break his faith,
With Ariadne and Antiopa?

---

[1] wanton: a lascivious woman.
[2] buskin'd: in high hunting-boots.
[3] glance at: hint.

Titania   These are the forgeries of jealousy. ...
(*A Midsummer Night's Dream* 2.1)

奥布朗　真不巧又在月光下碰见你，骄傲的提泰妮娅！

提泰妮娅　嘿，嫉妒的奥布朗！神仙们，快快走开；我已经发誓不和他同游同寝了。

奥布朗　等一等，坏脾气的女人[1]！我不是你的夫君吗？

提泰妮娅　那么我也一定是你的尊夫人了。但是你从前溜出了仙境，扮作牧人的样子，整天吹着麦笛，唱着情歌，向风骚的牧女调情，这种事我全知道。今番你为什么要从迢迢的印度平原上赶到这里来呢？无非是为着那位身材高大的阿玛宗女王，你的穿靴子的爱人，要嫁给忒修斯了，所以你得来向他们道贺道贺。

奥布朗　你怎么好意思说出这种话来，提泰妮娅，把我的名字和希波吕忒牵涉在一起侮蔑我？你自己知道你和忒修斯的私情瞒不过我。不是你在朦胧的夜里引导他离开被他所俘虏的佩丽古娜？不是你使他负心地遗弃了美丽的伊葛尔、爱丽亚邓和安提奥巴？

提泰妮娅　这些都是因为嫉妒而捏造出来的谎话。……

（朱生豪译《仲夏夜之梦》第2幕第1场）

评点

在人间情侣为爱而奋不顾身之时，森林里的仙王与仙后却在彼此斗气、互揭老底，指责对方不忠、出轨，并矢口否认对自己不利的控诉，就是为了争夺一个小侍童。这剧情毫不逊于凡尘生活，给剧本增添了喜剧元素。

---

[1] 梁实秋译为"泼妇"；原文的意思其实更接近于"荡妇"。

场景 7：顾影自怜

（"The more my prayer, the lesser is my grace."）

> 此时，赫米娅与拉山德已秘密私奔，狄米特律斯随即追入森林；海丽娜失望至极，却不肯罢休，非要尾随其后。狄米特律斯大为恼火，对她恶语相向。

Helena Stay, though thou kill me, sweet Demetrius!
Demetrius I charge[1] thee, hence, and do not haunt[2] me thus.
Helena O wilt thou darkling[3] leave me? Do not so.
Demetrius Stay, on thy peril; I alone will go. [*Exit.*]
Helena O, I am out of breath in this fond[4] chase!
　　　　　The more my prayer, the lesser is my grace.
　　　　　Happy is Hermia, wheresoe'er she lies,
　　　　　For she hath blessed and attractive eyes.
　　　　　How came her eyes so bright? Not with salt tears;
　　　　　If so, my eyes are oftener wash'd than hers.
　　　　　No, no; I am as ugly as a bear,
　　　　　For beasts that meet me run away for fear:
　　　　　Therefore no marvel though Demetrius
　　　　　Do, as[5] a monster, fly my presence thus.
　　　　　What wicked and dissembling glass of mine
　　　　　Made me compare with Hermia's sphery eyne?

(*A Midsummer Night's Dream* 2.2)

---

[1] charge: order, entreat.
[2] haunt: hang about.
[3] darkling: in the dark.
[4] fond: foolish; with the overtone "foolishly loving".
[5] as: as if I were.

海丽娜	你杀死了我也好,但是请你停步吧,亲爱的狄米特律斯!
狄米特律斯	我命令你走开,不要这样缠扰着我!
海丽娜	啊!你要把我丢在黑暗中吗?请不要这样!
狄米特律斯	站住!否则叫你活不成。我要独自走我的路。(下)
海丽娜	唉!这痴心的追赶使我乏得透不过气来。我越是千求万告,越是惹他憎恶。赫米娅无论在什么地方都是那么幸福,因为她有一双天赐的迷人的眼睛。她的眼睛怎么会这样明亮呢?不是为着泪水的缘故,因为我的眼睛被眼泪洗着的时候比她更多。不,不,我是像一头熊那么难看,就是野兽看见我也会因害怕而逃走;因此难怪狄米特律斯会这样逃避我,就像逃避一个丑妖怪一样。哪一面欺人的坏镜子使我居然敢把自己跟赫米娅的明星一样的眼睛相比呢?

(朱生豪译《仲夏夜之梦》第 2 幕第 2 场)

评点

海丽娜爱狄米特律斯,爱得卑微,尊严尽失,自我评价降到最低点——她将自己被拒归因于"我是像一头熊那么难看,就是野兽看见我也会因害怕而逃走"(I am as ugly as a bear, / For beasts that meet me run away for fear)。而她在第 1 幕第 1 场中还觉得"在全雅典大家都认为我跟她一样美"(Through Athens I am thought as fair as she)。

不过,下一个场景的局面陡然一变,文体风格也随之改变:从这一场景的素体诗到下一场景的英雄双韵体,内容与形式息息相关。

场景 8：连环误会

("Wherefore was I to this keen mockery born?")

> 迫克误给拉山德滴了爱情魔药，拉山德在醒来时对海丽娜一见倾心，大胆表白；海丽娜却无论如何也无法相信他突如其来的柔情蜜意，反而认为这是存心挖苦。

Helena　Do not say so, Lysander, say not so.
　　　　What though he love your Hermia? Lord, what though?
　　　　Yet Hermia still loves you; then be content.

Lysander　Content with Hermia? No. I do repent
　　　　The tedious minutes I with her have spent.
　　　　Not Hermia, but Helena I love:
　　　　Who will not change a raven for a dove?
　　　　The will of man is by his reason sway'd,
　　　　And reason says you are the worthier maid.
　　　　Things growing are not ripe until their season:
　　　　So I, being young, till now ripe not to reason;
　　　　And, touching now the point of human skill,
　　　　Reason becomes the marshal to my will,
　　　　And leads me to your eyes, where I o'erlook
　　　　Love's stories, written in love's richest book.

Helena　Wherefore was I to this keen mockery born?
　　　　When at your hands did I deserve this scorn?
　　　　Is't not enough, is't not enough, young man,
　　　　That I did never, no, nor never can
　　　　Deserve a sweet look from Demetrius' eye,
　　　　But you must flout[1] my insufficiency?
　　　　Good troth, you do me wrong, good sooth[2], you do,

---

[1] flout: mock, make a fool of.
[2] good troth / good sooth: really, truly.

> In such disdainful manner me to woo.
> But fare you well; perforce[1] I must confess
> I thought you lord of more true gentleness.
> O that a lady, of one man refus'd,
> Should of another therefore be abus'd!

(*A Midsummer Night's Dream* 2.2)

海丽娜　不要这样说，拉山德！不要这样说！即使他爱你的赫米娅又有什么关系？上帝！那又有什么关系？赫米娅仍旧是爱着你的，所以你应该心满意足了。

拉山德　跟赫米娅心满意足吗？不，我真悔恨和她在一起度着的那些可厌的时辰。我不爱赫米娅，我爱的是海丽娜；谁不愿意把一只乌鸦换一头白鸽呢？男人的意志是被理性所支配的，理性告诉我你比她更值得敬爱。凡是生长的东西，不到季节，总不会成熟：我过去由于年轻，我的理性也不曾成熟；但是现在我的智慧已经充分成长，理性指挥着我的意志，把我引到了你的眼前；在你的眼睛里我可以读到写在最丰美的爱情的经典上的故事。

海丽娜　我怎么忍受得下这种尖刻的嘲笑呢？我什么时候得罪了你，使你这样讥讽我呢？我从来不曾得到过，也永远不会得到，狄米特律斯的一瞥爱怜的眼光，难道那还不够，难道那还不够，年轻人，你必须再这样挖苦我的短处吗？真的，你侮辱了我；真的，用这种卑鄙的样子向我献假殷勤。但是再会吧！我还以为你是个较有教养的上流人哩。唉！一个女子受到了这一个男人的摈拒，还得忍受那一个男子的揶揄。

（朱生豪译《仲夏夜之梦》第2幕第2场）

评点

　　魔药进一步加强了爱情的"盲目"。海丽娜尽管在狄米特律斯面前几乎失去了自我，但是不乏自尊；当她认为拉山德在挖苦羞辱她时，就义愤填膺，一连三个反问，连连驳斥，极力捍卫自己的人格尊严。

　　拉山德则振振有词地为自己辩护，对魔药的影响毫无觉察，反而以"理性"自居——四次使用"理性"（reason）一词不无反讽意味。

---

[1] perforce: at any rate.

场景 9：驴头艳遇

("What angel wakes me from my flowery bed?")

> 仲夏夜的雅典森林上演着人间与仙界的各路爱恨情仇，在森林的另一个角落却有一帮工匠偷偷排戏，其中的织工波顿（Bottom）被精灵施了魔法，长出了驴耳朵。这吓跑了同伴，却令同样被施了魔药的仙后对他"一见钟情"。

Titania　What angel wakes me from my flowery bed?

……

Titania　I pray thee, gentle mortal, sing again:
　　　　Mine ear is much enamour'd of thy note;
　　　　So is mine eye enthralled to thy shape;
　　　　And thy fair virtue's force perforce doth move me
　　　　On the first view to say, to swear, I love thee.

Bottom　Methinks, mistress, you should have little reason for that: and yet, to say the truth, reason and love keep little company together now-a-days; the more the pity that some honest neighbours will not make them friends. Nay, I can gleek upon occasion.

Titania　Thou art as wise as thou art beautiful.

Bottom　Not so, neither: but if I had wit enough to get out of this wood, I have enough to serve mine own turn.

Titania　Out of this wood do not desire to go:
　　　　Thou shalt remain here, whether thou wilt or no.
　　　　I am a spirit of no common rate;
　　　　The summer still doth tend upon my state;
　　　　And I do love thee: therefore, go with me;
　　　　I'll give thee fairies to attend on thee,
　　　　And they shall fetch thee jewels from the deep,
　　　　And sing while thou on pressed flowers dost sleep;
　　　　And I will purge thy mortal grossness so

That thou shalt like an airy spirit go.
(*A Midsummer Night's Dream* 3.1)

提泰妮娅　什么天使使我从百花的卧榻上醒来呢?
....

提泰妮娅　温柔的凡人,请你唱下去吧!我的耳朵沉醉在你的歌声里,我的眼睛又为你的状貌所迷惑;在第一次见面的时候,你的美姿已使我不禁说出而且矢誓着我爱你了。

波顿　咱想,奶奶,您这可太没有理由。不过说老实话,现今世界上理性可真难得跟爱情碰头;也没有哪位正直的邻居大叔给他俩撮合撮合做朋友,真是抱歉得很。哈,我有时也会说说笑话。

提泰妮娅　你真是又聪明又美丽。

波顿　不见得,不见得。可是咱要是有本事跑出这座林子,那已经很够了。

提泰妮娅　请不要跑出这座林子!不论你愿不愿,你一定要留在这里。我不是一个平常的精灵,夏天永远听从我的命令;我真是爱你,因此跟我去吧。我将使神仙们侍候你,他们会从海底里捞起珍宝献给你;当你在花茵上睡去的时候,他们会给你歌唱;而且我要给你洗涤去俗体的污垢,使你身轻得像个精灵一样。

(朱生豪译《仲夏夜之梦》第3幕第1场)

评点

　　按照仙王的说法,那魔药源于"爱懒花"(love-in-idleness):"它的汁液如果滴在睡着的人的眼皮上,无论男女,醒来一眼看见什么生物,都会发疯似的对它恋爱。"魔药也许是一个隐喻:一见钟情的发生如此不可思议而且难以抗拒,不食人间烟火的仙后居然迷上了一个蠢汉。

　　仙后与波顿二人对话,文风截然不同:仙后采用素体诗,不时押韵,辞藻华丽,符合其高贵身份;出身平民的波顿则用散文体,体现小人物的平凡本色。

场景 10：匪夷所思

("Man is but an ass if he go about to expound this dream.")

> 最终，迫克之前乱点鸳鸯谱的各种"一见钟情"都恢复了正常。与此同时，波顿在森林里独自醒来，他的驴耳朵也消失了，之前发生的一切犹如梦境一般不可思议。

Bottom   [*Waking.*] When my cue comes, call me and I will answer.
My next is 'Most fair Pyramus'. Heigh-ho! Peter Quince!
Flute, the bellows-mender! Snout, the tinker! Starveling!
God's my life! Stolen hence, and left me asleep!
I have had a most rare vision. I have had a dream,
past the wit of man to say what dream it was.
Man is but an ass if he go about to expound this dream.
Methought[1] I was—there is no man can tell what.
Methought I was—and methought
I had—but man is but a patched fool[2] if he will
offer to say what methought I had.
The eye of man hath not heard, the ear of man hath not seen,
man's hand is not able to taste, his tongue to conceive,
nor his heart to report, what my dream was.
I will get Peter Quince to write a ballad of this dream:
it shall be called 'Bottom's Dream', because it hath no bottom;
and I will sing it in the latter end of a play, before the duke.
Peradventure[3], to make it the more gracious[4],
I shall sing it at her death.

(*A Midsummer Night's Dream* 4.1)

---

[1] methought: it seemed to me.
[2] a patched fool: a fool commonly wore a parti-colored costume.
[3] peradventure: perhaps.
[4] gracious: appealing.

波顿 （醒）轮到咱说尾白的时候，请你们叫咱一声，咱就会答应；咱下面的一句是，"最美丽的皮拉摩斯"。喂！喂！彼得·昆斯！弗鲁特，修风箱的！斯诺特，补锅子的！斯塔佛林！……悄悄地溜走了，把咱撇下在这儿一个人睡觉吗？咱看见了一个奇怪得了不得的幻象，咱做了一个梦。没有人说得出那是怎样的一个梦；要是谁想把这个梦解释一下，那他一定是一头驴子。咱好像是——没有人说得出那是什么东西；咱好像是——咱好像有——但要是谁敢说出来咱好像有什么东西，那他一定是一个蠢材。咱那个梦啊，人们的眼睛从来没有听到过，人们的耳朵从来没有看见过，人们的手也尝不出来是什么味道，人们的舌头也想不出来是什么道理，人们的心也说不出来究竟那是怎样的一个梦。咱要叫彼得·昆斯给咱写一首歌儿咏一下这个梦，题目就叫做"波顿的梦"，因为这个梦可没有个底儿；咱要在演完戏之后当着公爵大人的面前唱这个歌——或者更好些，还是等咱死了之后再唱吧。

（朱生豪译《仲夏夜之梦》第 4 幕第 1 场）

评点

波顿可谓《仲夏夜之梦》中最杰出的喜剧角色，其台词都是散文体的大白话。他一向自以为是，自命不凡，自告奋勇，自吹自擂。即便如此，他也觉得夜里的"艳遇"不可理喻、荒诞不经。

凡人与仙人两个世界在仲夏夜的短暂交集就此结束，回归并行不悖的状态。仙人染指凡尘，凡人却只当是一场梦。当局者迷，也许只有局外人才能看清。然而，谁又能保证自己不在局中？

场景 11：爱之疯狂

("Lovers and madmen have such seething brains ...")

> 一个离奇的仲夏夜就这样结束了。次日清晨，公爵忒修斯（Theseus）带着未婚妻希波吕忒（Hippolyta）及随员打猎，恰巧发现了这两对青年情侣，一切矛盾都得以化解。事后，公爵夫妇闲聊。

Hippolyta 'Tis strange, my Theseus, that these lovers speak of.
Theseus More strange than true. I never may believe
These antique fables, nor these fairy toys.
Lovers and madmen have such seething[1] brains,
Such shaping fantasies, that apprehend
More than cool reason ever comprehends.
The lunatic, the lover, and the poet
Are of imagination all compact[2]:
One sees more devils than vast hell can hold;
That is the madman: the lover, all as frantic,
Sees Helen's beauty in a brow of Egypt:
The poet's eye, in fine frenzy rolling,
Doth glance from heaven to earth, from earth to heaven;
And as imagination bodies[3] forth
The forms of things unknown, the poet's pen
Turns them to shapes, and gives to airy nothing
A local habitation and a name.
Such tricks hath strong imagination,
That if it would but apprehend some joy,
It comprehends some bringer of that joy:
Or, in the night, imagining some fear,

---

[1] seething: on the boil.
[2] all compact: entirely made up.
[3] bodies: embodies.

> How easy is a bush suppos'd a bear!
> (*A Midsummer Night's Dream* 5.1)

希波吕忒 忒修斯，这些恋人们所说的话真是奇怪得很。

忒修斯 奇怪得不像会是真实。我永不相信这种古怪的传说和胡扯的神话。情人们和疯子们都富于纷乱的思想和成形的幻觉，他们所理会到的永远不是冷静的理智所能充分了解。疯子、情人和诗人，都是幻想的产儿：疯子眼中所见的鬼，多过于广大的地狱所能容纳；情人，同样是那么疯狂，能从埃及人的黑脸上看见海伦的美貌；诗人的眼睛在神奇的狂放的一转中，便能从天上看到地下，从地下看到天上。想象会把不知名的事物用一种形式呈现出来，诗人的笔再使它们具有如实的形象，空虚的无物也会有了居处和名字。强烈的想象往往具有这种本领，只要一领略到一些快乐，就会相信那种快乐的背后有一个赐予的人；夜间一转到恐惧的念头，一株灌木一下子便会变成一头熊。

（朱生豪译《仲夏夜之梦》第 5 幕第 1 场）

评点

将坠入情网的人（lovers）与疯子（madmen / the lunatic）相提并论，正是为了调侃爱情的疯狂与不可思议。这一观点在《仲夏夜之梦》中屡屡出现，除了忒修斯之外，赫米娅与波顿也有过类似评论。此外，莎士比亚喜剧《皆大欢喜》也有一句台词："爱情不过是一种疯狂。"（Love is merely a madness.）

忒修斯所说的"疯子、情人和诗人，都是幻想的产儿"（The lunatic, the lover, and the poet / Are of imagination all compact）一句，还顺便揶揄了诗人想象力过于活跃，情感过于丰富，可谓莎士比亚的自嘲。

场景 12：滑稽悲剧

("Merry and tragical? Tedious and brief?")

> 在三对新人的婚庆大典上，工匠剧团献丑，众人嬉笑评论。全剧以这场"戏中戏"压轴。以下为公爵选戏的场景。

Theseus　'A tedious brief scene of young Pyramus
　　　　　And his love Thisbe, very tragical mirth'?
　　　　　Merry and tragical? Tedious and brief?
　　　　　That is hot ice, and wondrous strange snow!
　　　　　How shall we find the concord of this discord?
Philostrate　A play there is, my lord, some ten words long,
　　　　　Which is as brief as I have known a play;
　　　　　But by ten words, my lord, it is too long,
　　　　　Which makes it tedious; for in all the play
　　　　　There is not one word apt, one player fitted.
　　　　　And tragical, my noble lord, it is,
　　　　　For Pyramus therein doth kill himself;
　　　　　Which, when I saw rehears'd, I must confess
　　　　　Made mine eyes water; but more merry tears
　　　　　The passion of loud laughter never shed.
Theseus　What are they that do play it?
Philostrate　Hard-handed men that work in Athens here,
　　　　　Which never labour'd in their minds till now;
　　　　　And now have toil'd their unbreath'd[1] memories
　　　　　With this same play, against your nuptial.

(*A Midsummer Night's Dream* 5.1)

---

[1] unbreath'd: unexercised, unpractised.

忒修斯	"关于年轻的皮拉摩斯及其爱人提斯柏的冗长的短戏,非常悲哀的趣剧"。悲哀的趣剧!冗长的短戏!那简直是说灼热的冰,发烧的雪。这种矛盾怎么能调和起来呢?
菲劳斯特莱特	殿下,一出一共只有十来个字那么长的戏,当然是再短没有了;然而即使只有十个字,也会嫌太长,叫人看了厌倦;因为在全剧之中,没有一个字是用得恰当的,没有一个演员是支配得适如其分的。那本戏的确很悲哀,殿下,因为皮拉摩斯在戏里要把自己杀死。可是我看他们预演那一场的时候,我得承认确曾使我的眼中充满了眼泪;但那些泪都是在纵声大笑的时候忍俊不住而流下来的,再没有人流过比那更开心的泪水了。
忒修斯	扮演这戏的是些什么人呢?
菲劳斯特莱特	都是在这儿雅典城里作工过活的胼手胝足的汉子。他们从来不曾用过头脑,今番为了准备参加殿下的婚礼,才辛辛苦苦地把这本戏记诵起来。

(朱生豪译《仲夏夜之梦》第5幕第1场)

评点

工匠们的活动空间既不与四位贵族青年重合,也不与公爵重合。除了波顿与精灵有交集之外,这一组人物直到剧终时才与其他人物同台登场。

工匠们不乏热情与善意,却水平有限,他们拙劣演技硬生生地把传统悲剧演出了喜剧效果。节目单上对这些剧目的简介,诸如"冗长的短戏"(A tedious brief scene)、"悲哀的趣剧"(very tragical mirth),吊足了观众的胃口。所以,哪怕公爵有更多更精湛的剧目可供选择,他也指明要看工匠们的表演。

二、《罗密欧与朱丽叶》

(Romeo and Juliet)
(1596)

"罗密欧啊,罗密欧!为什么你偏偏是罗密欧呢?"
("O Romeo, Romeo, wherefore art thou Romeo?")

《罗密欧与朱丽叶》的故事背景设在意大利名城维罗纳：两个高贵而富有的大家族，势均力敌、旗鼓相当，却偏偏势不两立、不共戴天。整部剧自始至终都没有提及产生仇恨的根源，也从不探讨化解矛盾的可能性，似乎两家之间深仇大恨理所当然、亘古不变、非人力所能化解，结仇的原因反倒无关紧要了。

为了仇恨而仇恨，无休无止地冤冤相报，最终必然两败俱伤。凯普莱特家族的提伯尔特最为好斗，屡屡挑衅滋事，最终不仅葬送了他自己，而且让罗密欧与朱丽叶这一对金童玉女沦为家族仇恨的牺牲品……

不过，此剧风格并不全然悲伤或紧张，毕竟这是莎士比亚的早期悲剧，悲剧意味远不及莎士比亚晚期的四大悲剧。且不提罗密欧与朱丽叶至死不渝的爱情，就说剧终的"光明尾巴"——两家父母见子女双双殉情之后，幡然悔悟，握手言和，至少让人看到了维罗纳城获得安宁的希望。

此外，剧中不乏喜剧场景或温馨画面：两大家族尽管对外剑拔弩张，但是对内都井然有序、彬彬有礼，甚至颇有人情味。两家的男女主人（即罗密欧与朱丽叶的父母）都不是简单的反面人物，虽说其人性弱点促成了悲剧的发生，但并非出于恶意。

爱与恨、文明与野蛮、理智与情感……各种元素在《罗密欧与朱丽叶》一剧中交相辉映，令人不得不感慨人性的多面、世事的复杂！

《罗密欧与朱丽叶》（*Romeo and Juliet*）

场景 1： 情不知所起 （"Love is a smoke made with the fume of sighs."） 1.1

场景 2： 君子好逑 （"But woo her, gentle Paris, get her heart."） 1.2

场景 3： 完美佳婿 （"Read over the volume of young Paris' face …"） 1.3

场景 4： 一见钟情 （"O, she doth teach the torches to burn bright!"） 1.5

场景 5： 以吻涤罪 （"Thus from my lips, by yours, my sin is purged."） 1.5

场景 6： 玫瑰之名 （"What's in a name?"） 2.2

场景 7： 指月发誓 （"O, swear not by the moon …"） 2.2

场景 8： 情深似海 （"My bounty is as boundless as the sea …"） 2.2

场景 9： 善恶共生 （"Virtue itself turns vice, being misapplied."） 2.3

场景 10： 见异思迁 （"Is Rosaline … so soon forsaken?"） 2.3

场景 11： 飘风不终朝 （"These violent delights have violent ends."） 2.6

场景 12： 棒打鸳鸯 （"'Tis torture, and not mercy …"） 3.3

场景 13： 晨曦话别 （"Art thou gone so, love, lord, ay husband, friend?"） 3.5

场景 14： 贫穷致恶 （"The world affords no law to make thee rich."） 5.1

场景 15： 饮鸩殉情 （"Here's to my love."） 5.3

场景1：情不知所起

("Love is a smoke made with the fume of sighs.")

> 剧本一开场，蒙太古（Montague）家族与凯普莱特（Capulet）家族的仆人在集市上发生口角、械斗，冲突不断升级，直到亲王亲自出面制止并严重警告。
>
> 随即，蒙太古夫人一句"罗密欧何在"令画风陡然一变，将剧情从公共领域切换到私人空间，从紧张走向舒缓，从恨转为爱，从开头一座城、一群人的宏观视角聚焦于男主角……罗密欧上场伊始就是一个"情种"。

Romeo　　Alas, that love, whose view is muffled[1] still,
　　　　　Should without eyes see pathways to his will.
　　　　　Where shall we dine? O me, what fray was here?
　　　　　Yet tell me not, for I have heard it all.
　　　　　Here's much to do with hate, but more with love.
　　　　　Why then, O brawling love, O loving hate,
　　　　　O anything of nothing first create,
　　　　　O heavy lightness, serious vanity,
　　　　　Misshapen chaos of well-seeming forms,
　　　　　Feather of lead, bright smoke, cold fire, sick health,
　　　　　Still-waking[2] sleep that is not what it is.
　　　　　This love feel I that feel no love in this.

……

Romeo　　Love is a smoke made with the fume of sighs;
　　　　　Being purged, a fire sparkling in lovers' eyes;
　　　　　Being vexed[3], a sea nourished with loving tears.
　　　　　What is it else? A madness most discreet,

---

[1] muffled: blindfolded.
[2] still-waking: forever wakeful.
[3] vexed: troubled or suffering (rather than in the modern sense of annoyed).

> A choking gall[1] and a preserving sweet.
> (*Romeo and Juliet* 1.1)

罗密欧 唉！想不到爱神蒙着眼睛，却会一直闯进人们的心灵！我们在什么地方吃饭？嗳哟！又是谁在这儿打过架了？可是不必告诉我，我早就知道了。这些都是怨恨造成的后果，可是爱情的力量比它要大过许多。啊，吵吵闹闹的相爱，亲亲热热的怨恨！啊，无中生有的一切！啊，沉重的轻浮，严肃的狂妄，整齐的混乱，铅铸的羽毛，光明的烟雾，寒冷的火焰，憔悴的健康，永远觉醒的睡眠，否定的存在！我感觉到的爱情正是这么一种东西，可是我并不喜爱这一种爱情。

....

罗密欧 爱情是叹息吹起的一阵烟；恋人的眼中有它净化了的火星；恋人的眼泪是它激起的波涛。它又是最智慧的疯狂，哽喉的苦味，吃不到嘴的蜜糖。

（朱生豪译《罗密欧与朱丽叶》第 1 幕第 1 场）

评点

显然，罗密欧并不热衷于家族仇杀，尤其是此时正陷于单相思。需要注意的是，此时令罗密欧朝思暮想的心上人并非朱丽叶（此时罗密欧尚未见过朱丽叶），而是罗瑟琳——这位姑娘在剧中只被人偶尔提到名字，却始终都没上场露面。

不同于凯普莱特家争强好斗的提伯尔特，罗密欧一上场就饱受相思之苦，其独白大量运用英雄双韵体——诗行两两押韵（如 sighs 与 eyes, discreet 与 sweet），还采用了一连串矛盾修饰法（oxymoron），表达缠绵悱恻的相思（如 loving hate, cold fire 等）。

这一段开头提到了小爱神（Cupid）。《罗密欧与朱丽叶》一剧有多个人物都曾提及这个典故。在莎士比亚时期的欧洲传统文化中，小爱神的形象往往是被蒙蔽双眼，以示"爱情盲目"之意。

---

[1] gall: bitterness.

场景 2：君子好逑

("But woo her, gentle Paris, get her heart.")

> 正当罗密欧为罗瑟琳而害相思病之时，凯普莱特夫妇则在为爱女朱丽叶（Juliet）物色如意郎君。早在罗密欧见到朱丽叶之前，另一位贵族青年帕里斯（Paris）就已经向凯普莱特家提亲了。

Capulet　But saying o'er what I have said before:
　　　　My child is yet a stranger in the world;
　　　　She hath not seen the change of fourteen years[1],
　　　　Let two more summers wither in their pride
　　　　Ere we may think her ripe to be a bride.
Paris　　Younger than she are happy mothers made.
Capulet　And too soon marred are those so early married[2].
　　　　She is the hopeful[3] lady of my earth.
　　　　But woo her, gentle Paris, get her heart.
　　　　My will to her consent is but a part,
　　　　And, she agreed, within her scope of choice
　　　　Lies my consent and fair according voice.

(*Romeo and Juliet* 1.2)

---

[1] not seen the change of fourteen years: i.e. not yet fourteen years old.
[2] marred: injured, hurt, spoiled, ruined. As a common proverb of that time goes: "The maid that soon married is, soon marred is."
[3] hopeful: i.e. in whom my hopes are vested.

二、《罗密欧与朱丽叶》　035

凯普莱特　我的意思早就对您表示过了。我的女儿今年还没有满十四岁，完全是一个不懂事的孩子；再过两个夏天，才可以谈到亲事。

帕里斯　比她年纪更小的人，都已经做了幸福的母亲了。

凯普莱特　早结果的树木一定早雕[1]。我在这世上已经什么希望都没有了，只有她是我的唯一的安慰。可是向她求爱吧，善良的帕里斯，得到她的欢心；只要她愿意，我的同意是没有问题的。

（朱生豪译《罗密欧与朱丽叶》第1幕第2场）

评点

　　一老一少两位男士的这段对白基本上都采用两两对偶（couplet）的诗歌形式，朗朗上口，带有轻喜剧色彩。看似是家长里短、儿女情长的闲聊，却蕴含着一场丰富而微妙的心理战：一方面，凯普莱特有意摆出"惜嫁"的姿态，罗列了种种理由——也许是真心宠爱女儿，也许是在试探帕里斯的诚意，欲迎还拒；另一方面，帕里斯确实表现得无可挑剔，凯普莱特随后便松了口，不但对这位求婚者表达了认可与鼓励，而且还立马举办宴会，为两个年轻人彼此熟识而创造机会。

　　凯普莱特在表示只要朱丽叶同意就没问题（My will to her consent is but a part）时，显得非常尊重女儿的意愿。这也许只是他一厢情愿地认为朱丽叶不会不接受，毕竟帕里斯如此优秀——从最后一幕帕里斯为朱丽叶深夜守墓并因此付出生命代价来看，凯普莱特夫妇相中这位准女婿确实颇有眼光。

　　父母为独生女的终身大事操碎了心，可是偏偏事与愿违。朱丽叶在舞会上完全没有关注过帕里斯，却相中了罗密欧；即便后来在父母的施压下，她也拒不接受帕里斯——这可能不是因为帕里斯本人的问题，而是出于对大家长作风的强烈反感吧！

---

[1] 现代汉语通常用"凋"。

场景 3：完美佳婿

("Read over the volume of young Paris' face …")

> 女儿的婚姻大事非同小可。凯普莱特负责跟准女婿斡旋，而凯普莱特夫人则负责做女儿的思想工作。在凯普莱特家的舞会开始之前，凯普莱特夫人特地找来朱丽叶，极力夸赞求婚者帕里斯。

Lady Capulet　This night you shall behold him at our feast.
　　　　　　　Read o'er the volume of young Paris' face,
　　　　　　　And find delight writ there with beauty's pen;
　　　　　　　Examine every married[1] lineament[2],
　　　　　　　And see how one another lends content[3];
　　　　　　　And what obscured in this fair volume lies
　　　　　　　Find written in the margent[4] of his eyes.
　　　　　　　This precious book of love, this unbound lover,
　　　　　　　To beautify him only lacks a cover.
　　　　　　　The fish lives in the sea, and 'tis much pride
　　　　　　　For fair without the fair within to hide.
　　　　　　　That book in many's eyes doth share the glory
　　　　　　　That in gold clasps locks in the golden story.
　　　　　　　So shall you share all that he doth possess,
　　　　　　　By having him, making yourself no less.

(*Romeo and Juliet* 1.3)

---

[1] married：harmoniously blended.
[2] lineament: feature.
[3] content: satisfaction.
[4] margent: margin（西方国家的早期书籍常常有页面边缘的注释或点评）。上文将帕里斯这个人比作一卷好书（this fair volume），而书的内容可能隐晦（obscured），那么通常被视为"心灵之窗"（the window of the soul）的眼睛就能像页面边缘的注释那样，揭示其内涵。

凯普莱特夫人 今晚上在我们家里的宴会中间,你就可以看见他。从年轻的帕里斯的脸上,你可以读到用秀美的笔写成的迷人诗句;一根根齐整的线条,交织成整个一幅谐和的图画;要是你想探索这一卷美好的书中的奥秘,在他的眼角上可以找到微妙的诠释。这本珍贵的恋爱的经典,只缺少一帧可以使它相得益彰的封面;正像游鱼需要活水,美妙的内容也少不了美妙的外表陪衬。记载着金科玉律的宝籍,锁合在漆金的封面里,它的辉煌富丽为众目所共见;要是你做了他的封面,那么他所有的一切都属于你所有了。

(朱生豪译《罗密欧与朱丽叶》第1幕第3场)

评点

  凯普莱特夫人向女儿提前介绍当晚舞会即将见面的帕里斯,赞赏之辞溢于言表。不无讽刺的是,剧中的整场舞会却完全没有提到帕里斯,朱丽叶似乎只看见罗密欧——偏偏是仇家的独生子,不可不谓阴差阳错!

  朱丽叶的父母都十分关心女儿的幸福,用心良苦,但是与女儿的沟通不畅,彼此之间明显存在生疏感。凯普莱特夫人甚至需要奶妈在场辅助帮腔,才好开口跟女儿谈话。

  朱丽叶只是表面上乖巧、顺从,不敢忤逆父母的强权意志;她其实颇有主见,甚至叛逆,阳奉阴违,极力想摆脱父母对她的控制。朱丽叶与父母之间的疏远且紧张的关系给最后的悲剧埋下了一个伏笔。

  凯普莱特夫人的这番话辞藻华丽、精心雕琢,大量运用修辞手法,尤其是以书喻人。不过,在闺阁之内、母女之间,这番文绉绉、冠冕堂皇的话恐怕让人产生心理距离和不信任感。她说话的口吻也不免盛气凌人、居高临下,容易让女儿产生逆反心理。

场景 4：一见钟情

("O, she doth teach the torches to burn bright!")

> 罗密欧与朋友们混进了仇家的假面舞会，原本是为了瞻仰他心目中的女神罗瑟琳，却阴差阳错地看见一位陌生女郎美若天仙。罗密欧深陷爱河，却不知危险临近。

Romeo   O, she doth teach the torches to burn bright!
It seems she hangs upon the cheek of night
As a rich jewel in an Ethiope's[1] ear,
Beauty too rich for use, for earth too dear.
So shows a snowy dove trooping with crows
As yonder lady o'er her fellows shows.
The measure[2] done, I'll watch her place of stand[3],
And, touching hers, make blessed my rude[4] hand.
Did my heart love till now? Forswear[5] it, sight,
For I ne'er saw true beauty till this night.

Tybalt   This by his voice should be a Montague.
Fetch me my rapier[6], boy. What, dares the slave
Come hither, covered with an antic face[7],
To fleer and scorn at our solemnity?
Now by the stock and honor of my kin[8],

---

[1] Ethiop:（古）埃塞俄比亚人。Night is personified here as an Ethiop with Juliet as a lustrous pendant.
[2] measure: dance.
[3] stand: halt and rest.
[4] rude: rough, coarse, compared to Juliet's.
[5] forswear it: break the former oath (of undying love to Rosaline).
[6] rapier: sharp light sword.
[7] antic face: fantastical mask.
[8] stock and honor of my kin: pedigree（血统，家谱）and respect due to my ancestors.

To strike him dead I hold it not a sin.
(*Romeo and Juliet* 1.5)

罗密欧　　啊！火炬远不及她的明亮；
　　　　　她皎然悬在暮天的颊上，
　　　　　像黑奴耳边璀璨的珠环；
　　　　　她是天上明珠降落人间！
　　　　　瞧她随着女伴进退周旋，
　　　　　像鸦群中一头白鸽蹁跹。
　　　　　我要等舞阑后追随左右，
　　　　　握一握她那纤纤的素手。
　　　　　我从前的恋爱是假非真，
　　　　　今晚才遇见绝世的佳人！
提伯尔特　听这个人的声音，好像是一个蒙太古家里的人。孩子，拿我的剑来。哼！这不知死活的奴才，竟敢套着一个鬼脸，到这儿来嘲笑我们的盛会吗？为了保持凯普莱特家族的光荣，我把他杀死了也不算罪过。

（朱生豪译《罗密欧与朱丽叶》第1幕第5场）

评点

"情不知所起，一往而深"，罗密欧也许朝三暮四，但是正如他后来向劳伦斯神父辩解的那样，他之前并不真正理解"爱情"，直至遇见朱丽叶。

充满戏剧性的是，一边是罗密欧浪漫无比，满眼满心都是朱丽叶，身处危险却浑然不觉，另一边则是朱丽叶的表兄提伯尔特恶意满满、剑拔弩张，执着于维护家族荣誉。爱恨情仇，对比鲜明，极具戏剧性。

场景 5：以吻涤罪

("Thus from my lips, by yours, my sin is purged.")

> 在舞会上，罗密欧对朱丽叶一见钟情，朱丽叶也欣然接受。表白、牵手、初吻一气呵成。吟诗作对，二人势均力敌，配合高度默契，充满柔情蜜意。

Romeo　If I profane[1] with my unworthiest hand
　　　　This holy shrine[2], the gentle fine is this:
　　　　My lips, two blushing pilgrims, ready stand
　　　　To smooth that rough touch with a tender kiss.
Juliet　Good pilgrim, you do wrong your hand too much,
　　　　Which mannerly devotion shows in this;
　　　　For saints have hands that pilgrims' hands do touch,
　　　　And palm to palm is holy palmers' kiss.
Romeo　Have not saints lips, and holy palmers too?
Juliet　Ay, pilgrim, lips that they must use in prayer.
Romeo　O, then, dear saint, let lips do what hands do;
　　　　They pray, grant thou, lest faith turn to despair.
Juliet　Saints do not move, though grant for prayers' sake.
Romeo　Then move not, while my prayer's effect I take.　[*Kisses her.*]
　　　　Thus from my lips, by yours, my sin is purged.
Juliet　Then have my lips the sin that they have took.
Romeo　Sin from thy lips? O trespass sweetly urged!
　　　　Give me my sin again.　[*Kisses her.*]
Juliet　You kiss by the book.

(*Romeo and Juliet* 1.5)

---

[1] profane: defile, trespass on something sacred.
[2] this holy shrine: it refers to Juliet's hand.

罗密欧	要是我这俗手上的尘污
	亵渎了你的神圣的庙宇，
	这两片嘴唇，含羞的信徒，
	愿意用一吻乞求你宥恕。
朱丽叶	信徒，莫把你的手儿侮辱，
	这样才是最虔诚的礼敬；
	神明的手本许信徒接触，
	掌心的密合远胜如亲吻。
罗密欧	生下了嘴唇有什么用处？
朱丽叶	信徒的嘴唇要祷告神明。
罗密欧	那么我要祷求你的允许，
	让手的工作交给了嘴唇。
朱丽叶	你的祷告已蒙神明允准。
罗密欧	神明，请容我把殊恩受领。（吻朱丽叶）
	这一吻涤清了我的罪孽。
朱丽叶	你的罪却沾上我的唇间。
罗密欧	啊，我的唇间有罪？感谢你精心的指责！让我收回吧。
朱丽叶	你可以亲一下《圣经》。

（朱生豪译《罗密欧与朱丽叶》第1幕第5场）

评点

　　从形式上来看，这番对白由一首莎士比亚式十四行诗（sonnet）与一组四行诗（quatrain）构成。其中运用了大量比喻、双关等修辞手法，属于自中世纪以来的"典雅爱情"（courtly love）传统。例如，罗密欧把自己比作朝圣者，把朱丽叶比作神龛里的圣人，由此为亲吻朱丽叶找到了"光明正大"的理由。

场景 6：玫瑰之名

（"What's in a name?"）

> 舞会散场之后，罗密欧翻墙跳进朱丽叶家的后花园，而朱丽叶则在卧室阳台上感慨罗密欧的姓氏……爱其人，却恨其名，如何破解？名字与个人之间究竟有何干系？

Juliet   O Romeo, Romeo, wherefore art thou Romeo?
           Deny thy father and refuse thy name,
           Or if thou wilt not, be but sworn my love,
           And I'll no longer be a Capulet.

Remeo   Shall I hear more, or shall I speak at this?

Juliet   'Tis but thy name that is my enemy.
           Thou art thyself, though not a Montague.
           What's Montague? It is nor hand nor foot,
           Nor arm nor face nor any other part
           Belonging to a man. O be some other name!
           What's in a name? That which we call a rose
           By any other word would smell as sweet;
           So Romeo would, were he not Romeo called,
           Retain that dear[1] perfection which he owes[2]
           Without that title[3]. Romeo, doff[4] thy name,
           And for thy name, which is no part of thee,
           Take all myself.

(*Romeo and Juliet* 2.2)

---

[1] dear: precious.
[2] owes: owns, possesses.
[3] title: appellation, name.
[4] doff: get rid of, cast off.

朱丽叶　罗密欧啊，罗密欧！为什么你偏偏是罗密欧呢？否认你的父亲，抛弃你的姓名吧；也许你不愿意这样做，那么只要你宣誓做我的爱人，我也不愿再姓凯普莱特了。

罗密欧　我还是继续听下去呢，还是现在就对她说话？

朱丽叶　只有你的名字才是我的仇敌；你即使不姓蒙太古，仍然是这样的一个你。姓不姓蒙太古又有什么关系呢？它又不是手，又不是脚，又不是手臂，又不是脸，又不是身体上任何其他的部分。啊！换一个姓名吧！姓名本来是没有意义的；我们叫做玫瑰的这一种花，要是换了个名字，它的香味还是同样的芬芳；罗密欧要是换了别的名字，他的可爱的完美也决不会有丝毫改变。罗密欧，抛弃了你的名字吧；我愿意把我整个的心灵，赔偿你这一个身外的空名。

（朱生豪译《罗密欧与朱丽叶》第2幕第2场）

评点

　　二人年纪不大，却颇有主见。即便朱丽叶在舞会散场时已经得知情郎来自仇家，她也一意孤行，哪怕深知此路凶险——"昨天的仇敌，今日的情人，／这场恋爱怕要种下祸根"（Prodigious birth of love it is to me, / That I must love a loathed enemy）。罗密欧就更是如此，毫不犹豫地认命了，"我的生死现在操在我的仇人的手里了"（my life is my foe's debt）。二人也许有幼稚、任性之嫌，但他们的独立思考、勇敢追求、不畏艰险地坚守自己的自由意志，难能可贵。

　　朱丽叶关于"名实分离"的思考中采用了一个巧妙比喻："罗密欧"这个名字对于以此为名的人而言，就像"rose"一词对于以此为名的花那样，是身外之物，名字可以与人、物本身截然分离。花可以改其名而不改其香，罗密欧也可以改其名而不改其人。有此思想基础，朱丽叶就能坦然接受罗密欧的追求了，此后更是矢志不渝地坚持自己的选择。

场景 7：指月发誓

（"O, swear not by the moon …"）

> 月亮皎洁，佳人近在眼前。罗密欧指月发誓，试图让"月亮代表我的心"，可是被朱丽叶立马阻止。

Romeo   Lady, by yonder blessed moon I vow,
          That tips with silver all these fruit-tree tops—
Juliet   O swear not by the moon, th'inconstant moon[1],
          That monthly changes in her circled orb,
          Lest that thy love prove likewise variable[2].
Romeo   What shall I swear by?
Juliet   Do not swear at all,
          Or, if thou wilt, swear by thy gracious[3] self,
          Which is the god of my idolatry,
          And I'll believe thee.
Romeo   If my heart's dear love—
Juliet   Well, do not swear. Although I joy in thee,
          I have no joy of this contract tonight;
          It is too rash, too unadvised, too sudden,
          Too like the lightning which doth cease to be
          Ere one can say 'it lightens'. Sweet, good night.
          This bud of love by summer's ripening breath
          May prove a beauteous flower when next we meet.

(*Romeo and Juliet* 2.2)

---

[1] th'inconstant moon: The moon, because of its changes, was a common type of inconstancy.
[2] variable: changeable, uncertain.
[3] gracious: charming and attractive.

罗密欧 姑娘，凭着这一轮皎洁的月亮，它的银光涂染着这些果树的梢端，我发誓——

朱丽叶 啊！不要指着月亮起誓，它是变化无常的，每个月都有盈亏圆缺；你要是指着它起誓，也许你的爱情也会像它一样无常。

罗密欧 那么我指着什么起誓呢？

朱丽叶 不用起誓吧；或者要是你愿意的话，就凭着你优美的自身起誓，那是我所崇拜的偶像，我一定会相信你的。

罗密欧 要是我的出自深心的爱情——

朱丽叶 好，别起誓啦。我虽然喜欢你，却不喜欢今天晚上的密约；它太仓卒、太轻率、太出人意外了，正像一闪电光，等不及人家开一声口，已经消隐了下去。好人，再会吧！这一朵爱的蓓蕾，靠着夏天的暖风的吹拂，也许会在我们下次相见的时候，开出鲜艳的花来。

（朱生豪译《罗密欧与朱丽叶》第2幕第2场）

评点

相比罗密欧的情感冲动，朱丽叶则更为审慎而冷静，觉得感情问题不可仓促——"它太仓卒、太轻率、太出人意外了"（It is too rash, too unadvised, too sudden）。少女心思敏感微妙、矛盾重重：一方面希望山盟海誓，另一方面担心美好的爱情不能长久。

关于罗密欧拿来发誓的月亮，西方文化传统上是这样理解的：受托勒密宇宙观的影响，西方自古认为月亮之下的世界受月盈月亏的影响，因而阴晴不定、变化无常，与高高在上、恒定不变的恒星截然不同。朱丽叶不希望罗密欧的爱情有变，因而不愿罗密欧指月发誓。

在莎士比亚时代，北极星象征始终如一，正如莎士比亚笔下的凯撒（Caesar）所宣称的"我犹如北极星那样恒定"（I am constant as the northern star）。莎士比亚第116首十四行诗也以北极星比喻矢志不移的爱。不过，朱丽叶并不需要山盟海誓，因为她充分相信罗密欧的真心实意，甚至将罗密欧称为"我所崇拜的偶像"（the god of my idolatry）。

场景 8：情深似海

("My bounty is as boundless as the sea ...")

> 夜晚即将过去，这场秘密的阳台幽会随之结束。罗密欧与朱丽叶话别，情意绵绵，难舍难分……

Juliet　My bounty is as boundless as the sea,
　　　　My love as deep; the more I give to thee,
　　　　The more I have, for both are infinite.
　　　　…
Romeo　O blessed, blessed night! I am afeared,
　　　　Being in night, all this is but a dream,
　　　　Too flattering-sweet to be substantial.
……
Juliet　'Tis almost morning. I would have thee gone,
　　　　And yet no further than a wanton's[1] bird,
　　　　That lets it hop a little from her hand,
　　　　Like a poor prisoner in his[2] twisted gyves[3],
　　　　And with a silk thread plucks it back again,
　　　　So loving-jealous of his liberty.
Romeo　I would I were thy bird.
Juliet　　　　　　　　　　Sweet, so would I,
　　　　Yet I should kill thee with much cherishing.
　　　　Good night, good night! Parting is such sweet sorrow
　　　　That I shall say good night till it be morrow.

(*Romeo and Juliet* 2.2)

---

[1] wanton: naughty child. Juliet compares herself to a naughty boy and possessive master imprisoning a pet bird for love by keeping it on a silken thread.
[2] his: its.
[3] twisted gyves: interlaced shackles or fetters.

朱丽叶　我的慷慨像海一样浩渺，我的爱情也像海一样深沉；我给你的越多，我自己也越是富有，因为这两者都是没有穷尽的。……

罗密欧　幸福的，幸福的夜啊！我怕我只是在晚上做了一个梦，这样美满的事不会是真实的。

…………

朱丽叶　天快要亮了；我希望你快去；可是我就好比一个淘气的女孩子，像放松一个囚犯似的让她心爱的鸟儿暂时跳出她的掌心，又用一根丝线把它拉了回来，爱的私心使她不愿意给它自由。

罗密欧　我但愿我是你的鸟儿。

朱丽叶　好人，我也但愿这样；可是我怕你会死在我的过分的爱抚里。晚安！晚安！离别是这样甜蜜的凄清，我真要向你道晚安直到天明！

（朱生豪译《罗密欧与朱丽叶》第2幕第2场）

评点

　　朱丽叶与罗密欧一样擅作情诗，其台词甚至更加深情而动人。其中，"我的慷慨像海一样浩渺"（My bounty is as boundless as the sea）一句呼应了朱丽叶在婚礼前对罗密欧所说的"真诚的爱情充溢在我的心里，我无法估计自己享有的财富"（But my true love is grown to such excess / I cannot sum up sum of half my wealth）。

　　该选段末尾的鸟之喻，形象地突显了二人亲密程度。他们的爱情完美至极，令人隐隐有不祥之感——不仅罗密欧感觉如同梦幻，而且朱丽叶有意无意地提到"可是我怕你会死在我的过分的爱抚里"（Yet I should kill thee with much cherishing）。二人谈情说爱，大量使用死亡意象，一方面极言其爱，另一方面也预示着结局。

场景 9：善恶共生

("Virtue itself turns vice, being misapplied.")

> 罗密欧与朱丽叶告别之时已接近清晨。罗密欧径直去了教堂，等候大清早上教堂院子里采药的劳伦斯神父。这是劳伦斯神父在剧中的首次出场。

Friar Laurence Now, ere the sun advance[1] his burning eye,
The day to cheer and night's dank[2] dew to dry,
I must up-fill[3] this osier[4] cage[5] of ours
With baleful[6] weeds and precious-juiced[7] flowers.
The earth that's nature's mother is her tomb,
What is her burying grave, that is her womb;
And from her womb children of divers kind
We sucking on her natural bosom find,
Many for many virtues excellent,
None but for some, and yet all different.
O, mickle[8] is the powerful grace that lies
In herbs, plants, stones and their true qualities,
For nought[9] so vile that on the earth doth live
But to the earth some special good doth give,
Nor aught[10] so good but, strained[11] from that fair use,
Revolts from true birth, stumbling on abuse.
Virtue itself turns vice, being misapplied,
And vice sometimes by action dignified.

---

[1] advance: raise.
[2] dank: damp.
[3] up-fill: fill up.
[4] osier: i.e. made of willow twigs.
[5] cage: basket.
[6] baleful: deadly or noxious.
[7] precious-juiced: full of natural goodness.
[8] mickle: (archaic) great or much.
[9] nought: nothing.
[10] aught: anything.
[11] strained: perverted, used beyond its province.

> Within the infant rind of this weak flower
> Poison hath residence and medicine power,
> For this, being smelled, with that part cheers each part,
> Being tasted, slays all senses with the heart.
> Two such opposed kings encamp them still[1]
> In man as well as herbs, grace and rude will,
> And where the worser is predominant,
> Full soon the canker death eats up that plant.

(*Romeo and Juliet* 2.3)

劳伦斯 黎明笑向着含愠的残宵，金鳞浮上了东方的天梢；看赤轮驱走了片片乌云，像一群醉汉向四处狼奔。趁太阳还没有睁开火眼，晒干深夜里的涔涔露点，我待要采摘下满篮盈筐，毒草灵葩充实我的青囊。大地是生化万类的慈母，她又是掩藏群生的坟墓，试看她无所不载的胸怀，哺乳着多少的娇女婴孩！天生下的万物没有弃掷，什么都有它各自的特色，石块的冥顽，草木的无知，都含着玄妙的造化生机。莫看那蠢蠢的恶木莠蔓，对世间都有它特殊贡献；即使最纯良的美谷嘉禾，用得失当也会害性戕躯。美德的误用会变成罪过，罪恶有时反会造成善果。这一朵有毒的弱蕊纤苞，也会把淹煎的痼疾医疗；它的香味可以祛除百病，吃下腹中却会昏迷不醒。草木和人心并没有不同，各自有善意和恶念争雄；恶的势力倘然占了上风，死便会蛀蚀进它的心中。

（朱生豪译《罗密欧与朱丽叶》第 2 幕第 3 场）

评点

这番独白不仅展现了劳伦斯神父精通草药，为他后来用"假死药"帮助朱丽叶逃婚埋下了伏笔，而且神父通过对自然花草的理解臻至化境，从中洞悉人性与世界的复杂多样。

就语言文风而言，大量使用修辞手法，充满想象与哲思，成对的反义词层出不穷，具有鲜明的辩证色彩，例如 tomb/grave 与 womb、virtue/good 与 vile/vice、fair use 与 abuse、poison 与 medicine。

神父虽然睿智，但是他在帮助罗密欧与朱丽叶时，几乎好心办坏事。正如他在独白中所说："美德的误用会变成罪过，罪恶有时反会造成善果。"（Virtue itself turns vice, being misapplied, / And vice sometimes by action dignified.）

---

[1] still: always.

场景 10：见异思迁

("Is Rosaline … so soon forsaken?")

> 劳伦斯神父虽是配角，但是在剧中是一个至关重要的人物。罗密欧与朱丽叶都高度信赖劳伦斯神父，二人从秘密结婚到假死逃脱，再到墓地殉情，事事征求神父的意见。在此，罗密欧突然说要立马娶朱丽叶，令劳伦斯神父备感意外。

Friar Laurence　Holy Saint Francis[1], what a change is here!
　　　　　　　　Is Rosaline, that thou didst love so dear,
　　　　　　　　So soon forsaken? Young men's love then lies
　　　　　　　　Not truly in their hearts, but in their eyes.
　　　　　　　　Jesu Maria[2], what a deal of brine[3]
　　　　　　　　Hath washed thy sallow[4] cheeks for Rosaline!
　　　　　　　　How much salt water thrown away in waste,
　　　　　　　　To season love that of it doth not taste!
　　　　　　　　The sun not yet thy sighs from heaven clears,
　　　　　　　　Thy old groans ring yet in my ancient ears.
　　　　　　　　Lo, here upon thy cheek the stain doth sit
　　　　　　　　Of an old tear that is not washed off yet.
　　　　　　　　If e'er thou wast thyself and these woes thine,
　　　　　　　　Thou and these woes were all for Rosaline.
　　　　　　　　And art thou changed? Pronounce this sentence[5] then:
　　　　　　　　Women may fall when there's no strength in men.

(*Romeo and Juliet* 2.3)

---

[1] Holy Saint Francis：a mild oath suitable to a priest. 感叹语，相当于"天啊"。
[2] Jesu Maria: a distinctly Catholic exclamation or mild oath.
[3] brine: salt water, i.e. tears.
[4] sallow: brownish in complexion.
[5] sentence: maxim.

劳伦斯 圣芳济啊！多么快的变化！难道你所深爱着的罗瑟琳，就这样一下子被你抛弃了吗？这样看来，年轻人的爱情，都是见异思迁，不是发于真心的。耶稣，马利亚！你为了罗瑟琳的缘故，曾经用多少的眼泪洗过你消瘦的面庞！为了替无味的爱情添加一点辛酸的味道，曾经浪费掉多少的咸水！太阳还没有扫清你吐向苍穹的怨气，我这龙钟的耳朵里还留着你往日的呻吟；瞧！就在你自己的颊上，还剩着一丝不曾揩去的旧时的泪痕。要是你不曾变了一个人，这些悲哀都是你真实的情感，那么你是罗瑟琳的，这些悲哀也是为罗瑟琳而发的；难道你现在已经变心了吗？男人既然这样没有恒心，那就莫怪女人家朝三暮四了。

（朱生豪译《罗密欧与朱丽叶》第 2 幕第 3 场）

评点

　　劳伦斯神父的意外、不解与责备并不奇怪，不仅是因为罗密欧与朱丽叶来自不共戴天的仇家，而且此前让罗密欧害相思病的是罗瑟琳，怎么突然改成朱丽叶了？神父批评罗密欧草率、冲动："年轻人的爱情，都是见异思迁，不是发于真心的。"（Young men's love then lies / Not truly in their hearts, but in their eyes.）这一段采用非常工整的英雄双韵体，两两押韵，铿锵有力。

　　最终，劳伦斯神父同意为二人举办秘密婚礼。毋庸置疑，劳伦斯神父一片好心，希望两家仇敌从此化干戈为玉帛（To turn your households' rancour to pure love）。不过，世事难料，阴差阳错，如此秘密行动，当事人承担的责任及风险显然不小。

场景 11：飘风不终朝

（"These violent delights have violent ends."）

> 在举办秘密婚礼之前，劳伦斯神父不无顾虑，而罗密欧不顾一切，急不可耐。神父不免又耳提面命一番。一老一少，一缓一急，对比鲜明。

Friar Laurence　So smile the heavens upon this holy act
　　　　　　　That after-hours[1] with sorrow chide us not!
Romeo　　　　Amen, amen, but come what sorrow can,
　　　　　　　It cannot countervail[2] the exchange of joy
　　　　　　　That one short minute gives me in her sight.
　　　　　　　Do thou but close[3] our hands with holy words,
　　　　　　　Then love-devouring death[4] do what he dare,
　　　　　　　It is enough I may but call her mine.
Friar Laurence　These violent delights have violent ends
　　　　　　　And in their triumph die, like fire and powder,
　　　　　　　Which, as they kiss, consume. The sweetest honey
　　　　　　　Is loathsome in his[5] own deliciousness,
　　　　　　　And in the taste confounds[6] the appetite.[7]
　　　　　　　Therefore love moderately; long love doth so;
　　　　　　　Too swift arrives as tardy as too slow.

(*Romeo and Juliet* 2.6)

---

[1] after-hours: in times to come.
[2] countervail: match in value.
[3] close: join together.
[4] love-devouring death: proverbial, "Death devours all things".
[5] his: its.
[6] confound: ruin.
[7] The idea in this sentence is proverbial, "Too much honey cloys the stomach".

劳伦斯　愿上天祝福这神圣的结合，不要让日后的懊恨把我们谴责！

罗密欧　阿门，阿门！可是无论将来会发生什么悲哀的后果，都抵不过我在看见她这短短一分钟内的欢乐。不管侵蚀爱情的死亡怎样伸展它的魔手，只要你用神圣的言语，把我们的灵魂结为一体，让我能够称她一声我的人，我也就不再有什么遗恨了。

劳伦斯　这种狂暴的快乐将会产生狂暴的结局，正像火和火药的亲吻，就在最得意的一刹那烟消云散。最甜的蜜糖可以使味觉麻木；不太热烈的爱情才会维持久远；太快和太慢，结果都不会圆满。

（朱生豪译《罗密欧与朱丽叶》第 2 幕第 6 场）

评点

罗密欧爱情至上、无所顾忌，充满干柴烈火般的激情，其措辞中的 sorrow、short、death 等词有不祥之兆……劳伦斯神父作为稳重的长辈，则强调情感的克制，推崇细水长流，以期长久维持。例如，"这种狂暴的快乐将会产生狂暴的结局"（These violent delights have violent ends），"不太热烈的爱情才会维持久远"（love moderately; long love doth so），"太快和太慢，结果都不会圆满"（Too swift arrives as tardy as too slow）。

这些逆耳忠言都是老生常谈的箴言谚语，中国传统文化中也不乏类似的古训，在当今也毫不过时。上述第一句呼应着《道德经》中的"飘风不终朝，骤雨不终日"，第二句类似于"平平淡淡才是真，细水长流才是爱"，最后一句与我国成语"欲速则不达""过犹不及"异曲同工。

场景 12：棒打鸳鸯

("'Tis torture, and not mercy …")

> 罗密欧刚结婚，就被卷入一场与朱丽叶表哥提伯尔特的决斗，闹出人命官司，被判流放。罗密欧躲在劳伦斯神父那儿，尽情宣泄悲伤与绝望。

Romeo   'Tis torture, and not mercy. Heaven is here
Where Juliet lives, and every cat and dog
And little mouse, every unworthy thing,
Live here in heaven and may look on her;
But Romeo may not. More validity[1],
More honourable state, more courtship[2] lives
In carrion flies than Romeo. They may seize
On the white wonder[3] of dear Juliet's hand
And steal immortal[4] blessing from her lips,
Who even in pure and vestal[5] modesty,
Still blush, as thinking their own kisses sin.
But Romeo may not, he is banished:
Flies may do this, but I from this must fly;
They are free men, but I am banished:
And sayest thou yet that exile is not death?
Hadst thou no poison mixed, no sharp-ground knife,
No sudden mean of death, though ne'er so mean[6],
But 'banished' to kill me? Banished!

(*Romeo and Juliet* 3.3)

---

[1] validity: soundness.
[2] courtship: behavior befitting a courtier.
[3] white wonder: pale skin was a sign of upper-class origin, proof that a person was not engaged in manual or outdoor work such as farming.
[4] immortal: because "Heaven is here / Where Juliet lives".
[5] vestal: virginal.
[6] mean: 这一行有两个 mean。前一个是名词，表示 method；后一个是形容词，意为 base。

罗密欧　这是酷刑，不是恩典。朱丽叶所在的地方就是天堂；这儿的每一只猫、每一只狗、每一只小小的老鼠，都生活在天堂里，都可以瞻仰到她的容颜，可是罗密欧却看不见她。污秽的苍蝇都可以接触亲爱的朱丽叶的皎洁的玉手，从她的嘴唇上偷取天堂中的幸福，那两片嘴唇是这样的纯洁贞淑，永远含着娇羞，好像觉得它们自身的相吻也是一种罪恶；苍蝇可以这样做，我却必须远走高飞，它们是自由人，我却是一个放逐的流徒。你还说放逐不是死吗？难道你没有配好的毒药、锋锐的刀子或者无论什么致命的利器，而必须用"放逐"两个字把我杀害吗？放逐！

（朱生豪译《罗密欧与朱丽叶》第3幕第3场）

评点

尽管凯普莱特家族（尤其是朱丽叶之母）极力要求罗密欧以命偿命——罗密欧杀死了提伯尔特（Tybalt），但是亲王仅宣判罗密欧流放。这不是简单地偏袒蒙太古家族，因为提伯尔特作为这场恶性斗殴的挑起人，也有命案在身——罗密欧的好友、亲王的亲戚茂丘西奥（Mercutio）就丧生于提伯尔特的剑下。

无论是综合考虑事件本身的公正问题，还是为了平衡两大家族的势力、安抚人性，亲王的这一判决都是合情合理的，连劳伦斯神父都称为"mercy"。然而，罗密欧无法忍受即将背井离乡的未来，因为那意味着与爱人长期隔绝，重逢时日遥遥无期。

罗密欧的这番悲痛欲绝的言辞堪比《李尔王》中的李尔王哀悼爱女考狄利娅（Cordelia）：罗密欧说自己还不如牲畜幸福，因为畜生都能跟朱丽叶一起待在城里，而自己却被流放（every cat and dog / And little mouse, every unworthy thing, / Live here in heaven and may look on her）；李尔王则哀叹为什么卑贱的牲畜都有生命而爱女却死了（Why should a dog, a horse, a rat have life / And thou no breath at all？）。二者都以牲畜来反衬人的不幸，罗列排比的手法更显悲伤。

场景 13：晨曦话别

("Art thou gone so, love, lord, ay husband, friend?")

> 罗密欧结婚当天即因杀人而被流放。虽然朱丽叶的表兄是罗密欧所杀，但是朱丽叶并没因此疏远罗密欧。二人共度新婚之夜，随即罗密欧必须在天亮之前出城。二人离别之时，难舍难分，朱丽叶心中充满了不祥的预感……

Juliet	Art thou gone so, love, lord, ay husband, friend?
	I must hear from thee every day in the hour,
	For in a minute there are many days.
	O, by this count I shall be much in years
	Ere I again behold my Romeo.
Romeo	Farewell.
	I will omit no opportunity
	That may convey my greetings, love, to thee.
Juliet	O, think'st thou we shall ever meet again?
Romeo	I doubt it not, and all these woes shall serve
	For sweet discourses in our times to come.
Juliet	O God, I have an ill-divining soul!
	Methinks I see thee now, thou art so low,
	As one dead in the bottom of a tomb.
	Either my eyesight fails, or thou look'st pale.
Romeo	And trust me, love, in my eye so do you.
	Dry sorrow drinks our blood. Adieu, adieu!

(*Romeo and Juliet* 3.5)

朱丽叶	你就这样走了吗？我的夫君，我的爱人，我的朋友！我必须在每一小时内的每一天听到你的消息，因为一分钟就等于许多天。啊！照这样计算起来，等我再看见我的罗密欧的时候，我不知道已经老到怎样了。
罗密欧	再会！我决不放弃任何的机会，爱人，向你传达我的衷忱。
朱丽叶	啊！你想我们会不会再有见面的日子？
罗密欧	一定会有的；我们现在这一切悲哀痛苦，到将来便是握手谈心的资料。
朱丽叶	上帝啊！我有一颗预感不祥的灵魂；你现在站在下面，我仿佛望见你像一具坟墓底下的尸骸。也许是我的眼光昏花，否则就是你的面容太惨白了。
罗密欧	相信我，爱人，在我的眼中你也是这样；忧伤吸干了我们的血液。再会！再会！

（朱生豪译《罗密欧与朱丽叶》第 3 幕第 5 场）

评点

尽管朱丽叶的表兄死于罗密欧之手，但是朱丽叶决定不受家族仇杀的影响，依然选择做罗密欧的妻子，罗密欧与朱丽叶的爱情经受住了一次重大考验。朱丽叶年纪虽小，却头脑清醒，情绪稳定，且极有主见。

这是一番令人柔肠寸断的漫长道别：朱丽叶问了不止一次"你就这样走了吗"，一留再留，想尽可能地延长与罗密欧相处的时间；后来发现时间不早了，留不住了，即便罗密欧一再承诺，朱丽叶也依然追问"会不会再有见面的日子"。日后谁也无法预料，即便当事人做出了种种努力，结果却是永别。

当朱丽叶俯身张望阳台下的罗密欧，她眼中的爱人就像"一具坟墓底下的尸骸"（one dead in the bottom of a tomb），这与剧终的墓地场景遥相呼应，可谓一语成谶。

场景 14：贫穷致恶

("The world affords no law to make thee rich.")

> 面对父母逼婚，朱丽叶凭借劳伦斯神父给她的假死药而成功逃婚。原本下一步就是远走高飞，偏偏劳伦斯神父的密信被耽误了，而罗密欧抢先一步回来了！罗密欧误以为朱丽叶已死，顿时万念俱灰，去买毒药。

Romeo   Art thou so bare[1] and full of wretchedness,
          And fearest to die? Famine is in thy cheeks,
          Need and oppression starveth in thine eyes,
          Contempt and beggary hangs upon thy back,
          The world is not thy friend, nor the world's law;
          The world affords no law to make thee rich;
          Then be not poor, but break it, and take this.
Apothecary   My poverty, but not my will, consents.
Romeo   I pay thy poverty, and not thy will.
Apothecary   Put this in any liquid thing you will,
          And drink it off; and, if you had the strength
          Of twenty men, it would dispatch you straight.
Romeo   There is thy gold, worse poison to men's souls,
          Doing more murders in this loathsome world,
          Than these poor compounds[2] that thou mayst not sell.
          I sell thee poison; thou hast sold me none.
          Farewell: buy food, and get thyself in flesh.

(*Romeo and Juliet* 5.1)

---

[1] bare: naked, exposed.
[2] compounds: drugs (chemical compounds).

二、《罗密欧与朱丽叶》

罗密欧　难道你这样穷苦，还怕死吗？饥寒的痕迹刻在你的面颊上，贫乏和迫害在你的眼睛里射出了饿火，轻蔑和卑贱重压在你的背上；这世间不是你的朋友，这世间的法律也保护不到你，没有人为你定下一条法律使你富有；那么你何必苦耐着贫穷呢？违犯了法律，把这些钱收下吧。

卖药人　我的贫穷答应了你，可是那是违反我的良心的。

罗密欧　我的钱是给你的贫穷，不是给你的良心的。

卖药人　把这一服药放在无论什么饮料里喝下去，即使你有二十个人的气力，也会立刻送命。

罗密欧　这儿是你的钱，那才是害人灵魂的更坏的毒药，在这万恶的世界上，它比你那些不准贩卖的微贱的药品更会杀人；你没有把毒药卖给我，是我把毒药卖给你。再见；买些吃的东西，把你自己喂得胖一点。

（朱生豪译《罗密欧与朱丽叶》第5幕第1场）

评点

　　买毒药一段只是整个剧情的细枝末节，莎士比亚却不是一笔带过，而是借题发挥地谈论贫困与罪恶的关系，以及金钱对人性的腐蚀，由此突破了贵族阶层的爱恨情仇与才子佳人的卿卿我我，叠加了更为广阔的人生百态、更为幽暗的复杂人性，增添了作品的维度与内涵。此时的罗密欧可谓亡命之徒，一改往日的温文尔雅，措辞尖刻犀利，毫不留情。

　　"金钱乃万恶之源"是西方文学传统上的一大主题。罗密欧认为金钱比毒药更毒，这在莎士比亚戏剧中并不罕见。无论喜剧《威尼斯商人》，还是悲剧《雅典的泰门》，就此话题都有长篇论述，与罗密欧相比，有过之而无不及。不过，罗密欧不是单纯批判金钱之罪，他还看到贫穷之恶——穷人经不起金钱的诱惑，容易被金钱收买，为了金钱铤而走险，甚至不惜违背良心与法律。这个卖药人就是一个典型。

场景15：饮鸩殉情

（"Here's to my love."）

> 罗密欧带着毒药连夜赶到凯普莱特家族的墓室。在极度悲伤绝望之中，他杀死了一位守墓人——同样哀悼朱丽叶的帕里斯！罗密欧在一番柔肠寸断的抒情独白之后，饮鸩而亡……

Romeo　O my love, my wife,
Death, that hath sucked the honey of thy breath
Hath had no power yet upon thy beauty.
Thou art not conquered. Beauty's ensign[1] yet
Is crimson in thy lips and in thy cheeks,
And death's pale flag is not advanced there.
Tybalt, liest thou there in thy bloody sheet?
O, what more favour can I do to thee
Than with that hand that cut thy youth in twain
To sunder his that was thine enemy?
Forgive me, cousin! Ah, dear Juliet,
Why art thou yet so fair? Shall I believe
That unsubstantial death is amorous,
And that the lean abhorred monster keeps
Thee here in dark to be his paramour?
For fear of that I still[2] will stay with thee;
And never from this palace of dim night
Depart again. Here, here will I remain
With worms that are thy chambermaids. O, here
Will I set up my everlasting rest,
And shake the yoke of inauspicious stars
From this world-wearied flesh. Eyes, look your last;
Arms, take your last embrace, and lips, O you
The doors of breath, seal with a righteous kiss

---

[1] ensign: banner, standard.
[2] still: always.

A dateless[1] bargain to engrossing[2] death.
Come, bitter conduct[3], come, unsavoury guide.
Thou desperate pilot, now at once run on
The dashing rocks thy seasick weary bark[4]!
Here's to my love.

(*Romeo and Juliet* 5.3)

罗密欧　啊，我的爱人！我的妻子！死虽然已经吸去了你呼吸中的芳蜜，却还没有力量摧残你的美貌；你还没有被他征服，你的嘴唇上、面庞上，依然显着红润的美艳，不曾让灰白的死亡进占。提伯尔特，你也裹着你的血淋淋的殓衾躺在那儿吗？啊！你的青春葬送在你仇人的手里，现在我来替你报仇来了，我要亲手杀死那杀害你的人。原谅我吧，兄弟！啊！亲爱的朱丽叶，你为什么仍然这样美丽？难道那虚无的死亡，那枯瘦可憎的妖魔，也是个多情种子，所以把你藏匿在这幽暗的洞府里做他的情妇吗？为了防止这样的事情，我要永远陪伴着你，再不离开这漫漫长夜的幽宫；我要留在这儿，跟你的侍婢，那些蛆虫们在一起；啊！我要在这儿永久安息下来，从我这厌倦人世的凡躯上挣脱恶运的束缚。眼睛，瞧你的最后一眼吧！手臂，作你最后一次的拥抱吧！嘴唇，啊！你呼吸的门户，用一个合法的吻，跟网罗一切的死亡订立一个永久的契约吧！来，苦味的向导，绝望的领港人，现在赶快把你的厌倦于风涛的船舶向那巉岩上冲撞过去吧！为了我的爱人，我干了这一杯！

（朱生豪译《罗密欧与朱丽叶》第 5 幕第 3 场）

评点

　　在罗密欧饮鸩殉情之时，朱丽叶其实并没有死，而是处于正在苏醒之中。等她醒来，发现罗密欧真的死了，她也不愿独存于世了……阴差阳错之间，二人失之交臂，令人扼腕叹息。无论古今中外，双双殉情的爱情故事最为动人，中国也有《梁祝》《孔雀东南飞》等传统经典。

　　罗密欧的这番悼词中运用了不少修辞手法，尤其是拟人与比喻，哪怕描述死亡，也充满了诗情画意。西方文化历来有将抽象的死亡具象化为死神的传统。在罗密欧看来，朱丽叶死了，就是因为死神爱上了朱丽叶而把她劫去冥府了；罗密欧则视死神为情敌，表示要不惜一切代价守护朱丽叶。

---

[1] dateless: everlasting.
[2] engrossing: devouring.
[3] conduct: i.e. the poison.
[4] thy seasick weary bark: It refers to Romeo's own body.

三、《裘力斯·凯撒》

(Julius Caesar)
(1599)

"并不是我不爱凯撒,可是我更爱罗马。"
(Not that I loved Caesar less, but that I loved Rome more.)

　　莎士比亚悲剧《裘力斯·凯撒》取材于古罗马历史,既有波澜壮阔的战争场面,又有微妙细腻的儿女情长,更有"刺杀独裁者"是否正义之举、是否明智之选的伦理哲思。一如"吾爱吾师,吾更爱真理"的亚里士多德,莎翁笔下的勃鲁托斯(Marcus Brutus)宣称"并不是我不爱凯撒,可是我更爱罗马"——千百年来,勃鲁托斯的"大义灭亲"令人莫衷一是,见仁见智。

　　虽然这部剧以凯撒(Julius Caesar)命名,但是剧中的真正主角是刺杀凯撒的两个主谋——罗马贵族领袖勃鲁托斯与凯歇斯(Caius Cassius)。其中,勃鲁托斯在此二人关系中起主导作用,是该剧真正的主人公。

　　在这部5幕剧中,凯撒死于正当中——第3幕第1场,凯歇斯死于第5幕第3场,勃鲁托斯死于剧终一场——第5幕第5场。与其说《裘力斯·凯撒》展现凯撒的人生,不如说这是一部以勃鲁托斯为焦点、展现古罗马城共和制下统治精英的集体悲剧。

《裘力斯·凯撒》（*Julius Caesar*）

场景 1：危机四伏（"Let no images be hung with Caesar's trophies."）1.1

场景 2：以人为镜（"Tell me, good Brutus, can you see your face?"）1.2

场景 3：荣誉至上（"I love the name of honour more than I fear death."）1.2

场景 4：独霸天下（"He doth bestride the narrow world like a Colossus."）1.2

场景 5：大义灭亲（"And therefore think him as a serpent's egg …"）2.1

场景 6：宗教献祭（"Let's be sacrificers but not butchers."）2.1

场景 7：家有贤妻（"I grant I am a woman, but …"）2.1

场景 8：无所畏惧（"The valiant never taste of death but once."）2.2

场景 9：凯撒遇刺（"Et tu, Brute？— Then fall, Caesar."）3.1

场景 10：留名青史（"The men who gave their country liberty"）3.1

场景 11：报仇雪恨（"Caesar's spirit, ranging for revenge …"）3.1

场景 12：取信于民（"Believe me for mine honour."）3.2

场景 13：欲擒故纵（"Brutus is an honourable man."）3.2

场景 14：群情激昂（"… move the stones of Rome to rise and mutiny."）3.2

场景 15：亡灵索命（"… thou shalt see me at Philippi."）4.3

场景 16：生离死别（"… 'tis true this parting was well made."）5.1

场景1：危机四伏

("Let no images be hung with Caesar's trophies.")

> 开篇伊始，古罗马城表面上一片欢腾，其实却剑拔弩张。两位护民官（tribunes）在街头严厉斥责欢迎凯撒（Caesar）凯旋的罗马民众……凯撒如日中天之时，也是危机四伏之秋。

Murellus　Wherefore rejoice? What conquest brings he home?
　　　　　What tributaries[1] follow him to Rome
　　　　　To grace in captive bonds his chariot wheels?
　　　　　You blocks, you stones, you worse than senseless[2] things!
　　　　　O you hard hearts, you cruel men of Rome,
　　　　　Knew you not Pompey[3]? …

Flavius　… See where their basest mettle[4] be not moved.
　　　　　They vanish tongue-tied in their guiltiness.
　　　　　Go you down that way towards the Capitol[5].
　　　　　This way will I. Disrobe the images[6],
　　　　　If you do find them decked[7] with ceremonies.

Murellus　May we do so?
　　　　　You know it is the feast of Lupercal[8].

Flavius　It is no matter. Let no images
　　　　　Be hung with Caesar's trophies. I'll about,

---

[1] tributaries: payers of tribute.
[2] senseless: incapable of sense, both as feeling and as wisdom.
[3] Pompey: Gnaeus Pompeius (106 BC–48 BC), is an outstanding general and a first triumvir with Caesar and Crassus. Later Caesar defeated him and Pompey fled and died.
[4] their basest mettle: The commoners have the basest spirit, rapidly affected; they are also of the basest metal in creation, lead, which melts most quickly.
[5] Capitol: It was the great national temple of Rome, dedicated to Jupiter, overlooking the Forum.
[6] images: i.e. statues of Caesar.
[7] decked: adorned.
[8] Lupercal: 15 February. Lupercus, a rural deity associated with Pan and the legendary history of the founding of Rome, brought fertility. The Lupercal was also a cave where a wolf suckled Romulus and Remus.

And drive away the vulgar[1] from the streets.
So do you too, where you perceive them thick.
These growing feathers plucked from Caesar's wing
Will make him fly an ordinary pitch[2],
Who else[3] would soar above the view of men
And keep us all in servile fearfulness.

(*Julius Caesar* 1.1)

马鲁勒斯　为什么要庆祝呢？他带了些什么胜利回来？他的战车后面缚着几个纳土称臣的俘囚君长？你们这些木头石块，冥顽不灵的东西！冷酷无情的罗马人啊，你们忘记了庞贝吗？……

弗莱维斯　……瞧这些下流的材料也会天良发现；他们因为自知有罪，一个个哑口无言地去了。您打那一条路向圣殿走去；我打这一条路走。要是您看见他们在偶像上披着锦衣彩饰，就把它撕下来。

马鲁勒斯　我们可以这样做吗？您知道今天是卢柏克节。

弗莱维斯　别管它；不要让偶像身上悬挂着凯撒的胜利品。我要去驱散街上的愚民；您要是看见什么地方有许多人聚集在一起，也要把他们赶散。我们应当趁早剪拔凯撒的羽毛，让他无力高飞；要是他羽毛既长，一飞冲天，我们大家都要在他的足下俯伏听命了。

（朱生豪译《裘力斯·凯撒》第1幕第1场）

评点

　　凯撒凯旋，古罗马城因此撕裂为两种截然不同的立场：民众大多支持凯撒，而古罗马城的不少政治精英则反对凯撒。于是，凯撒与政治精英之间、政治精英与普通民众之间产生了难以调和的尖锐矛盾。

　　古罗马政治演讲在这部剧中得到充分体现：剧中几个关键政治领袖都有精彩发言。开场发言的两位护民官（古罗马公民选举出来以保护民众权利的官员）虽然是小角色，但是也充分展现了公众演讲的强大震撼力与说服力。不过，二人对普通民众的态度显得居高临下、趾高气扬，他们在高度警惕专制集权的同时，不免表露出过强的精英意识，为后来的内战埋下了伏笔。

---

[1] the vulgar: the common people (less pejorative than today).
[2] pitch: the highest point a falcon reaches before swooping on prey.
[3] else: otherwise.

场景 2：以人为镜

("Tell me, good Brutus, can you see your face?")

凯撒凯旋，两位罗马贵族凯歇斯（Cassius）与勃鲁托斯（Brutus）在一旁冷眼旁观、忧心忡忡。凯歇斯积极拉拢勃鲁托斯，以期结成反凯撒联盟。

Cassius … Tell me, good Brutus, can you see your face?

Brutus No, Cassius; for the eye sees not itself
But by reflection, by some other things.

Cassius 'Tis just[1],
And it is very much lamented, Brutus,
That you have no such mirrors as will turn
Your hidden worthiness into your eye,
That you might see your shadow[2]: I have heard
Where many of the best respect[3] in Rome
(Except immortal Caesar) speaking of Brutus,
And groaning underneath this age's yoke,
Have wished that noble Brutus had his eyes.

Brutus Into what dangers would you lead me, Cassius,
That you would have me seek into myself
For that which is not in me?

Cassius Therefore[4], good Brutus, be prepared to hear.
And since you know you cannot see yourself
So well as by reflection, I your glass

---

[1] just: true.
[2] shadow: reflection.
[3] best respect: highest rank.
[4] therefore: as to that.

Will modestly discover[1] to yourself

That of yourself which you yet know not of.

(*Julius Caesar* 1.2)

凯歇斯	……告诉我，好勃鲁托斯，您能够瞧见您自己的脸吗？
勃鲁托斯	不，凯歇斯；因为眼睛不能瞧见它自己，必须借着反射，借着外物的力量。
凯歇斯	不错，勃鲁托斯，可惜您却没有这样的镜子，可以把您隐藏着的贤德照到您的眼里，让您看见您自己的影子。我曾经听见那些在罗马最有名望的人——除了不朽的凯撒以外——说起勃鲁托斯，他们呻吟于当前的桎梏之下，都希望高贵的勃鲁托斯睁开他的眼睛。
勃鲁托斯	凯歇斯，您要我在我自己身上寻找我所没有的东西，到底是要引导我去干什么危险的事呢？
凯歇斯	所以，好勃鲁托斯，留心听着吧；您既然知道您不能瞧见您自己，像在镜子里照得那样清楚，我就可以做您的镜子，并不夸大地把您自己所不知道的自己揭露给您看。

（朱生豪译《裘力斯·凯撒》第1幕第2场）

评点

凯歇斯深谙人性：哪怕他明知勃鲁托斯颇受凯撒器重，他也能劝说勃鲁托斯参与刺杀凯撒的计划。在凯歇斯的诸多劝说技巧之中，其镜子之喻颇为巧妙、摄人心魄，就连勃鲁托斯也不得不引起警惕。

---

[1] modestly discover: disclose without exaggeration.

场景 3：荣誉至上

("I love the name of honour more than I fear death.")

> 勃鲁托斯向来高度注重个人荣誉。于是，凯歇斯便强调凯撒的权力过分膨胀，威胁到个人的尊严与自由。这样有针对性的循循善诱对游说勃鲁托斯颇为有效。

Brutus　What means this shouting? I do fear the people
　　　　Choose Caesar for their king.

Cassius　　　　　　　　　　　Ay, do you fear it?
　　　　Then must I think you would not have it so.

Brutus　I would not, Cassius, yet I love him well.
　　　　But wherefore do you hold me here so long?
　　　　What is it that you would impart to me?
　　　　If it be aught toward the general good,
　　　　Set honour in one eye, and death i'th' other,
　　　　And I will look on both indifferently[1].
　　　　For let the gods so speed[2] me as I love
　　　　The name of honour more than I fear death.

Cassius　I know that virtue to be in you, Brutus,
　　　　As well as I do know your outward favour[3].
　　　　Well, honour is the subject of my story.
　　　　I cannot tell what you and other men
　　　　Think of this life; but for my single self
　　　　I had as lief[4] not be as live to be In awe of such a thing as
　　　　I myself[5]. I was born free as Caesar, so were you;

---

[1] indifferently: impartially.
[2] speed: make prosper, echoing "God speed".
[3] favour: appearance, countenance.
[4] lief: soon.
[5] such a thing as I myself: a human being like me.

> We both have fed as well, and we can both
> Endure the winter's cold as well as he.
> …
> Ye gods, it doth amaze me
> A man of such a feeble temper[1] should
> So get the start of the majestic world
> And bear the palm[2] alone.

(*Julius Caesar* 1.2)

勃鲁托斯　这一阵欢呼是什么意思？我怕人民会选举凯撒做他们的王。
凯歇斯　嗯，您怕吗？那么看来您是不赞成这回事了。
勃鲁托斯　我不赞成，凯歇斯；虽然我很敬爱他。可是您为什么拉住我在这儿？您有什么话要对我说？倘然那是对大众有利的事，那么让我的一只眼睛看见光荣，另一只眼睛看见死亡，我也会同样无动于衷地正视着它们；因为我喜爱光荣的名字，甚于恐惧死亡，这自有神明作证。
凯歇斯　我知道您有那样内心的美德，勃鲁托斯，正像我知道您的外貌一样。好，光荣正是我的谈话的题目。我不知道您和其他的人对于这一个人生抱着怎样的观念；可是拿我个人而论，假如要我为了自己而担惊受怕，那么我还是不要活着的好。我生下来就跟凯撒同样的自由；您也是一样。我们都跟他同样地享受过，同样地能够忍耐冬天的寒冷。……神啊，像这样一个心神软弱的人，却会征服这个伟大的世界，独占着胜利的光荣，真是我再也想不到的事。

（朱生豪译《裘力斯·凯撒》第 1 幕第 2 场）

评点

　　作为一位出身高贵的古罗马人，勃鲁托斯视荣誉高于一切，甚至高于生命。他后来刺杀凯撒并最终自杀，都是为不惜一切代价捍卫其荣誉。
　　勃鲁托斯不同于凯歇斯：凯歇斯与凯撒一向不和，彼此都心存芥蒂；勃鲁托斯则不但与凯撒无冤无仇，而且凯撒还有恩于他，二人私交甚好，就连凯撒本人都没有料到后来的刺杀者中居然有勃鲁托斯。

---

[1] temper: physical condition; but also mental constitution.
[2] palm: palm leaf or branch as symbol of victory.

场景 4：独霸天下

("He doth bestride the narrow world like a Colossus.")

> 凯撒受到民众一阵又一阵喝彩欢呼。一旁的勃鲁托斯对此深感不安，凯歇斯趁机游说勃鲁托斯推翻凯撒。

Brutus   Another general shout?
I do believe that these applauses are
For some new honours that are heaped on Caesar.

Cassius   Why, man, he doth bestride the narrow world
Like a colossus[1], and we petty men
Walk under his huge legs and peep about
To find ourselves dishonourable graves.
Men at some time are masters of their fates.
The fault, dear Brutus, is not in our stars
But in ourselves, that we are underlings.
…
Now, in the names of all the gods at once,
Upon what meat[2] doth this our Caesar feed
That he is grown so great? Age, thou art shamed!
Rome, thou hast lost the breed[3] of noble bloods!
When went there by an age, since the great flood[4],
But it was famed with[5] more than with one man?
When could they say, till now, that talked of Rome,
That her wide walks encompassed but one man?

---

[1] colossus: a huge statue. The most famous in the ancient world was the bronze statue of Apollo at Rhodes, one of the Seven Wonders of the World.
[2] meat: food in general.
[3] breed: ability to generate.
[4] the great flood: In Greek mythology, Zeus sent a universal flood, and only Deucalion and Pyrrha were saved. In Bible, there is also a story about the flood and Noah's ark (Genesis,6–8).
[5] famed with: renowned for.

Brutus …
　　　　Till then, my noble friend, chew upon this:
　　　　Brutus had rather be a villager
　　　　Than to repute himself a son of Rome
　　　　Under these hard conditions as this time
　　　　Is like to lay upon us.

(*Julius Caesar* 1.2)

勃鲁托斯　又是一阵大众的欢呼！我相信他们一定又把新的荣誉加在凯撒的身上，所以才有这些喝彩的声音。

凯歇斯　嘿，老兄，他像一个巨人似的跨越这狭隘的世界；我们这些渺小的凡人一个个在他粗大的两腿下行走，四处张望着，替自己寻找不光荣的坟墓。人们有时可以支配他们自己的命运；要是我们受制于人，亲爱的勃鲁托斯，那错处并不在我们的命运，而在我们自己。……凭着一切天神的名字，我们这位凯撒究竟吃些什么美食，才会长得这样伟大？可耻的时代！罗马啊，你的高贵的血统已经中断了！自从洪水以后，什么时代你不曾产生比一个更多的著名人物？直到现在为止，什么时候人们谈起罗马，能够说，她的广大的城墙之内，只是一个人的世界？要是罗马给一个人独占了去，那么它真的变成无人之境了。

勃鲁托斯　……在那个时候没有到来以前，我的好友，请您记住这一句话：勃鲁托斯宁愿做一个乡野的贱民，不愿在这种将要加到我们身上来的难堪的重压之下自命为罗马的儿子。

（朱生豪译《裘力斯·凯撒》第1幕第2场）

评点

凯歇斯极为警惕凯撒与日俱增的威望与影响力，唯恐凯撒独揽大权，威胁罗马的民主政治——尤其是可能损害元老院的权威，此外也不乏嫉妒心理作祟。因而，凯歇斯视凯撒为敌，试图除之而后快。他自己力量不够，必须争取更有权势的盟友，首当其冲的是勃鲁托斯。

凯歇斯擅长察言观色，也深谙说服的艺术。既然勃鲁托斯如此看重荣誉，那么凯歇斯就以荣誉与自由为名，投其所好。勃鲁托斯也是一位举足轻重的政治家，深知事关重大。对于凯歇斯的游说，他没有立即表态，但重申了自己捍卫古罗马传统和个人自由的决心。

场景 5：大义灭亲

("And therefore think him as a serpent's egg …")

> 是否干掉凯撒，这是一个问题。勃鲁托斯回家以后，继续思考凯撒日益膨胀的权威，最终拿定主意——刺杀凯撒。

Brutus　It must be by his death: and for my part
　　　　I know no personal cause to spurn[1] at him
　　　　But for the general[2]. He would be crowned:
　　　　How that might change his nature, there's the question.
　　　　It is the bright day that brings forth the adder,
　　　　And that craves[3] wary walking. Crown him that,
　　　　And then I grant we put a sting in him
　　　　That at his will he may do danger[4] with.
　　　　Th'abuse of greatness is when it disjoins
　　　　Remorse[5] from power; and to speak truth of Caesar
　　　　I have not known when his affections[6] swayed
　　　　More than his reason. But 'tis a common proof[7]
　　　　That lowliness[8] is young ambition's ladder
　　　　Whereto the climber upward turns his face;
　　　　But when he once attains the upmost round[9].
　　　　He then unto the ladder turns his back,
　　　　Looks in the clouds, scorning the base degrees
　　　　By which he did ascend. So Caesar may.
　　　　Then, lest he may, prevent[10]. And since the quarrel[11]

---

[1] spurn: kick violently.
[2] general: common, collective good.
[3] craves: calls for.
[4] danger: damage.
[5] remorse: compassion, with an older sense of conscience.
[6] affections: feelings, passions.
[7] proof: experience.
[8] lowliness: humility as an affectation to win popularity.
[9] round: rung.
[10] prevent: act before, forestall.
[11] quarrel: cause of complaint.

Will bear no colour[1] for the thing he is,
Fashion[2] it thus: that what he is, augmented,
Would run to these and these extremities[3].
And therefore think him as a serpent's egg
Which hatched, would as his kind[4] grow mischievous[5],
And kill him in the shell.

(*Julius Ceasar* 2.1)

勃鲁托斯　只有叫他死这一个办法；我自己对他并没有私怨，只是为了大众的利益。他将要戴上王冠；那会不会改变他的性格是一个问题；蝮蛇是在光天化日之下出现的，所以步行的人必须刻刻提防。让他戴上王冠？——不！那等于我们把一个毒刺给了他，使他可以随意加害于人。把不忍之心和威权分开，那威权就会被人误用；讲到凯撒这个人，说一句公平话，我还不曾知道他什么时候曾经一味感情用事，不受理智的支配。可是微贱往往是初期野心的阶梯，凭借着它一步步爬上了高处；当他一旦登上了最高的一级之后，他便不再回顾那梯子，他的眼光仰望着云霄，瞧不起他从前所恃为凭借的低下的阶段。凯撒何尝不会这样？所以，为了怕他有这一天，必须早一点防备。既然我们反对他的理由，不是因为他现在有什么可以指责的地方，所以就得这样说：照他现在的地位要是再扩大些权力，一定会引起这样这样的后患；我们应当把他当作一颗蛇蛋，与其让他孵出以后害人，不如趁他还在壳里的时候就把他杀死。

（朱生豪译《裘力斯·凯撒》第 2 幕第 1 场）

评点

　　勃鲁托斯面临艰难抉择：对他而言，刺杀凯撒是以天下为公、防患于未然，而非为了个人私利。他本人与凯撒私交深厚，历史上甚至有"勃鲁托斯是凯撒的私生子"的说法。

　　史书上对勃鲁托斯的看法颇有争议，这一点也同样表现在文学作品中：既有人欣赏他为了捍卫罗马的民主自由而大义灭亲，也有人将他视为恩将仇报、罪大恶极的人物——无论但丁的《神曲》还是乔叟的《坎特伯雷故事集》，都将勃鲁托斯视为叛徒。

---

[1] colour: excuse.
[2] fashion: transform.
[3] extremities: conclusions; severities.
[4] kind: nature.
[5] mischievous: harmful.

场景 6：宗教献祭

("Let's be sacrificers but not butchers.")

> 德高望重的勃鲁托斯顺理成章地被推举为刺杀行动的首领。当凯歇斯提议除了除掉凯撒，还要干掉凯撒的左膀右臂安东尼（Antony）时，勃鲁托斯立马表示反对。

Brutus Our course will seem too bloody, Caius Cassius,
To cut the head off and then hack the limbs —
Like wrath in death and envy afterwards —
For Antony is but a limb of Caesar.
Let's be sacrificers but not butchers, Caius.
We all stand up against the spirit of Caesar,
And in the spirit of men there is no blood.
O that we then could come by Caesar's spirit
And not dismember Caesar! But, alas,
Caesar must bleed for it. And, gentle[1] friends,
Let's kill him boldly, but not wrathfully:
Let's carve him as a dish fit for the gods,
Not hew him as a carcass fit for hounds.
And let our hearts, as subtle masters do,
Stir up their servants to an act of rage
And after seem to chide 'em. This shall make
Our purpose necessary and not envious,
Which so appearing to the common eyes,
We shall be called purgers[2], not murderers.
And for Mark Antony, think not of him;
For he can do no more than Caesar's arm

---

[1] gentle: with the courteous generosity of nobility.
[2] purgers: surgeons who treat a patient by bleeding.

When Caesar's head is off.

(*Julius Ceasar* 2.1)

勃鲁托斯 卡厄斯·凯歇斯，我们割下了头，再去切断肢体，不但泄愤于生前，而且迁怒于死后，那瞧上去未免太残忍了；因为安东尼不过是凯撒的一只胳膊。让我们做献祭的人，不要做屠夫，卡厄斯。我们一致奋起反对凯撒的精神，我们的目的并不是要他流血；啊！要是我们能够直接战胜凯撒的精神，我们就可以不必戕害他的身体。可是唉！凯撒必须因此而流血。所以，善良的朋友们，让我们勇敢地，却不是残暴地，把他杀死；让我们把他当作一盘祭神的牺牲而宰割，不要把他当作一具饲犬的腐尸而脔切；让我们的心像聪明的主人一样，在鼓动他们的仆人去行暴以后，再在表面上装作责备他们的神气。这样可以昭示世人，使他们知道我们采取如此步骤，只是迫不得已，并不是出于私心的嫉恨；在世人的眼中，我们将被认为恶势力的清扫者，而不是杀人的凶手。至于玛克·安东尼，我们尽可不必把他放在心上，因为凯撒的头要是落了地，他这条凯撒的胳臂是无能为力的。

（朱生豪译《裘力斯·凯撒》第 2 幕第 1 场）

评点

勃鲁托斯将刺杀凯撒的行动视为宗教献祭，充满了神圣崇高的仪式感；他丝毫不认为刺杀行动卑鄙或罪恶，反而认为自己捍卫罗马传统的壮举是高贵无私的。勃鲁托斯只将凯撒一人视为罗马的威胁，因而放了安东尼一马，显得宽宏大量，却低估了安东尼构成的潜在威胁。

凯撒死后，正是安东尼联合手握重兵的屋大维（Octavius），打败了勃鲁托斯与凯歇斯。可见，老谋深算的凯歇斯此时对安东尼的担心并非多余。相比勃鲁托斯的理想主义与政治上的不成熟，凯歇斯更加精明务实，只是凯歇斯没有勃鲁托斯那么大的话语权，每每都得对勃鲁托斯让步。

场景 7: 家有贤妻

("I grant I am a woman, but …")

> 勃鲁托斯在家寝食难安,却守口如瓶。其妻鲍西亚(Portia)出身名门,以贤惠著称,情真意切地恳请勃鲁托斯信赖她,向她敞开心扉,让她一同分担他的忧愁。

Portia Within the bond of marriage, tell me, Brutus,
Is it excepted I should know no secrets
That appertain[1] to you? Am I your self
But as it were in sort or limitation,
To keep[2] with you at meals, comfort[3] your bed
And talk to you sometimes? Dwell I but in the suburbs[4]
Of your good pleasure? If it be no more,
Portia is Brutus' harlot, not his wife.

Brutus You are my true and honourable wife,
As dear to me as are the ruddy drops
That visit my sad heart.

Portia If this were true, then should I know this secret.
I grant I am a woman: but withal
A woman that Lord Brutus took to wife.
I grant I am a woman: but withal
A woman well-reputed, Cato's daughter[5].
Think you I am no stronger than my sex
Being so fathered and so husbanded?

---

[1] appertain: belong.
[2] keep: keep company.
[3] comfort: bring pleasure to.
[4] suburbs: outskirts.
[5] Cato's daughter: Marcus Porcius Cato was conspicuous for his stern morality. An ally of Pompey, he killed himself rather than fall into Caesar's hands. Father to Portia, he was also uncle to Brutus.

> Tell me your counsels. I will not disclose 'em:
> I have made strong proof of my constancy,
> Giving myself a voluntary wound
> Here in the thigh. Can I bear that with patience
> And not my husband's secrets?

(*Julius Ceasar* 2.1)

鲍西娅	在我们夫妇的名分之内，告诉我，勃鲁托斯，难道我是不应该知道您的秘密的吗？我虽然是您自身的一部分，可是那只是有限制的一部分，除了陪着您吃饭，在枕席上安慰安慰您，有时候跟您谈谈话以外，没有别的任务了吗？难道您只要我跟着您的好恶打转吗？假如不过是这样，那么鲍西娅只是勃鲁托斯的娼妓，不是他的妻子了。
勃鲁托斯	你是我的忠贞的妻子，正像滋润我悲哀的心的鲜红血液一样宝贵。
鲍西娅	这句话倘然是真的，那么我就应该知道您的心事。我承认我只是一个女流之辈，可是我却是勃鲁托斯娶为妻子的一个女人；我承认我只是一个女流之辈，可是我却是凯图的女儿，不是一个碌碌无名的女人。您以为我有了这样的父亲和丈夫，还是跟一般女人同样不中用吗？把您的心事告诉我，我一定不向人泄漏。我为了保证对你的坚贞，曾经自愿把我的贞操献给了你[1]；难道我能够忍耐那样的痛苦，却不能保守我丈夫的秘密吗？

（朱生豪译《裘力斯·凯撒》第2幕第1场）

评点

《裘力斯·凯撒》这部以政治、军事、历史为题材的戏剧由男性角色主导，其中虽然只有两位女性人物，但是她们也极具特色，引人注目：一个是勃鲁托斯的妻子鲍西娅，另一个是凯撒的妻子凯尔弗妮娅（Calphurnia）。在凯撒遇刺之前，刺杀者的妻子与被刺杀者的妻子都怀有强烈的不祥预感，都为夫君的安危而担忧，展现了古罗马贤妻的忠诚与明智。

鲍西娅的这番话也衬托出夫妻情深。在爱妻及仆人的衬托下，勃鲁托斯展现出他在家庭生活中温情脉脉的一面，与随后的血腥刺杀形成鲜明对比。

---

[1] 对照原文，不应该译为"曾经自愿把我的贞操献给了你"，而是"我自愿给自己扎上一刀伤口，就在大腿这里"。

场景 8：无所畏惧

("The valiant never taste of death but once.")

> 刺杀者们多为罗马贵族元老，他们亲自登门邀请凯撒，声称元老院要将王冠授予凯撒。而凯撒的妻子凯尔弗妮娅前一夜噩梦连连，因此极力劝阻凯撒。凯撒经不起众人的怂恿诱惑，最终还是出门了……

Caesar Caesar shall forth. The things that threatened me
    Ne'er looked but on my back: when they shall see
    The face of Caesar, they are vanished.

……

Caesar   What can be avoided
    Whose end is purposed by the mighty gods?
    Yet Caesar shall go forth, for these predictions
    Are to the world in general as to Caesar.

Calphurnia When beggars die, there are no comets seen;
    The heavens themselves blaze forth the death of princes.

Caesar Cowards die many times before their deaths;
    The valiant never taste of death but once.
    Of all the wonders that I yet have heard,
    It seems to me most strange that men should fear,
    Seeing that death, a necessary end,
    Will come when it will come.

(*Julius Ceasar* 2.2)

凯撒	凯撒一定要出去。恐吓我的东西只敢在我背后装腔作势；它们一看见凯撒的脸，就会销声匿迹。

....

凯撒	天意注定的事，难道是人力所能逃避的吗？凯撒一定要出去；因为这些预兆不是给凯撒一个人看，而是给所有的世人看的。
凯尔弗妮娅	乞丐死了的时候，天上不会有彗星出现；君王们的凋殒才会上感天象。
凯撒	懦夫在未死以前，就已经死过好多次；勇士一生只死一次。在我所听到过的一切怪事之中，人们的贪生怕死是一件最奇怪的事情，因为死本来是一个人免不了的结局，它要来的时候谁也不能叫它不来。

（朱生豪译《裘力斯·凯撒》第2幕第2场）

评点

凯撒久经沙场、英勇无畏，即便已经出现了各种不祥的异象，他也满不在乎。也许因为他太自负，低估了潜在危险，也许因为他的宿命，冥冥之中，一切有定，凡人无法逃离命运，那还畏惧什么？哈姆莱特在最后接受比剑挑战时也持相似观点——There's a special providence in the fall of a sparrow（见本书第五章最后一个场景"命中注定"）。

凯撒在自称时常常直呼自己的大名，而不用代词"我"，这种独特的措辞习惯似乎表明他颇以自己的名字为荣，其自信甚至自负程度可见一斑。

场景 9：凯撒遇刺

("Et tu, Brute?— Then fall, Caesar.")

> 凯撒被人簇拥着，前往元老院，路上又遇见一个月之前警告他"当心三月十五"（Beware the Ides of March）的那个预言家。凯撒奚落他"三月十五已经来了"（The Ides of March are come），预言家则回应"是的，凯撒，可是它还没有去"（Ay, Caesar, but not gone）。随后在大殿之上，准备刺杀凯撒的元老贵族们找借口激怒凯撒，争辩之中就动手了……

Caesar I could be well moved if I were as you:
If I could pray to move, prayers would move me.
But I am constant as the northern star[1],
Of whose true-fixed and resting quality
There is no fellow in the firmament.
The skies are painted with unnumbered sparks:
They are all fire, and every one doth shine;
But there's but one in all doth hold his place.
So in the world: 'tis furnished well with men,
And men are flesh and blood, and apprehensive[2].
Yet in the number I do know but one
That unassailable holds on his rank[3]
Unshaked of motion. And that I am he
Let me a little show it even in this,
That I was constant Cimber should be banished
And constant do remain to keep him so.

Cinna O Caesar,—

Caesar Hence! Wilt thou lift up Olympus[4]?

---

[1] northern star: the unmoving Pole Star.
[2] apprehensive: capable of apprehension, perceptive.
[3] holds on his rank: keeps his position.
[4] Olympus: the mountain home of the gods in Greek mythology, signifying an impossibility.

Decius	Great Caesar—
Caesar	Doth not Brutus bootless[1] kneel?
Casca	Speak hands for me! [*They stab Caesar.*]
Caesar	Et tu, Brute? — Then fall, Caesar. [*Dies.*]

(*Julius Ceasar* 3.1)

凯撒	要是我也跟你们一样,我就会被你们所感动;要是我也能够用哀求打动别人的心,那么你们的哀求也会打动我的心;可是我是像北极星一样坚定,它的不可动摇的性质,在天宇中是无与伦比的。天上布满了无数的星辰,每一个星辰都是一个火球,都有它各自的光辉,可是在众星之中,只有一个星卓立不动。在人世间也是这样;无数的人生活在这世间,他们都是有血肉有知觉的,可是我知道只有一个人能够确保他的不可侵犯的地位,任何力量都不能使他动摇。我就是他;让我在这件小小的事上向你们证明,我既然已经决定把辛伯放逐,就要贯彻我的意旨,毫不含糊地执行这一个成命,而且永远不让他再回到罗马来。
西那	啊,凯撒——
凯撒	去!你想把俄林波斯山一手举起吗?
狄歇斯	伟大的凯撒——
凯撒	勃鲁托斯不是白白地下跪吗?
凯斯卡	好,那么让我的手代替我说话!(率众刺凯撒)
凯撒	勃鲁托斯,你也在内吗?那么倒下吧,凯撒!(死)

(朱生豪译《裘力斯·凯撒》第3幕第1场)

评点

凯撒不是没有得到各路预警消息,但是他将各种警告置若罔闻。凯撒的自负,从他将自己比作天上岿然不动的北极星(the northern star)与奥林匹斯山(Olympus)上的神明可见一斑。

一切出乎凯撒的意料,尤其是他颇为器重的勃鲁托斯也在刺杀者之列。凯撒死前的那句反问"Et tu, Brute?"只有半截,显然话没说完。此处特地保留了古罗马时代的拉丁文原句,可见这一句话多么耐人寻味。

---

[1] bootless: in vain, without success.

场景 10：留名青史

（"The men who gave their country liberty"）

> 勃鲁托斯与凯歇斯在刺杀凯撒之后，向刺杀行动的同盟者们豪情万丈地展望这一"壮举"将世世代代为后人所牢记与敬仰。

Brutus Fates, we will know your pleasures.
That we shall die, we know; 'tis but the time
And drawing days out, that men stand upon.

Caska Why, he that cuts off twenty years of life
Cuts off so many years of fearing death.

Brutus Grant that, and then is death a benefit.
So are we Caesar's friends, that have abridged
His time of fearing death. Stoop, Romans, stoop,
And let us bathe our hands in Caesar's blood
Up to the elbows, and besmear our swords.
Then walk we forth even to the market-place,
And waving our red weapons o'er our heads,
Let's all cry, 'Peace, freedom and liberty!'

Cassius Stoop, then, and wash. How many ages hence
Shall this our lofty scene be acted over
In states unborn and accents yet unknown?

Brutus How many times shall Caesar bleed in sport
That now on Pompey's basis[1] lies along,
No worthier than the dust?

Cassius So oft as that shall be,
So often shall the knot[2] of us be called

---

[1] Pompey's basis: the base of Pompey's statue, against which the body of Caesar lies stretched out.
[2] knot: a small band (of men).

The men that gave their country liberty.

(*Julius Caesar* 3.1)

勃鲁托斯　命运，我们等候着你的旨意。我们谁都免不了一死；与其在世上偷生苟活，拖延着日子，还不如轰轰烈烈地死去。

凯斯卡　嘿，切断了二十年的生命，等于切断了二十年在忧生畏死中过去的时间。

勃鲁托斯　照这样说来，死还是一件好事。所以我们都是凯撒的朋友，帮助他结束了这一段忧生畏死的生命。弯下身去，罗马人，弯下身去；让我们把手浸在凯撒的血里，一直到我们的肘上；让我们用他的血抹我们的剑。然后我们就迈步前进，到市场上去；把我们鲜红的武器在我们头顶挥舞，大家高呼着，"和平，自由，解放！"

凯歇斯　好，大家弯下身去，洗你们的手吧。多少年代以后，我们这一场壮烈的戏剧，将要在尚未产生的国家用我们所不知道的语言表演！

勃鲁托斯　凯撒将要在戏剧中流多少次的血，他现在却长眠在庞贝的像座之下，他的尊严化成了泥土！

凯歇斯　后世的人们搬演今天这一幕的时候，将要称我们这一群为祖国的解放者。

（朱生豪译《裘力斯·凯撒》第3幕第1场）

点评

凯歇斯与勃鲁托斯认为他们冒着巨大的政治风险，奋不顾身地扼杀了潜在的独裁者，捍卫了古罗马传统及共和政体，因而留名青史。确实，这场著名的政变被载入史册了，两位主谋因而赫赫有名。不过，后世对刺杀凯撒的看法颇为复杂。尤其是，刺杀行动不但没有让罗马得到自由与和平，而且还爆发了内乱与仇杀。刺杀凯撒似乎只是徒劳，反而吞噬了刺杀者自己，罗马共和国最终还是转变为一人（屋大维，即奥古斯都）独揽大权的罗马帝国……

尽管但丁对勃鲁托斯与凯歇斯进行了妖魔化描述，但是在莎士比亚笔下，二人在人性弱点之外，也不乏人性光辉，人物形象立体而丰满。

场景 11：报仇雪恨

("Caesar's spirit, ranging for revenge …")

> 凯撒遇刺之后，其心腹安东尼得到了勃鲁托斯的宽恕与和解。安东尼在哀悼凯撒之时，暗暗谋划叛乱，为凯撒报仇……

Antony O pardon me, thou bleeding piece of earth,
That I am meek and gentle with these butchers.
Thou art the ruins of the noblest man
That ever lived in the tide of times[1].
Woe to the hand that shed this costly[2] blood.
Over thy wounds now do I prophesy
(Which like dumb mouths do ope their ruby lips
To beg the voice and utterance of my tongue)
A curse shall light upon the limbs of men:
Domestic fury and fierce civil strife
Shall cumber[3] all the parts of Italy:
Blood and destruction shall be so in use,
And dreadful objects so familiar,
That mothers shall but smile when they behold
Their infants quartered[4] with[5] the hands of war:
All pity choked with custom of fell deeds[6],
And Caesar's spirit, ranging for revenge,
With Ate[7] by his side come hot from hell,

---

[1] tide of times: stream of history.
[2] costly: of great value; causing excessive expenditure.
[3] cumber: overwhelm.
[4] quartered: cut into pieces.
[5] with: by.
[6] with custom of fell deeds: because of the familiarity of cruel deeds.
[7] Ate: Greek goddess of blind infatuation, daughter of Zeus in Homer, of Strife in Hesiod, and sister of lawlessness.

Shall in these confines[1], with a monarch's voice[2],
Cry havoc[3] and let slip[4] the dogs of war[5],
That this foul deed shall smell above the earth
With carrion men, groaning for burial.

(*Julius Caesar* 3.1)

安东尼 啊！你这一块流血的泥土，你这有史以来最高贵的英雄的遗体，恕我跟这些屠夫们曲意周旋。愿灾祸降于溅泼这样宝贵的血的凶手！你的一处处伤口，好像许多无言的嘴，张开了它们殷红的嘴唇，要求我的舌头替它们向世人申诉；我现在就在这些伤口上预言：一个咒诅将要降临在人们的肢体上；残暴惨酷的内乱将要使意大利到处陷于混乱；流血和破坏将要成为一时的风尚，恐怖的景象将要每天接触到人们的眼睛，以至于做母亲的人看见她们的婴孩被战争的魔手所肢解，也会毫不在乎地付之一笑；人们因为习惯于残杀，一切怜悯之心将要完全灭绝；凯撒的冤魂借着从地狱的烈火中出来的阿提的协助，将要用一个君王的口气，向罗马的全境发出屠杀的号令，让战争的猛犬四出蹂躏，为了这一个万恶的罪行，大地上将要弥漫着呻吟求葬的臭皮囊。

（朱生豪译《裘力斯·凯撒》第3幕第1场）

评点

安东尼绝非勃鲁托斯所判断的那样头脑简单、意志薄弱，他也不因凯撒遇刺而见风使舵地归顺于凯撒的反对派。在隐忍外表的遮蔽之下，复仇烈火正在安东尼的心头熊熊燃烧……

该选段展现安东尼矗立于凯撒尸体面前的内心独白，由哀悼逝者，转而想象复仇的腥风血雨。各种修辞意象淋漓尽致地渲染出恢宏而恐怖的场面，战争的序幕即将拉开……

---

[1] these confines: regions of Italy.
[2] monarch's voice: only a monarch or his representative could cry havoc.
[3] cry havoc: signal slaughter and pillage without mercy.
[4] let slip: unleash.
[5] dogs of war: the hounds of famine, sword and fire.

场景 12：取信于民

（"Believe me for mine honour."）

> 勃鲁托斯向来受人爱戴，颇具社会影响力。在凯撒被刺杀之后，他当即向罗马民众发表演说，以自己的人品名誉做担保，动之以情，晓之以理，论述杀死凯撒的必要性与正当性。

Brutus Be patient till the last. Romans, countrymen, and lovers[1]! hear me for my cause[2] and be silent, that you may hear. Believe me for mine honour, and have respect to[3] mine honour, that you may believe. Censure[4] me in your wisdom, and awake your senses[5], that you may the better judge. If there be any in this assembly, any dear friend of Caesar's, to him I say, that Brutus' love to Caesar was no less than his. If then that friend demand why Brutus rose against Caesar, this is my answer: Not that I loved Caesar less, but that I loved Rome more. Had you rather Caesar were living and die all slaves, than that Caesar were dead, to live all free men? As Caesar loved me, I weep for him; as he was fortunate, I rejoice at it; as he was valiant, I honour him: but as he was ambitious, I slew him. There is tears for his love; joy for his fortune; honour for his valour; and death for his ambition. Who is here so base, that would be a bondman? If any, speak, for him have I offended. Who is here so rude, that would not be a Roman? If any, speak, for him have I offended. Who is here so vile, that will not love his country? If any, speak, for him have I offended. I pause for a reply.

All None, Brutus, none.

(*Julius Caesar* 3.2)

---

[1] lovers: friends.
[2] cause: subject of concern; position pressed to you; grounds for action.
[3] have respect to: bear in mind.
[4] censure: judge.
[5] senses: reason.

勃鲁托斯 请耐心听我讲完。各位罗马人，各位亲爱的同胞们！请你们静静地听我解释。为了我的名誉，请你们相信我；尊重我的名誉，这样你们就会相信我的话。用你们的智慧批评我；唤起你们的理智，给我一个公正的评断。要是在今天在场的群众中间，有什么人是凯撒的好朋友，我要对他说，勃鲁托斯也是和他同样地爱着凯撒。要是那位朋友问我为什么勃鲁托斯要起来反对凯撒，这就是我的回答：并不是我不爱凯撒，可是我更爱罗马。你们宁愿让凯撒活在世上，大家做奴隶而死呢，还是让凯撒死去，大家做自由人而生？因为凯撒爱我，所以我为他流泪；因为他是幸运的，所以我为他欣慰；因为他是勇敢的，所以我尊敬他；因为他有野心，所以我杀死他。我用眼泪报答他的友谊，用喜悦庆祝他的幸运，用尊敬崇扬他的勇敢，用死亡惩戒他的野心。这儿有谁愿意自甘卑贱，做一个奴隶？要是有这样的人，请说出来；因为我已经得罪他了。这儿有谁愿意自居化外，不愿做一个罗马人？要是有这样的人，请说出来；因为我已经得罪他了。这儿有谁愿意自处下流，不爱他的国家？要是有这样的人，请说出来；因为我已经得罪他了。我等待着答复。

众市民 没有，勃鲁托斯，没有。

（朱生豪译《裘力斯·凯撒》第3幕第2场）

评点

　　勃鲁托斯的公众演讲简短有力，大量使用排比与反问，气势磅礴。他在认为凯撒"野心勃勃"的同时，也由衷敬佩与深切爱戴凯撒，并不全盘否定或抹黑凯撒。刺杀凯撒不是出于个人私利，而是为了捍卫罗马的民主传统。勃鲁托斯的自我牺牲赢得了民众的认可。

场景 13：欲擒故纵

("Brutus is an honourable man.")

> 勃鲁托斯的演说在一片欢呼中圆满结束，随后安东尼手托凯撒尸体出场。安东尼虽然得到勃鲁托斯的许可，得以在此面向公众发表演讲，但是他阳奉阴违，明褒实贬地评价勃鲁托斯，逐步颠覆了公众舆论的导向。

Antony   Friends, Romans, countrymen, lend me your ears:
I come to bury Caesar, not to praise him.
The evil that men do lives after them:
The good is oft interred with their bones.
So let it be with Caesar. The noble Brutus
Hath told you Caesar was ambitious:
If it were so, it was a grievous fault,
And grievously hath Caesar answered[1] it.
Here, under leave[2] of Brutus and the rest
(For Brutus is an honourable man;
So are they all, all honourable men)
Come I to speak in Caesar's funeral.
He was my friend, faithful and just to me;
But Brutus says he was ambitious,
And Brutus is an honourable man.
He hath brought many captives home to Rome,
Whose ransoms did the general coffers[3] fill.
Did this in Caesar seem ambitious?
When that the poor have cried, Caesar hath wept:
Ambition should be made of sterner stuff.
Yet Brutus says he was ambitious,
And Brutus is an honourable man.
You all did see that on the Lupercal.
I thrice presented him a kingly crown,
Which he did thrice refuse. Was this ambition?
Yet Brutus says he was ambitious,

---

[1] answered: paid the penalty for.
[2] under leave: by permission.
[3] general coffers: the state's money-chests.

And, sure, he is an honourable man.
I speak not to disprove what Brutus spoke,
But here I am to speak what I do know.
You all did love him once, not without cause:
What cause withholds you then, to mourn for him?
O judgment! thou art fled to brutish beasts
And men have lost their reason.

(*Julius Caesar* 3.2)

安东尼　各位朋友，各位罗马人，各位同胞，请你们听我说；我是来埋葬凯撒，不是来赞美他。人们做了恶事，死后免不了遭人唾骂，可是他们所做的善事，往往随着他们的尸骨一齐入土；让凯撒也这样吧。尊贵的勃鲁托斯已经对你们说过，凯撒是有野心的；要是真有这样的事，那诚然是一个重大的过失，凯撒也为了它付出惨酷的代价了。现在我得到勃鲁托斯和他的同志们的允许——因为勃鲁托斯是一个正人君子，他们也都是正人君子——到这儿来在凯撒的丧礼中说几句话。他是我的朋友，他对我是那么忠诚公正；然而勃鲁托斯却说他是有野心的，而勃鲁托斯是一个正人君子。他曾经带许多俘虏回到罗马来，他们的赎金都充实了公家的财库；这可以说是野心者的行径吗？穷苦的人哀哭的时候，凯撒曾经为他们流泪；野心者是不应当这样仁慈的。然而勃鲁托斯却说他是有野心的，而勃鲁托斯是一个正人君子。你们大家看见在卢柏克节的那天，我三次献给他一顶王冠，他三次都拒绝了；这难道是野心吗？然而勃鲁托斯却说他是有野心的，而勃鲁托斯的的确确是一个正人君子。我不是要推翻勃鲁托斯所说的话，我所说的只是我自己所知道的事实。你们过去都曾爱过他，那并不是没有理由的；那么什么理由阻止你们现在哀悼他呢？唉，理性啊！你已经遁入了野兽的心中，人们已经失去辨别是非的能力了。

（朱生豪译《裘力斯·凯撒》第3幕第2场）

评点

　　安东尼的演讲一开始处于守势，而且一再称赞勃鲁托斯"正人君子"，就是为了消除听众对他的敌意与轻蔑。然而，随着"honourable"一词一而再、再而三地反复强调，这个褒义词逐渐变成了揶揄讽刺。与此同时，勃鲁托斯指责凯撒的"野心"一词却在安东尼一遍遍的强调之中变得越来越令人生疑，直到最后安东尼反问："这是野心吗？"（Was this ambition?）

　　安东尼与勃鲁托斯在凯撒葬礼上的演讲针锋相对，都展示出古罗马时期的高超水平。短短一席话，他就严重动摇了听众们对勃鲁托斯的认可与好感。接下来，安东尼就要进一步煽动听众的情绪了……

场景 14：群情激昂

("… move the stones of Rome to rise and mutiny.")

> 安东尼在第一阶段演讲之后，向罗马民众展示了凯撒的遗嘱。当民众看到凯撒将巨额财产都分给罗马人民，深受感动，这彻底扭转了舆论，民众开始将刺杀者称为叛徒。安东尼随即又发表了一番演说，呈现凯撒尸体的惨状，控诉勃鲁托斯的"忘恩负义"。

Antony　If you have tears, prepare to shed them now.
　　　　You all do know this mantle[1]. I remember
　　　　The first time ever Caesar put it on.
　　　　'Twas on a summer's evening, in his tent,
　　　　That day he overcame the Nervii.
　　　　Look, in this place ran Cassius' dagger through:
　　　　See what a rent the envious[2] Casca made:
　　　　Through this the well-beloved Brutus stabb'd,
　　　　And as he plucked his cursed steel away,
　　　　Mark how the blood of Caesar followed it,
　　　　As rushing out of doors, to be resolved
　　　　If Brutus so unkindly knocked or no;
　　　　For Brutus, as you know, was Caesar's angel.
　　　　Judge, O you gods, how dearly Caesar loved him.
　　　　This was the most unkindest cut of all:
　　　　For when the noble Caesar saw him stab,
　　　　Ingratitude, more strong than traitors' arms,
　　　　Quite vanquished him: then burst his mighty heart;
　　　　And, in his mantle muffling up his face,
　　　　Even at the base of Pompey's statue,
　　　　Which all the while ran blood, great Caesar fell.
　　　　O, what a fall was there, my countrymen!
　　　　Then I, and you, and all of us fell down,
　　　　Whilst bloody treason flourished[3] over us.

---

[1] mantle: cloak.
[2] envious: malicious.
[3] flourished: triumphed.

……
Antony　　　　　　　　But were I Brutus,
And Brutus Antony, there were an Antony
Would ruffle up your spirits and put a tongue
In every wound of Caesar that should move
The stones of Rome to rise and mutiny.

All　We'll mutiny.

(*Julius Caesar* 3.2)

安东尼　要是你们有眼泪，现在准备流起来吧。你们都认识这件外套；我记得凯撒第一次穿上它，是在一个夏天的晚上，在他的营帐里，就在他征服纳维人的那一天。瞧！凯歇斯的刀子是从这地方穿过的；瞧那狠心的凯斯卡割开了一道多深的裂口；他所深爱的勃鲁托斯就从这儿刺了一刀进去，当他拔出他那万恶的武器的时候，瞧凯撒的血是怎样汩汩不断地跟着它出来，好像急于涌到外面来，想要知道究竟是不是勃鲁托斯下这样无情的毒手；因为你们知道，勃鲁托斯是凯撒心目中的天使。神啊，请你们判断判断凯撒是多么爱他！这是最无情的一击，因为当尊贵的凯撒看见他行刺的时候，负心，这一柄比叛徒的武器更锋锐的利剑，就一直刺进了他的心脏，那时候他的伟大的心就碎裂了；他的脸给他的外套蒙着，他的血不停地流着，就在庞贝像座之下，伟大的凯撒倒下了。啊！那是一个多么惊人的殒落，我的同胞们；我、你们，我们大家都随着他一起倒下，残酷的叛逆却在我们头上耀武扬威。

…………

安东尼　可是假如我是勃鲁托斯，而勃鲁托斯是安东尼，那么那个安东尼一定会激起你们的愤怒，让凯撒的每一处伤口里都长出一条舌头来，即使罗马的石块也将要大受感动，奋身而起，向叛徒们抗争了。

众市民　我们要暴动！

（朱生豪译《裘力斯·凯撒》第 3 幕第 2 场）

> **评点**

　　安东尼的措辞与口吻都貌似谦卑，以一个弱者的姿态登场，更能博得民众的同情。在其演讲末尾，安东尼使用虚拟句式鼓动叛乱，给自己留下了进退自如的回旋空间。果然，民众群情激昂，由此拉开了为凯撒报仇的序幕……

　　自始至终，安东尼的演说都颇为煽情，号召民众哀哭凯撒。在他的演说过程中，凯撒的遗嘱与尸体都成为舞台道具，进一步加强其说服力与感染力。语言的力量、舆论的操控、民众的盲从，在勃鲁托斯与安东尼针锋相对的演说中都得到了淋漓尽致的体现。

场景 15：亡灵索命

（"... thou shalt see me at Philippi."）

> 即便凯撒在剧本正中间（第 3 幕第 1 场）就已遇刺，他在后半部剧中也依然亡魂不散。无论其拥护者还是其刺杀者，都在冥冥之中深感凯撒的强大影响力。在安东尼煽动暴乱之后，内战打响。在腓利比战役的前一夜，有鬼魂出现于勃鲁托斯的大帐之中。

[*Enter the Ghost of Caesar.*]

Brutus How ill this taper burns. Ha! Who comes here?
         I think it is the weakness of mine eyes
         That shapes this monstrous apparition.
         It comes upon me. Art thou any thing?
         Art thou some god, some angel, or some devil,
         That mak'st my blood cold, and my hair to stare[1]?
         Speak to me what thou art.

Caesar Thy evil spirit, Brutus.

Brutus   Why com'st thou?

Caesar To tell thee thou shalt see me at Philippi.

Brutus Well: then I shall see thee again?

Caesar Ay, at Philippi.

Brutus Why, I will see thee at Philippi, then. [*Exit Ghost.*]
         Now I have taken heart thou vanishest.
         Ill spirit, I would hold more talk with thee.

(*Julius Caesar* 4.3)

---

[1] stare: stand on end.

（凯撒幽灵上）

勃鲁托斯　这蜡烛的光怎么这样暗！嘿！谁来啦？我想我的眼睛有点昏花，所以会看见鬼怪。它走近我的身边来了。你是什么东西？你是神呢，天使呢，还是魔鬼，吓得我浑身冷汗，头发直竖？对我说你是什么。

幽灵　你的冤魂，勃鲁托斯。

勃鲁托斯　你来干什么？

幽灵　我来告诉你，你将在腓利比看见我。

勃鲁托斯　好，那么我将要再看见你吗？

幽灵　是的，在腓利比。

勃鲁托斯　好，那么我们在腓利比再见。（幽灵隐去）我刚鼓起一些勇气，你又不见了；冤魂，我还要跟你谈话。

（朱生豪译《裘力斯·凯撒》第4幕第3场）

评点

安东尼在第3幕第1场中独自哀悼凯撒时所提到的"凯撒的灵魂"（Caesar's spirit）在第4幕第3场真的上场了，一如《哈姆雷特》中的鬼魂。鬼魂在莎士比亚悲剧与历史剧中频频出现，往往都只出现在凶手面前，旁人却不一定能看到。勃鲁托斯询问侍与守卫，除他之外，谁都没看到鬼魂。凯撒的鬼魂告知勃鲁托斯一个谜一般的预言——"你将在腓利比（Philippi）看见我"，含蓄地影射着勃鲁托斯将战死沙场……

场景 16：生离死别

("… 'tis true this parting was well made.")

> 对于势力强大的叛军，勃鲁托斯与凯歇斯仓促应战，但是无论在军事补给上，还是在作战策略上，都纷争不断。而后彼此妥协，握手言和，并肩作战。在腓利比战场上，二人互表决心：一旦战败，绝不苟且偷生。

Cassius　　　　　Then, if we lose this battle,
　　　　　　　　You are contented to be led in triumph
　　　　　　　　Thorough the streets of Rome?
　Brutus　No, Cassius, no: think not, thou noble Roman,
　　　　　　That ever Brutus will go bound to Rome.
　　　　　　He bears too great a mind. But this same day
　　　　　　Must end that work the ides of March begun;
　　　　　　And whether we shall meet again I know not:
　　　　　　Therefore our everlasting farewell take:
　　　　　　For ever and for ever farewell, Cassius.
　　　　　　If we do meet again, why, we shall smile;
　　　　　　If not, why then, this parting was well made.
Cassius　For ever and for ever farewell, Brutus!
　　　　　　If we do meet again, we'll smile indeed;
　　　　　　If not, 'tis true this parting was well made.

(*Julius Caesar* 5.1)

凯歇斯	那么，要是我们失败了，你愿意被凯旋的敌人拖来拖去，在罗马的街道上游行吗？
勃鲁托斯	不，凯歇斯，不。尊贵的罗马人，你不要以为勃鲁托斯会有一天被人绑着回到罗马；他是有一颗太高傲的心的。可是今天这一天必须结束三月十五所开始的工作；我不知道我们能不能再有见面的机会，所以让我们从此永诀吧。永别了，永别了，凯歇斯！要是我们还能相见，那时候我们可以相视而笑；否则今天就是我们生离死别的日子。
凯歇斯	永别了，永别了，勃鲁托斯！要是我们还能相见，那时候我们一定相视而笑；否则今天真的是我们生离死别的日子了。

（朱生豪译《裘力斯·凯撒》第5幕第1场）

评点

在与安东尼等人率领的大军决一死战之前，勃鲁托斯与凯歇斯部署军队，并道别——他们深知这一别极可能就是永别。尽管二人此前不乏矛盾，但他们在根本价值观上保持一致，都展现了古罗马贵族的品质：勇于战斗，绝不屈服，视死如归。后来二人见战场失利，便双双自杀，场景颇为悲壮。凯撒的鬼魂前一夜所说的预言也就成为现实。

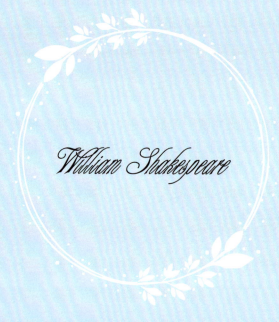

四、《皆大欢喜》

As You Like It
(1599)

"逆运也有它的好处。"
("Sweet are the uses of adversity.")

莎士比亚喜剧《皆大欢喜》的男主角奥兰多与女主角罗瑟琳都是贵族出身的公子小姐，却因家庭变故而被迫逃亡，不约而同地来到阿登森林。一开场，男女主角各为一条独立的剧情线索，两条线索在剧中几番交织，逐渐合成一股，上演一场浪漫爱情故事。

罗瑟琳之父是剧中的第三条线索（剧终与前两条线索汇合），他与其随员在阿登森林里享受罗宾汉式的自由生活，猎鹿、会餐、唱歌、闲聊……其中有一位人送绰号"忧郁的杰奎斯"，特立独行，金句连连，即便只是一个小配角，却也令人印象深刻。

此外，还有其他可圈可点的小配角，比如苦苦相思的牧羊人与心高气傲的牧羊女，以及小丑试金石与其单纯无知却不乏自尊的牧羊女女友。他们的爱情故事独立于剧本主线之外，却不断与主线交织，最终"皆大欢喜"。

《皆大欢喜》以悲剧开头，以集体婚礼结束。剧中主要人物历经坎坷，却患难见真情，可谓"好事多磨"。

《皆大欢喜》（*As You Like It*）

场景 1：远走高飞（"Why, whither shall we go?"）1.3

场景 2：苦中作乐（"Sweet are the uses of adversity."）2.1

场景 3：世态炎凉（"… misery doth part the flux of company."）2.1

场景 4：绿林欢歌（"Under the greenwood tree …"）2.5

场景 5：畅所欲言（"Give me leave to speak my mind …"）2.7

场景 6：以柔克刚（"Your gentleness shall force …"）2.7

场景 7：人生如戏（"All the world's a stage."）2.7

场景 8：寒风凛冽（"Blow, blow, thou winter wind!"）2.7

场景 9：田园哲学（"Hast any philosophy in thee, shepherd?"）3.2

场景 10：痴心一片（"Love is merely a madness …"）3.2

场景 11：美言不信（"… the truest poetry is the most faining …"）3.3

场景 12：多愁善感（"… it is a melancholy of mine own …"）4.1

场景 13：爱情神话（"Men have died … but not for love."）4.1

场景 14：天壤之别（"… the sky changes when they are wives."）4.1

场景 15：离群索居（"I am for other than for dancing measures."）5.4

场景 1：远走高飞

("Why, whither shall we go?")

> 第 1 幕的前两场是关于不甘平庸的少年奥兰多（Orlando）的。他不听劝阻，舍命参加摔跤比赛，却出人意料地反败为胜，不仅受到公爵的赏赐，而且还与罗瑟琳（Rosalind）一见钟情。
>
> 罗瑟琳的父亲原本是公爵，却被叔父篡位。虽然父亲被流放至阿登森林，但罗瑟琳得以获准留在宫廷与叔父的独生女西莉娅（Celia）做伴。在第 1 幕第 3 场中，叔父突然改变主意，勒令罗瑟琳离开。两姐妹情同手足，不忍分离，打算乔装打扮，一起出逃。

Rosalind Why, whither shall we go?

Celia To seek my uncle in the Forest of Arden.

Rosalind Alas, what danger will it be to us,
　　　　　Maids as we are, to travel forth so far!
　　　　　Beauty provoketh thieves sooner than gold.

Celia I'll put myself in poor and mean[1] attire,
　　　　And with a kind of umber smirch my face —
　　　　The like do you[2]; so shall we pass along
　　　　And never stir assailants[3].

Rosalind Were it not better,
　　　　　Because that I am more than common tall,
　　　　　That I did suit me[4] all points[5] like a man?
　　　　　A gallant curtle-axe[6] upon my thigh,
　　　　　A boar spear in my hand, and in my heart,
　　　　　Lie there what hidden woman's fear there will,

---

[1] mean: shabby.
[2] The like do you: You do the same.
[3] assailants: attackers.
[4] suit me: dress and equip myself.
[5] all points: in every respect.
[6] curtle-axe: cutlass, a short broad-bladed sword; 短剑、弯刀。

> We'll have a swashing[1] and a martial outside,
> As many other mannish[2] cowards have
> That do outface[3] it with their semblances[4].

(*As You Like It* 1.3)

罗瑟琳　但是我们要到哪儿去呢?
西莉娅　到亚登森林找我的伯父去。
罗瑟琳　唉,像我们这样的姑娘家,走这么远路,该是多么危险! 美貌比金银更容易引起盗心呢。
西莉娅　我可以穿了破旧的衣裳,用些黄泥涂在脸上,你也这样;我们便可以通行过去,不会遭人家算计了。
罗瑟琳　我的身材特别高,完全打扮得像个男人岂不更好? 腰间插一把出色的匕首,手里拿一柄刺野猪的长矛;心里尽管隐藏着女人家的胆怯,俺要在外表上装出一副雄赳赳气昂昂的样子来,正像那些冒充好汉的懦夫一般。

(朱生豪译《皆大欢喜》第 1 幕第 3 场)

评点

两位贵族小姐即将离开原生家庭,独闯世界,不但失去了养尊处优的生活,而且还脱离了人身保护,难免顾虑重重。不过,姐妹俩总能以积极乐观的心态面对一切困难。剧中的罗瑟琳一贯聪明活泼,伶牙俐齿,即便谈论自己女扮男装的计划,她也能借此讽刺"表里不一"的社会风气。

---

[1] swashing: swash-buckling, flamboyantly adventurous and boastful.
[2] mannish: ostentatiously manly (usually applied to masculine women).
[3] outface it: brave it out.
[4] semblances: appearances.

场景 2：苦中作乐

（"Sweet are the uses of adversity."）

> 第 1 幕展示了奥兰多与罗瑟琳各自逃亡的起因，第 2 幕则切换到了阿登森林——第 1 幕里几次提到的流亡公爵（即罗瑟琳的父亲）就坐镇阿登森林。

Duke Senior　Now, my co-mates and brothers in exile,
　　　　　　　Hath not old custom[1] made this life more sweet
　　　　　　　Than that of painted pomp[2]? Are not these woods
　　　　　　　More free from peril than the envious court?
　　　　　　　Here feel we not the penalty of Adam[3],
　　　　　　　The seasons' difference — as the icy fang[4]
　　　　　　　And churlish chiding[5] of the winter's wind,
　　　　　　　Which when it bites and blows upon my body,
　　　　　　　Even till I shrink with cold, I smile and say:
　　　　　　　'This is no flattery. These are counsellors
　　　　　　　That feelingly persuade me what I am.'
　　　　　　　Sweet are the uses of adversity,
　　　　　　　Which, like the toad, ugly and venomous[6],
　　　　　　　Wears yet a precious jewel in his head[7];
　　　　　　　And this our life, exempt from public haunt,

---

[1] old custom: ancient traditions of pastoral innocence.
[2] painted pomp: ceremonial display.
[3] the penalty of Adam: According to Genesis（《圣经·创世纪》）, God punished Adam for eating the forbidden fruit. As a result, Adam and Eve were driven out of Eden and into the fallen world where human beings have to work very hard in order to make a living.
[4] fang: tooth.
[5] churlish chiding: rude scolding.
[6] venomous: poisonous.
[7] Toadstones（蟾蜍石）are mythical stones that were thought to be found inside the head of a toad. They were believed to sweat, change colour or even heat up in the presence of poison. It was thought that a toadstone placed on bites from snakes, insects, spiders and shrews would extract poison from the wound.

  Finds tongues in trees, books in the running brooks,
  Sermons in stones, and good in everything.
(*As You Like It* 2.1)

公爵 我的流放生涯中的同伴和弟兄们，我们不是已经习惯了这种生活，觉得它比虚饰的浮华有趣得多吗？这些树林不比猜嫉的朝廷更为安全吗？我们在这儿所感觉到的，只是时序的改变，那是上帝加于亚当的惩罚；冬天的寒风张舞着冰雪的爪牙，发出暴声的呼啸，即使当它砭刺着我的身体，使我冷得发抖的时候，我也会微笑着说："这不是谄媚啊；它们就像是忠臣一样，谆谆提醒我所处的地位。"逆运也有它的好处，就像丑陋而有毒的蟾蜍，它的头上却顶着一颗珍贵的宝石。我们的这种生活，虽然远离尘嚣，却可以听树木的谈话，溪中的流水便是大好的文章，一石之微，也暗寓着教训；每一件事物中间，都可以找到些益处来。我不愿改变这种生活。

（朱生豪译《皆大欢喜》第2幕第1场）

评点

  老公爵及其随员被迫在阿登森林里生活。虽然条件艰苦，但也能苦中作乐，在大自然里感悟人生真谛，获得精神上的宁静与自由，甚至不乏诗情画意与浪漫情怀。这种返璞归真、拒斥世俗纷扰的田园牧歌是西方文学史上的一大常见主题，其中也不乏西方基督教传统上的禁欲苦修精神。

  不过，这种安贫乐道的心态也许主要因为老公爵处于人生低谷期，而不是真心自愿选择隐居生活。否则，剧终爵位失而复得之时，他怎么就立马打道回府了呢？

场景 3：世态炎凉

("… misery doth part the flux of company.")

> 阿登森林里的流放生活主要以打猎为主。老公爵与其随员笑谈杰奎斯（Jaques）因一只受伤的鹿而感慨万千、针砭时弊……

Duke Senior　　　　　　　But what said Jaques?
　　　　　　　　Did he not moralize this spectacle?
First Lord　O yes, into a thousand similes.
　　　　　First, for his weeping into the needless stream:
　　　　　'Poor deer,' quoth he, 'thou mak'st a testament
　　　　　As worldlings[1] do, giving thy sum of more
　　　　　To that which had too much[2].' Then being there alone,
　　　　　Left and abandoned of his velvet friends[3]:
　　　　　''Tis right,' quoth he, 'thus misery doth part[4]
　　　　　The flux[5] of company.' Anon a careless[6] herd,
　　　　　Full of the pasture[7], jumps along by him
　　　　　And never stays to greet him. 'Ay,' quoth Jaques,
　　　　　'Sweep on, you fat and greasy citizens!
　　　　　'Tis just the fashion. Wherefore do you look
　　　　　Upon that poor and broken bankrupt there?'

---

[1] worldlings: people whose values are shaped by their worldly wealth and consequence.
[2] giving thy sum of more / To that which had too much: According to Matthew（《圣经·马太福音》）, 25:29, "For unto every one that hath shall be given, and he shall have abundance; but from him that hath not shall be taken away even that which he hath". 此即"马太效应"的名称由来。
[3] velvet friends: other deer. The term may also refer to the Elizabethan aristocrats who were allowed to wear velvet.
[4] part: set apart from.
[5] flux: superfluity, excess.
[6] careless: unconcerned.
[7] full of the pasture: having newly grazed.

> Thus most invectively[1] he pierceth through
> The body of the country, city, court,
> Yea, and of this our life, swearing that we
> Are mere[2] usurpers, tyrants, and what's worse,
> To fright the animals, and to kill them up
> In their assigned and native dwelling-place.

(*As You Like It* 2.1)

公爵 但是杰奎斯怎样说呢？他见了此情此景，不又要讲起一番道理来了吗？

臣甲 啊，是的，他作了一千种的譬喻。起初他看见那鹿把眼泪浪费地流下了水流之中，便说，"可怜的鹿，他就像世人立遗嘱一样，把你所有的一切给了那已经有得太多的人。"于是，看它孤苦零丁，被它那些皮毛柔滑的朋友们所遗弃，便说，"不错，人倒了霉，朋友也不会来睬你了。"不久又有一群吃得饱饱的、无忧无虑的鹿跳过它的身边，也不停下来向它打个招呼；"嗯，"杰奎斯说，"奔过去吧，你们这批肥胖而富于脂肪的市民们；世事无非如此，那个可怜的破产的家伙，瞧他作什么呢？"他这样用最恶毒的话来辱骂着乡村、城市和宫廷的一切，甚至于骂着我们的这种生活；发誓说我们只是些篡位者、暴君或者比这更坏的人物，到这些畜生们的天然的居处来惊扰它们，杀害它们。

（朱生豪译《皆大欢喜》第2幕第1场）

评点

剧中第一次提及杰奎斯，就给他贴上了"忧郁"标签——"忧郁的杰奎斯"（the melancholy Jaques）。此人愤世嫉俗，总有惊人之语。此处，杰奎斯表面上惜鹿，其实是在叹人，以鹿为喻，洞悉世态炎凉与人间丑恶。

大自然是一本无言的大书。既然老公爵能在石头里看到训诫（"Sermons in stones"）——见本章场景2"苦中作乐"，杰奎斯也能在鹿群中看到人情冷暖。在大自然中参禅悟道是西方文化传统中的常用操作，尤其是中世纪离群索居的隐修士。《皆大欢喜》剧终，杰奎斯拒绝随公爵回城，选择继续隐居山林——见本章场景15"离群索居"。

---

[1] invectively: with satirical thrusts.
[2] mere: downright, absolute.

场景 4：绿林欢歌

("Under the greenwood tree ...")

> 阿登森林的浪漫生活少不了弹琴唱歌。以下这一曲描绘了绿林生活的自由与美好，却也提到了寒风凛冽的恶劣天气。

Amiens   [*Sings.*] Under the greenwood tree
                     Who loves to lie with me,
                     And turn his merry note
                     Unto the sweet bird's throat[1],
                     Come hither, come hither, come hither!
     All   [*Sings.*] Here shall he see no enemy
                     But winter and rough weather.

……

Amiens   [*Sings.*] Who doth ambition shun,
                     And loves to live i'th' sun[2],
                     Seeking the food he eats
                     And pleased with what he gets,
                     Come hither, come hither, come hither!
     All   [*Sings.*] Here shall he see no enemy
                     But winter and rough weather.

(*As You Like It* 2.5)

---

[1] throat: voice, warbling.
[2] i'th' sun: in the open air, away from the confines of the indoor and envious court.

阿米恩斯（唱）　绿树高张翠幕，
　　　　　　　　谁来偕我偃卧，
　　　　　　　　翻将欢乐心声，
　　　　　　　　学唱枝头鸟鸣：
　　　　　　　　盍来此？盍来此？盍来此？
　　众　（和）　目之所接，精神契一，
　　　　　　　　唯忧雨雪之将至。
…………
阿米恩斯（唱）　孰能敝屣尊荣，
　　　　　　　　来沐丽日光风，
　　　　　　　　觅食自求果腹，
　　　　　　　　一饱欣然意足：
　　　　　　　　盍来此？盍来此？盍来此？
　　众　（和）　目之所接，精神契一，
　　　　　　　　唯忧雨雪之将至。

（朱生豪译《皆大欢喜》第 2 幕第 5 场）

评点

　　这两段歌词均为 7 行：前 5 行赞美风景如画、自由快乐的田园生活，后两行强调这里"没有敌人"（no enemy），尽管这里有"寒冬与恶劣天气"（winter and rough weather）。歌者宁可忍受自然界的寒冬，也不愿卷入错综复杂的人际纷争；人类社会里的"敌人"比自然界的"寒冬"更可怕。遗憾的是，朱生豪对后两行的翻译并没忠实于原文，而是基于原作的再创作，含义有别。

　　这首歌词与老公爵的出场独白（见本章场景 2 "苦中作乐"）一脉相承：在诗情画意的浪漫人生的表象之下，掩藏着一段争名夺利、尔虞我诈的不堪往事，表达了厌倦尘世纷争的心声。

场景 5：畅所欲言

（"Give me leave to speak my mind …"）

> 在阿登森林里，杰奎斯第一次偶遇罗瑟琳姐妹的随从——宫廷小丑试金石（Touchstone），兴奋不已，随即向老公爵表达了自己也想当小丑的愿望（O that I were a fool! / I am ambitious for a motley coat[1]），理由如下。

Jaques It is my only suit[2],
Provided that you weed your better judgments
Of all opinion that grows rank[3] in them
That I am wise. I must have liberty
Withal[4], as large a charter[5] as the wind
To blow on whom I please, for so fools have,
And they that are most galled[6] with my folly,
They most must laugh. And why, sir, must they so?
The why is plain as way to parish church.
He that a fool doth very wisely hit
Doth very foolishly, although he smart,
Not to seem senseless of the bob[7]. If not,
The wise man's folly is anatomized
Even by the squandering[8] glances of the fool.
Invest[9] me in my motley. Give me leave
To speak my mind, and I will through and through
Cleanse the foul body of th'infected world,
If they will patiently receive my medicine.

(*As You Like It* 2.7)

---

[1] a motley coat: a fool's costume.
[2] suit: plea, i.e. legal suit, and a suit of clothes. 此为双关语。
[3] rank: gross, often including foul smells.
[4] withal: in addition.
[5] charter: licence, contract.
[6] galled: provoked.
[7] bob: knock, light glancing blow; jibe, taunt.
[8] squandering: extravagant.
[9] invest: clothe in official robes.

杰奎斯 这是我唯一的要求；只要殿下明鉴，除掉一切成见，别把我当聪明人看待；同时要准许我有像风那样广大的自由，高兴吹着谁便吹着谁：傻子们是有这种权利的，那些最被我的傻话所挖苦的人也最应该笑。殿下，为什么他们必须这样呢？这理由正和到教区礼拜堂去的路一样清楚：被一个傻子用俏皮话讥刺了的人，即使刺痛了，假如不装出一副若无其事的样子来，那么就显出聪明人的傻气，可以被傻子不经意一箭就刺穿，未免太傻了。给我穿一件彩衣，准许我说我心里的话；我一定会痛痛快快地把这染病的世界的丑恶的身体清洗个干净，假如他们肯耐心接受我的药方。

（朱生豪译《皆大欢喜》第 2 幕第 7 场）

评点

莎士比亚戏剧不乏宫廷小丑（jester / fool / clown，亦可译为"弄臣"或"傻子"）这一喜剧角色，比如《李尔王》《第十二夜》《皆大欢喜》等。《哈姆莱特》一剧甚至还上演了哈姆莱特手捧小丑头骨的一幕，足以可见这种角色在西方传统文化中的重要性。

小丑原本就是取乐的对象，社会地位不高，却因职业之故而拥有嬉笑怒骂、插科打诨而且不会因言获罪的特权。相比而言，其他有头有脸的人往往顾虑重重，说话慎重，难以一吐为快。因此，愤世嫉俗的杰奎斯十分羡慕这种口无遮拦的自由。

场景 6：以柔克刚

（"Your gentleness shall force …"）

奥兰多为了逃避兄长的迫害，不得不带着老仆人逃入阿登森林，他们饥渴难耐。一见老公爵等人在林中聚餐，奥兰多就拔剑威胁，企图强取豪夺。

Duke Art thou thus boldened[1], man, by thy distress?
   Or else a rude despiser of good manners,
   That in civility thou seem'st so empty?
Orlando You touched my vein[2] at first. The thorny point
   Of bare distress hath ta'en from me the show
   Of smooth civility; yet am I inland bred[3]
   And know some nurture[4]. But forbear, I say !
   He dies that touches any of this fruit
   Till I and my affairs are answered.
Jaques An[5] you will not be answered with reason, I must die.
Duke What would you have? Your gentleness shall force
   More than your force move us to gentleness.
Orlando I almost die for food, and let me have it.
Duke Sit down and feed, and welcome to our table.
Orlando Speak you so gently[6]? Pardon me, I pray you.
   I thought that all things had been savage here
   And therefore put I on the countenance
   Of stern commandment. But whate'er you are,
   That in this desert inaccessible,
   Under the shade of melancholy boughs,
   Lose and neglect the creeping hours of time —
   If ever you have looked on better days,
   If ever been where bells have knolled[7] to church,

---

[1] boldened: emboldened.
[2] touched my vein: hit upon my condition, as of a surgeon opening a vein.
[3] inland bred: brought up in the court.
[4] nurture: good breeding.
[5] an: if.
[6] gently: kindly, but also as a nobleman.
[7] knolled: the word "knoll" combines the tolling of the bell to summon the faithful to the church, and the knell for the dead.

> If ever sat at any good man's feast,
> If ever from your eyelids wiped a tear,
> And know what 'tis to pity[1] and be pitied —
> Let gentleness my strong enforcement be,
> In the which hope, I blush and hide my sword.

(*As You Like It* 2.7)

公爵　朋友，你是因为落难而变得这样强横吗？还是因为生来就是瞧不起礼貌的粗汉子，一点儿不懂得规矩？

奥兰多　你第一下就猜中我了，困苦逼迫着我，使我不得不把温文的礼貌抛在一旁；可是我却是在都市生长，受过一点儿教养的。但是我吩咐你们停住；在我的事情没有办完之前，谁碰一碰这些果子，就得死。

杰奎斯　你要是无理可喻，那么我准得死。

公爵　你要什么？假如你不用暴力，客客气气地向我们说，我们一定会更客客气气地对待你的。

奥兰多　我快饿死了；给我吃。

公爵　请坐请坐，随意吃吧。

奥兰多　你说得这样客气吗？请你原谅我，我以为这儿的一切都是野蛮的，因此才装出这副暴横的威胁神气来。可是不论你们是些什么人，在这儿人踪不到的荒野里，躺在凄凉的树荫下，不理会时间的消逝；假如你们曾经见过较好的日子，假如你们曾经到过鸣钟召集礼拜的地方，假如你们曾经参加过上流人的宴会，假如你们曾经揩过你们眼皮上的泪水，懂得怜悯和被怜悯的，那么让我的温文的态度格外感动你们：我抱着这样的希望，惭愧地藏好我的剑。

（朱生豪译《皆大欢喜》第 2 幕第 7 场）

评点

暴力不可取，以暴制暴为君子不齿；相反温文尔雅是一种强大的无形力量，强过唇枪舌剑或真刀真枪。面对不速之客，老公爵表现得沉稳而宽厚，主动邀请奥兰多落座就餐，尽显大度风范，令奥兰多不禁为自己的鲁莽失礼而羞愧不已。

老公爵教导奥兰多的一句"客客气气地向我们说，我们一定会更客客气气地对待你的"（Your gentleness shall force / More than your force move us to gentleness）采用了交错配列（chiasmus）修辞手法："文雅"（gentleness）与"武力"（force）截然对立，相映成趣；"文雅"可能比"武力"更能有效达到目的，甚至化敌为友。

---

[1] pity: in both chivalric and Christian sense.

场景7：人生如戏

（"All the world's a stage."）

> 走投无路的奥兰多在阿登森林被流放于此的老公爵接纳，随即去接他那奄奄一息的老仆人。公爵与杰奎斯眼看奥兰多的窘迫，又听闻奥兰多对自己仆人惨状的描述，不由得感慨万千。

Duke   Thou seest we are not all alone unhappy.
This wide and universal theatre
Presents more woeful pageants than the scene
Wherein we play in.

Jaques   All the world's a stage,
And all the men and women merely players.
They have their exits and their entrances,
And one man in his time plays many parts,
His acts[1] being seven ages. At first the infant,
Mewling and puking[2] in the nurse's arms;
Then the whining school-boy, with his satchel
And shining morning face, creeping like snail
Unwillingly to school; and then the lover,
Sighing like furnace, with a woeful ballad
Made to his mistress' eyebrow[3]; then a soldier,
Full of strange[4] oaths and bearded like the pard[5],
Jealous in honour, sudden[6] and quick in quarrel,
Seeking the bubble reputation
Even in the cannon's mouth; and then the justice,

---

[1] acts: divisions as in a play. 一部剧通常分为若干幕（act），每一幕分为若干场（scene）。
[2] mewling and puking: wailing and vomiting.
[3] mistress' eyebrow: a typically Petrarchan extravagance on courtly love poetry.
[4] strange: outlandish.
[5] pard: leopard.
[6] sudden: impetuous, unpredictable.

In fair round belly with good capon[1] lined,
With eyes severe and beard of formal cut[2],
Full of wise saws[3] and modern[4] instances[5];
And so he plays his part. The sixth age shifts
Into the lean and slippered pantaloon[6],
With spectacles on nose and pouch[7] on side,
His youthful hose[8] well saved, a world[9] too wide
For his shrunk shank, and his big manly voice,
Turning again toward childish treble[10], pipes
And whistles in his sound. Last scene of all,
That ends this strange eventful history,
Is second childishness and mere[11] oblivion,
Sans[12] teeth, sans eyes, sans taste, sans everything.

(*As You Like It* 2.7)

公爵　你们可以看到不幸的不只是我们；这个广大的宇宙的舞台上，还有比我们所演出的更悲惨的场景呢。

杰奎斯　全世界是一个舞台，所有的男男女女不过是一些演员；他们都有下场的时候，也都有上场的时候。一个人的一生中扮演着好几个角色，他的表演可以分为七个时期。最初是婴孩，在保姆的怀中啼哭呕吐。然后是背着书包、满脸红光的学童，像蜗牛一样慢腾腾地拖着脚步，不情愿地呜咽着上学堂。然后是情人，像炉灶一样叹着气，写了一首悲哀的诗歌咏着他恋人的眉毛。然后是一个军人，满口发着古怪的誓，胡须长得像豹子一样，爱惜着名誉，动不动就要打架，在炮口上寻求

---

[1] capon: a castrated cock.

[2] formal cut: trimmed appropriately for the dignity of his office.
[3] saws: sayings, precepts.
[4] modern: recent, new.
[5] instances: arguments or examples, used to defend a legal case.
[6] pantaloon: baggy trousers.
[7] pouch: purse.
[8] hose: stockings or tight trousers worn by men in the past.
[9] a world: much.
[10] childish treble: the high-pitched voice of a child.
[11] mere: total.
[12] sans: without.

着泡沫一样的荣名。然后是法官，胖胖圆圆的肚子塞满了阉鸡，凛然的眼光，整洁的胡须，满嘴都是格言和老生常谈；他这样扮了他的一个角色。第六个时期变成了精瘦的趿着拖鞋的龙钟老叟，鼻子上架着眼镜，腰边悬着钱袋；他那年轻时候节省下来的长袜子套在他皱瘪的小腿上显得宽大异常；他那朗朗的男子的口音又变成了孩子似的尖声，像是吹着风笛和哨子。终结着这段古怪的多事的历史的最后一场，是孩提时代的再现，全然的遗忘，没有牙齿，没有眼睛，没有口味，没有一切。

（朱生豪译《皆大欢喜》第2幕第7场）

评点

这是莎士比亚戏剧中最为经典、最脍炙人口的台词之一，呈现了两位饱经沧桑的没落贵族的人生感悟。公爵尽管沦落荒野，但是他安贫乐道，依然保持善良本质与平和心态，对他人的不幸充满同情。他把世界比作戏台，把个人比作演员，人生如戏，既有开场，也有落幕。

戏剧与人生的相关比喻在莎士比亚戏剧中屡屡出现。比如，在莎士比亚另一部喜剧《第十二夜》的第3幕第4场中，一个仆人角色这样评论难以置信的现实情况："要是这种情形在舞台上表演起来，我一定要批评它捏造得出乎情理之外。"（If this were played upon a stage now, I could condemn it as an improbable fiction.）

杰奎斯的上述长段台词不仅呼应公爵的人生感慨，而且也颇为符合他对人生与社会的深刻洞察力及忧郁个性。按照他的说法，人生分为七个时期（seven ages）：婴儿、学童、情郎、士兵、法官、老人，以及最终的行将就木。针对每个时期，杰奎斯都进行了一番个性化描述与犀利评论：各个时段各有特色，或可笑，或辛酸，或无奈，没有哪个人生时段是绝对的好或不好，人最终都将无可避免地走向衰亡，其中不乏无奈与讽刺。

这番人生感悟也许体现了杰奎斯的清醒睿智，其实却是西方文化传统上的老生常谈。从古典时期到文艺复兴时期，人生阶段论都是一个经久不衰的话题，有多种不同的划分方式：除了七阶段论之外，还有五阶段论、九阶段论、十二阶段论等，在诗文画作中多有所体现。杰奎斯（或者说剧作家莎士比亚）的这一名段以语言修辞、意象刻画见长，因此流芳百世。

其中，那行将就木的最后阶段被称为"孩提时代的再现"（second childishness）——这种说法在莎士比亚时期已成为谚语，莎士比亚的其他作品中也有所体现。比如在《哈姆莱特》第2幕第2场中，哈姆莱特跟两个老同学私下里嘲讽御前大臣波洛涅斯的对话。

Hamlet Hark you, Guildenstern, and you too at each ear a hearer. That great baby you see there is not yet out of his swaddling clouts[1].

Rosencrantz Happily[2] he is the second time come to them, for they say an old man is twice a child.

---

[1] swaddling clouts: swathing clothes, narrow strips of cloth wrapped around a baby to restrict its movement.
[2] happily: perhaps.

场景 8：寒风凛冽

("Blow, blow, thou winter wind!")

> 奥兰多与其仆人加入了老公爵的宴席。在众人大快朵颐之时，老公爵请同伴唱歌助兴。

Amiens (*Sings.*) Blow, blow, thou winter wind,
　　　　　　　　Thou art not so unkind[1]
　　　　　　　　As man's ingratitude.
　　　　　　　　Thy tooth is not so keen[2]
　　　　　　　　Because thou art not seen,
　　　　　　　　Although thy breath be rude[3].
　　　　　　　　Hey-ho, sing hey-ho, unto the green holly.
　　　　　　　　Most friendship is feigning[4], most loving mere folly.
　　　　　　　　Then hey-ho, the holly!
　　　　　　　　This life is most jolly.

　　　　　　　　Freeze, freeze, thou bitter sky,
　　　　　　　　That dost not bite so nigh[5]
　　　　　　　　As benefits forgot.
　　　　　　　　Though thou the waters warp[6],
　　　　　　　　Thy sting is not so sharp
　　　　　　　　As friend remembered not[7].
　　　　　　　　Hey-ho, sing hey-ho, unto the green holly[8].

---

[1] unkind: cruel, but also unnatural.
[2] keen: sharp.
[3] rude: rough, but also unmannerly.
[4] feigning: pretending.
[5] nigh: near.
[6] warp: ruffle.
[7] friend remembered not: the act of forgetting a friend, as well as the friend who is forgotten.
[8] green holly: evocative both of Christmas and of many pagan festivities and superstitions, as well as of Robin Hood's greenwood.

Most friendship is feigning, most loving mere folly.
Then hey-ho, the holly!
This life is most jolly.

(*As You Like It* 2.7)

阿米恩斯（唱）　不惧冬风凛冽，
　　　　　　　　风威远难遽及
　　　　　　　　人世之寡情；
　　　　　　　　其为气也虽厉，
　　　　　　　　其牙尚非甚锐，
　　　　　　　　风体本无形。
　　　　　　　　噫嘻乎！且向冬青歌一曲：
　　　　　　　　友交皆虚妄，恩爱痴人逐。
　　　　　　　　噫嘻乎冬青！
　　　　　　　　可乐唯此生。

　　　　　　　　不愁沍天冰雪，
　　　　　　　　其寒尚难遽及，
　　　　　　　　受施而忘恩；
　　　　　　　　风皱满池碧水，
　　　　　　　　利刺尚难遽比
　　　　　　　　捐旧之友人。
　　　　　　　　噫嘻乎！且向冬青歌一曲：
　　　　　　　　友交皆虚妄，恩爱痴人逐。
　　　　　　　　噫嘻乎冬青！
　　　　　　　　可乐唯此生。

（朱生豪译《皆大欢喜》第 2 幕第 7 场）

评点

　　这一首歌与前面那首《绿林欢歌》都是由同一个人物角色所唱，同样歌唱户外生活，同样借景抒情、感叹世事复杂，侧重点却有所不同：前面那首以绿树成荫、鸟语花香的正面描绘为主，即便提到寒冬，也只是一笔带过；这一首则重点突显寒风刺骨，借此抒发愤世嫉俗之情。

场景 9：田园哲学

（"Hast any philosophy in thee, shepherd?"）

> 罗瑟琳姐妹在阿登森林购置了一座农舍，雇人放羊，由此过上了悠闲的田园生活。她俩的随从试金石与老牧羊人闲聊生活哲学，处处标榜自己的优越性，却不得不折服于老牧羊人的朴实理念。

Corin　　　And how like you this shepherd's life, Master Touchstone?

Touchstone　Truly, shepherd, in respect of itself, it is a good life; but in respect that it is a shepherd's life, it is naught[1]. In respect that it is solitary[2], I like it very well; but in respect that it is private[3], it is a very vile[4] life. Now in respect it is in the fields, it pleaseth me well; but in respect it is not in the court, it is tedious. As it is a spare[5] life, look you, it fits my humour[6] well; but as there is no more plenty in it, it goes much against my stomach. Hast any philosophy in thee, shepherd?

Corin　　　No more but[7] that I know the more one sickens the worse at ease he is; and that he that wants money, means[8] and content, is without three good friends; that the property[9] of rain is to wet and fire to burn; that good pasture makes fat sheep; and that a great cause of the night is lack of the sun; that he that hath learned no wit[10] by nature nor art[11] may complain of poor breeding or comes of a very dull

---

[1] naught: worthless.
[2] solitary: as in the contemplative life.
[3] private: lacking company, i.e. without access to public life and therefore unappealing for a court jester.
[4] vile: low, despised.
[5] spare: frugal.
[6] humour: constitution, mood.
[7] no more but: only.
[8] means: capacity.
[9] property: innate character.
[10] wit: understanding.
[11] art: skill.

kindred[1].

Touchstone Such a one is a natural philosopher[2].

(*As You Like It* 3.2)

柯林　您喜欢不喜欢这种牧人的生活，试金石先生？

试金石　说老实话，牧人，按着这种生活的本身说起来，倒是一种很好的生活；可是按着这是一种牧人的生活说起来，那就毫不足取了。照它的清静而论，我很喜欢这种生活；可是照它的寂寞而论，实在是一种很坏的生活。看到这种生活是在田间，很使我满意；可是看到它不是在宫廷里，那简直很无聊。你瞧，这是一种很经济的生活，因此倒怪合我的脾胃；可是它未免太寒伧了，因此我过不来。你懂不懂得一点哲学，牧人？

柯林　我只知道这一点儿：一个人越是害病，他越是不舒服；钱财、资本和知足，是人们缺少不来的三位好朋友；雨湿淋衣，火旺烧柴；好牧场产肥羊，天黑是因为没有了太阳；生来愚笨怪祖父，学而不慧师之情。

试金石　这样一个人是天生的哲学家了。

（朱生豪译《皆大欢喜》第 3 幕第 2 场）

评点

尽管田园牧歌是莎士比亚时代的一大文艺风尚，公子小姐热衷于扮演牧羊人与牧羊女，但是在阿登森林里真正过上牧羊生活的宫廷小丑试金石深知艺术与现实的差距：在理想化、浪漫化、诗意化的田园牧歌背后，是单调、平庸、无趣的乡野现实生活。

试金石问老牧羊人是否懂哲学，话题转换颇为突兀。二人的对话展现了宫廷与乡村的文化对比与思想碰撞：宫廷小丑精明且俏皮，却在村姑、农民面前处处标榜自身的优越感；老牧羊人虽然没有多少文化，但是淳朴忠厚，不乏务实的经验常识与朴素的处世智慧，在趾高气扬的宫廷小丑面前表现得沉稳宽厚、不卑不亢。二者的语言交锋颇具喜剧色彩。

---

[1] dull kindred: stupid family.

[2] natural philosopher: a pun on the "natural" wisdom of the uneducated, and the insight of a philosopher of the Natural or Libertine school, with elevated Reason and Nature above divine revelation in accordance with Stoic and Epicurean thought. It also encompassed the pioneering study of the physical universe by Montaigne, Donne, Bacon, Harriot and Harington.

场景 10：痴心一片

("Love is merely a madness …")

> 在阿登森林里，奥兰多把写给罗瑟琳的情诗挂在树上，恰巧被罗瑟琳撞见；而奥兰多没有认出女扮男装的罗瑟琳。罗瑟琳隐瞒真实身份，变着法子试探、捉弄奥兰多。

Rosalind　But are you so much in love as your rhymes speak?

Orlando　Neither rhyme nor reason can express how much.

Rosalind　Love is merely a madness, and I tell you deserves as well a dark house and a whip as madmen do; and the reason why they are not so punished and cured is that the lunacy is so ordinary that the whippers are in love too. Yet I profess curing it by counsel.

Orlando　Did you ever cure any so?

Rosalind　Yes, one, and in this manner. He was to imagine me his love, his mistress, and I set him every day to woo me. At which time would I — being but a moonish[1] youth — grieve, be effeminate[2], changeable, longing and liking[3], proud, fantastical[4], apish[5], shallow, inconstant, full of tears, full of smiles; for every passion something and for no passion truly anything, as boys and women are for the most part cattle of this colour[6]; would now like him, now loathe him; then entertain him, then forswear him; now weep for him, then spit at him; that I drave[7] my suitor from his mad humour of love to a living[8] humour of madness, which was to forswear the full stream of the world and to live in a nook[9] merely

---

[1] moonish: moody, governed by the moon.
[2] effeminate: (of a man or a boy) looking, behaving or sounding like a woman or a girl.
[3] liking: loving.
[4] fantastical: full of extravagant fancies.
[5] apish: inclined to imitate.
[6] cattle of this colour: creatures of this kind.
[7] drave: (archaic, north-country form) drove.
[8] living: vital.
[9] nook: corner.

monastic. And thus I cured him, and this way will I take upon me to wash your liver[1] as clean as a sound sheep's heart, that there shall not be one spot of love in't.

(*As You Like It* 3.2)

罗瑟琳　可是你真的像你诗上所说的那样热恋着吗？
奥兰多　什么也不能表达我的爱情的深切。
罗瑟琳　爱情不过是一种疯狂；我对你说，有了爱情的人，是应该像对待一个疯子一样，把他关在黑屋子里用鞭子抽一顿的。那么为什么他们不用这种处罚的方法来医治爱情呢？因为那种疯病是极其平常的，就是拿鞭子的人也在恋爱哩。可是我有医治它的法子。
奥兰多　你曾经医治过什么人吗？
罗瑟琳　是的，医治过一个；法子是这样的：他假想我是他的爱人，他的情妇，我叫他每天都来向我求爱；那时我是一个善变的少年，便一会儿伤心，一会儿温存，一会儿翻脸，一会儿思慕，一会儿欢喜；骄傲、古怪、刁钻、浅薄、轻浮，有时满眼的泪，有时满脸的笑。什么情感都来一点儿，但没有一种是真切的，就像大多数的孩子们和女人们一样；有时欢喜他，有时讨厌他，有时讨好他，有时冷淡他，有时为他哭泣，有时把他唾弃：我这样把我这位求爱者从疯狂的爱逼到真个疯狂起来，以至于抛弃人世，做起隐士来了。我用这种方法治好了他，我也可以用这种方法把你的心肝洗得干干净净，像一颗没有毛病的羊心一样，再没有一点爱情的痕迹。

（朱生豪译《皆大欢喜》第 3 幕第 2 场）

评点

　　此时的罗瑟琳扮作一个乡村美少年，机智而俏皮，对爱情不屑一顾，对朝思暮想她的奥兰多百般打趣。她所称的"爱情不过是一种疯狂"（Love is merely madness），在莎士比亚的其他剧本也有类似说法，比如《仲夏夜之梦》也常常将爱与疯狂挂钩。

　　罗瑟琳在一番试探之后，见奥兰多真心爱她，便打着为他治相思病的名义，要与奥兰多一起玩"谈恋爱"的游戏：奥兰多可以把罗瑟琳扮演的这个美少年想象成罗瑟琳，天天来向她求爱。

---

[1] liver: believed to be the seat of the passions.

场景 11：美言不信

("… the truest poetry is the most faining.")

> 在罗瑟琳与奥兰多谈情说爱的同时，小丑试金石与牧羊女奥德蕾也谈起恋爱。不过，后二者的关系并不平等，试金石总爱取笑牧羊女单纯无知，处处表现自己高人一等的优越感。

Touchstone　　I am here with thee and thy goats, as the most capricious poet, honest Ovid, was among the Goths.

……

Touchstone　　When a man's verses cannot be understood, nor a man's good wit seconded with[1] the forward[2] child, understanding, it strikes a man more dead than a great reckoning in a little room. Truly, I would the gods had made thee poetical.

Audrey　　I do not know what poetical is. Is it honest in deed and word? Is it a true thing?

Touchstone　　No, truly; for the truest poetry is the most faining[3], and lovers are given to poetry, and what they swear in poetry may be said, as lovers, they do feign.

Audrey　　Do you wish then that the gods had made me poetical?

Touchstone　　I do truly, for thou swear'st to me thou art honest. Now if thou wert a poet, I might have some hope thou didst feign.

Audrey　　Would you not have me honest?

Touchstone　　No, truly, unless thou wert hard-favoured[4]; for honesty coupled to beauty is to have honey a sauce to sugar[5].

(*As You Like It* 3.3)

---

[1]　seconded with: reinforced by.
[2]　forward: precocious.
[3]　faining: desiring or longing. It is punned with "feign", meaning to pretend, or to create fictions.
[4]　hard-favoured: ugly.
[5]　to have honey a sauce to sugar: i.e. to have too much of a good thing.

试金石　我陪着你和你的山羊在这里，就像那最会梦想的诗人奥维德在一群哥特人中间一样。

……………

试金石　要是一个人写的诗不能叫人懂，他的才情不能叫人理解，那比之小客栈里开出一张大账单来还要命。真的，我希望神们把你变得诗意一点。

奥德蕾　我不懂得什么叫做"诗意一点"。那是一句好话，一件好事情吗？那是诚实的吗？

试金石　老实说，不，因为最真实的诗是最虚妄的；情人们都富于诗意，他们在诗里发的誓，可以说都是情人们的假话。

奥德蕾　那么您愿意天爷爷们把我变得诗意一点吗？

试金石　是的，不错；因为你发誓说你是贞洁的，假如你是个诗人，我就可以希望你说的是假话了。

奥德蕾　您不愿意我贞洁吗？

试金石　对了，除非你生得难看；因为贞洁跟美貌碰在一起，就像在糖里再加蜜。

（朱生豪译《皆大欢喜》第 3 幕第 3 场）

评点

　　试金石喜欢牧羊女，却采用屈尊与垂青的姿态，比如他感叹牧羊女与他不在同一个文化层次（I would the gods had made thee poetical）；他明知牧羊女不擅长文字游戏，却满嘴俏皮话，振振有词地卖弄名言警句，故意让牧羊女掉进文字圈套。

　　牧羊女固然无知，却不乏自尊，于是，二人的对话近乎性别的较量、社会阶层的交锋、价值观的碰撞。比如二人争辩美貌与贞洁的关系，莎士比亚时代不乏有观点认为二者此消彼长、难以并存。

　　试金石的打趣嘲笑往往体现了文艺复兴时期的思想潮流。例如，"最真实的诗是最虚妄的"（The truest poetry is the most faining）一句谈到诗歌与真理之间的关系，这个话题自从古希腊柏拉图的《理想国》到 16 世纪西德尼爵士的《为诗一辩》，一直都是文化传统上的重要议题。

场景 12：多愁善感

("… it is a melancholy of mine own …")

> 杰奎斯结识了女扮男装的罗瑟琳，罗瑟琳则对杰奎斯的"忧郁"早有耳闻，由此展开一番关于忧郁的讨论。

Jaques　　I prithee, pretty youth, let me be better acquainted with thee.

Rosalind　They say you are a melancholy fellow.

Jaques　　I am so; I do love it better than laughing.

Rosalind　Those that are in extremity of either are abominable fellows and betray themselves to every modern censure worse than drunkards.

Jaques　　Why, 'tis good to be sad and say nothing.

Rosalind　Why then, 'tis good to be a post.

Jaques　　I have neither the scholar's melancholy, which is emulation; nor the musician's, which is fantastical[1]; nor the courtier's, which is proud; nor the soldier's, which is ambitious; nor the lawyer's, which is politic[2]; nor the lady's, which is nice[3]; nor the lover's, which is all these; but it is a melancholy of mine own, compounded[4] of many simples[5], extracted from many objects, and indeed the sundry[6] computation[7] of my travels, in which my often rumination[8] wraps me in a most humorous[9] sadness.

---

[1] fantastical: indulging in fantasies.
[2] politic: expedient; usually a pejorative, associated with Machiavelli.
[3] nice: fastidious, particular.
[4] compound: constituted, made up or combined.
[5] simples: medicinal herbs.
[6] sundry: consisting of different elements, of mixed composition.
[7] computation: reckoning.
[8] my often rumination: my frequent reflection.
[9] humorous sadness: volatile melancholy or heaviness.

Rosalind　A traveller! By my faith, you have great reason to be sad. I fear you have sold your own lands to see other men's. Then to have seen much and to have nothing is to have rich eyes and poor hands.

(*As You Like It* 4.1)

杰奎斯　可爱的少年，请你许我跟你结识结识。
罗瑟琳　他们说你是个多愁的人。
杰奎斯　是的，我喜欢发愁不喜欢笑。
罗瑟琳　这两件事各趋极端，都会叫人讨厌，比之醉汉更容易招一般人的指摘。
杰奎斯　发发愁不说话，有什么不好？
罗瑟琳　那么何不做一根木头呢？
杰奎斯　我没有学者的忧愁，那是好胜；也没有音乐家的忧愁，那是幻想；也没有侍臣的忧愁，那是骄傲；也没有军人的忧愁，那是野心；也没有律师的忧愁，那是狡猾；也没有女人的忧愁，那是挑剔；也没有情人的忧愁，那是集上面一切之大成；我的忧愁全然是我独有的，它是由各种成分组成的，是从许多事物中提炼出来的，是我旅行中所得到的各种观感，因为不断沉思，终于把我笼罩在一种十分古怪的悲哀之中。
罗瑟琳　是一个旅行家吗？噢，那你就有应该悲哀的理由了。我想你多半是卖去了自己的田地去看别人的田地；看见的这么多，自己却一无所有；眼睛是看饱了，两手却是空空的。

（朱生豪译《皆大欢喜》第4幕第1场）

评点

"忧郁的杰奎斯"对别人给自己打上的"忧郁"标签不但非常坦然，而且还有几分自豪，特地强调自己的"忧郁"与众不同。确实，忧郁堪称文艺复兴时期的精英品位，在当时的文艺作品中多有体现——莎士比亚戏剧中就有不少忧郁人物，比如哈姆莱特。

杰奎斯认为自己游历广、见识多，而女扮男装的罗瑟琳则从世俗价值观的角度，嘲笑他饱了眼福，却亏了家产。二人的思想交锋体现截然不同的人生观：如果杰奎斯代表的是感性、理想、精神追求，那么罗瑟琳的嘲讽则代表了一种理性、务实、世俗的心态。

场景 13：爱情神话

(" Men have died ... but not for love. ")

> 阿登森林里的田园生活相当悠闲，女扮男装的罗瑟琳在奥兰多面前，扮演他的心上人罗瑟琳，可谓本色出演了！

Rosalind ... Am not I your Rosalind?

Orlando I take some joy to say you are because I would be talking of her.

Rosalind Well, in her person[1], I say I will not have you.

Orlando Then, in mine own person, I die.

Rosalind No, faith, die by attorney[2]. The poor world is almost six thousand years old[3], and in all this time there was not any man died in his own person (videlicet, in a love-cause[4]). Troilus[5] had his brains dashed out with a Grecian club[6], yet he did what he could to die before, and he is one of the patterns of love. Leander, he would have lived many a fair year though Hero had turned nun, if it had not been for a hot midsummer night; for, good youth, he went but forth to wash him in the Hellespont and, being taken with the cramp, was drowned, and the foolish chroniclers of that age found it was Hero of Sestos. But these are all lies. Men have died from time to time and worms have eaten them, but not for love.

(*As You Like It* 4.1)

---

[1] in her person: playing the part of the true Rosalind; ironic, as it also means "playing myself".
[2] by attorney: by proxy (代理人). Here is a contrast between "in person" and "by attorney".
[3] six thousand years old: Shakespeare's contemporaries believed that the world was around 6,000 years old.
[4] love-cause: case (legal), cause (the reason for love) and course (the progress of the love affair).
[5] Troilus: a Trojan prince famous for his fidelity to Cressida.
[6] Grecian club: a blunt (wooden) weapon wielded by a Greek adversary.

罗瑟琳　……我不是你的罗瑟琳吗？
奥兰多　我很愿意把你当作罗瑟琳，因为这样我就可以讲着她了。
罗瑟琳　好，我代表她说我不愿接受你。
奥兰多　那么我代表我自己说我要死去。
罗瑟琳　不，真的，还是请个人代死吧。这个可怜的世界差不多有六千年的岁数了，可是从来不曾有过一个人亲自殉情而死。特洛伊罗斯是被一个希腊人的棍棒砸出了脑浆的；可是在这以前他就已经寻过死，而他是一个模范的情人。即使希罗当了尼姑，里昂德也会活下去活了好多年的，倘不是因为一个酷热的仲夏之夜；因为，好孩子，他本来只是要到赫勒斯滂海峡里去洗个澡的，可是在水中害起抽筋来，因而淹死了：那时代的愚蠢的史家却说他是为了塞斯托斯的希罗而死。这些全都是谎；人们一代一代地死去，他们的尸体都给蛆虫吃了，可是决不会为爱情而死的。

（朱生豪译《皆大欢喜》第4幕第1场）

评点

奥兰多把爱情看得比生命更重，罗瑟琳心中窃喜，嘴上却笑话他痴情傻冒，声称自古以来的痴情汉其实都并非为爱而死，那些殉情的故事只是杜撰加工而已。她大胆解构原有故事情节的因果逻辑，完全颠覆了传统解读。

罗瑟琳列举的两个爱情悲剧都是文艺复兴时期大众耳熟能详的古希腊传说：一个关于特洛伊王子特洛伊罗斯与投靠希腊阵营的心上人克瑞西达之间的爱情纠葛——莎士比亚就此写有一部剧本《特洛伊罗斯与克瑞西达》（*Troilus and Cressida*）；另一个故事讲的是青年里昂德为了与心上人希罗幽会，夜渡海峡，却淹死在暴风雨中——莎士比亚同龄人马洛（Marlowe）就此写有一篇著名的叙事诗《希罗与里昂德》（*Hero and Leander*）。

场景 14：天壤之别

("… the sky changes when they are wives.")

> 罗瑟琳让堂妹扮演牧师，与奥兰多举办了一个假模假样的婚礼，随后又提问考验奥兰多。奥兰多越是把心目中的罗瑟琳完美化、理想化，男扮女装的罗瑟琳就越是故意贬损女性，嘲讽婚姻。

Rosalind　Now tell me how long you would have her after you have possessed her.
Orlando　For ever and a day.
Rosalind　Say 'a day' without the 'ever'. No, no, Orlando, men are April[1] when they woo, December when they wed. Maids are May[2] when they are maids, but the sky changes when they are wives. I will be more jealous[3] of thee than a Barbary cock-pigeon[4] over his hen, more clamorous than a parrot against rain, more new-fangled[5] than an ape, more giddy[6] in my desires than a monkey. I will weep for nothing, like Diana in the fountain, and I will do that when you are disposed to be merry. I will laugh like a hyena[7], and that when thou art inclined to sleep.
Orlando　But will my Rosalind do so?
Rosalind　By my life, she will do as I do.
Orlando　O, but she is wise.
Rosalind　Or else she could not have the wit to do this — the wiser, the waywarder. Make the doors upon a woman's wit, and it will out at the casement[8].

---

[1] April: the prime of life and love.
[2] May: a month of brilliant but unreliable weather. As Sonnet 18 goes, "Rough winds do shake the darling buds of May."
[3] jealous: possessive, demanding of exclusive rights.
[4] Barbary cock-pigeon: a special variety of black or dun-coloured pigeon, introduced from Barbary in North Africa.
[5] new-fangled: obsessed with novelty.
[6] giddy: volatile generally, but also in sexual matters.
[7] hyena（鬣狗）: A hyena's bark sounds like a laugh.
[8] casement: window.

Shut that and 'twill out at the key-hole. Stop that, 'twill fly with the smoke out at the chimney.

(*As You Like It* 4.1)

罗瑟琳　现在你告诉我你占有了她之后，打算保留多久？

奥兰多　永久再加上一天。

罗瑟琳　说一天，不用说永久。不，不，奥兰多，男人们在未婚的时候是四月天，结婚的时候是十二月天；姑娘们做姑娘的时候是五月天，一做了妻子，季候便改变了。我要比一头巴巴里雄鸽对待它的雌鸽格外多疑地对待你；我要比下雨前的鹦鹉格外吵闹，比猢狲格外弃旧怜新，比猴子格外反复无常；我要在你高兴的时候像喷泉上的狄安娜女神雕像一样无端哭泣；我要在你想睡的时候像土狼一样纵声大笑。

奥兰多　但是我的罗瑟琳会做出这种事来吗？

罗瑟琳　我可以发誓她会像我一样做出来的。

奥兰多　啊！但是她是个聪明人哩。

罗瑟琳　她倘不聪明，怎么有本领做这等事？越是聪明，越是淘气。假如用一扇门把一个女人的才情关起来，它会从窗子里钻出来的；关了窗，它会从钥匙孔里钻出来的；塞住了钥匙孔，它会跟着一道烟从烟囱里飞出来的。

（朱生豪译《皆大欢喜》第4幕第1场）

评点

罗瑟琳的调侃之词在很大程度上表现了欧洲自中世纪以来的"厌女"（misogyny）讽刺文学，尤其针对已婚妇女——我国也有类似表述，比如贾宝玉所说的"死鱼眼睛"。

虽然角色与身份的变化可能带来言行举止的变化，但是罗瑟琳所描述的婚前与婚后女人的天壤之别未免夸张。罗瑟琳作为女性，不会真的这么性别歧视，只是模仿传统上的"厌女"口吻，试探甚至教育年轻的奥兰多，不要对妻子抱有不切实际的幻想，以免日后接受不了理想与现实之间的落差。

场景 15：离群索居

("I am for other than for dancing measures.")

> 全剧以一场集体婚礼结束，老公爵也即将结束流亡生涯。在这双喜临门的时刻，杰奎斯却声明自己不参加婚礼庆典，并且拒绝随老公爵回城享福，反而与众人一一道别。

Jaques　To him will I; out of these convertites[1]

There is much matter[2] to be heard and learned.

[*To Duke Senior*] You to your former honour I bequeath:

Your patience and your virtue well deserves it.

[*To Orlando*] You to a love that your true faith doth merit;

[*To Oliver*] You to your land and love and great allies;

[*To Silvius*] You to a long and well-deserved bed;

[*To Touchstone*] And you to wrangling, for thy loving voyage

Is but for two months victualled[3]. — So to your pleasures,

I am for other than for dancing measures[4].

Duke　Stay, Jaques, stay.

Jaques　To see no pastime, I. What you would have

I'll stay[5] to know at your abandoned cave. [*Exit.*]

Duke　Proceed, proceed! We will begin these rites[6],

As we do trust they'll end, in true delights.

(*As You Like It* 5.4)

---

[1] convertites: the recently converted.
[2] matter: information of substance.
[3] voyage / Is but for two months victualled: the food supply will only hold out for two months.
[4] measures: concerns, activities.
[5] stay: wait.
[6] rites: ceremonies, both the festivities and the wedding rituals.

杰奎斯　我就找他去；从这种悟道者的地方，很可以得到一些绝妙的教训。（向公爵）我让你去享受你那从前的光荣吧；那是你的忍耐和德行的酬报。（向奥兰多）你去享受你那用忠心赢得的爱情吧。（向奥列佛）你去享有你的土地、爱人和权势吧。（向西尔维斯）你去享用你那用千辛万苦换来的老婆吧。（向试金石）至于你呢，我让你去口角吧；因为在你的爱情的旅程上，你只带了两个月的粮草。好，大家各人去找各人的快乐；跳舞可不是我的份。

公爵　别走，杰奎斯，别走！

杰奎斯　我不想看你们的作乐；你们要有什么见教，我就在被你们遗弃了的山窟中恭候。（下）

公爵　进行下去吧，开始我们的嘉礼；我们相信始终都会很顺利。

（朱生豪译《皆大欢喜》第 5 幕第 4 场）

> [!NOTE] 评点
>
> 　　这是《皆大欢喜》一剧在谢幕词之前的最后场景和台词。在阿登森林里的流亡者否极泰来、皆大欢喜之时，杰奎斯却不愿参加婚礼庆典，甚至不愿离开阿登森林；哪怕老公爵一再挽留，杰奎斯也断然拒绝，成为大团圆结尾一个不和谐的音符，令人回味无穷，也许是为了提醒世人在享受世俗快乐的同时也不忘独立思考与精神追求。
>
> 　　杰奎斯是真心要远离尘嚣，他那与众不同的"忧郁"不是附庸风雅装出来的，自始至终都表现得特立独行。他在剧中一直表现为看破红尘、超然世外的旁观者形象，甚至在众人为回城而欢呼时，他却向众人告别，并表示自己要留在阿登森林，与隐士做伴。可见，杰奎斯此前待在阿登森林不一定是为老公爵之故，而只是为了隐居在阿登森林。

五、《哈姆莱特》

(Hamlet)

(1600)

"我所看见的幽灵也许是魔鬼的化身。"

("The spirit that I have seen may be a devil.")

《哈姆莱特》契合英国文艺复兴时期的"复仇剧"（revenge tragedy）传统，剧中人物无论大小，大多或迟或早地死于非命。剧中的主要人物有丹麦国王一家三口与御前大臣一家三口。在这六人中，大臣及其女儿在剧中横死，另四人则在剧终暴亡；除了大臣女儿之死是由王后告知之外，其余五人都"死"于舞台，不可不谓血腥。

除了这六人之外，哈姆莱特的两位同窗也稀里糊涂地成为权力斗争的牺牲品。还有剧中鬼魂所说的老国王之死，犹如一片挥之不去的阴云，时刻笼罩在哈姆莱特的心头。

这些人物之死直接或间接地与哈姆莱特的复仇相关。这位丹麦王子出身高贵，教养良好，其复仇计划绝非一时冲动、意气用事，而是深思熟虑并且阴差阳错的结果。

即便他最终杀死了叔父，得以报仇雪恨，却也是同归于尽，还造成连环悲剧。不知那位呼唤复仇的鬼魂能否预见整个丹麦王室乃至整个宫廷即将遭受灭顶之灾？

《哈姆莱特》（*Hamlet*）

场景 1：午夜显灵（"Lo, where it comes again …"）1.1

场景 2：笼络人心（"'Tis sweet and commendable in your nature …"）1.2

场景 3：脆弱之名（"Frailty, thy name is Woman!"）1.2

场景 4：谆谆教诲（"Do not believe his vows …"）1.3

场景 5：发誓报仇（"… one may smile and smile and be a villain."）1.5

场景 6：身陷囹圄（"Denmark's a prison."）2.2

场景 7：人生何为（"What piece of work is a man!"）2.2

场景 8：窥探人心（"I'll catch the conscience of the King."）2.2

场景 9：两难抉择（"To be, or not to be …"）3.1

场景 10：今非昔比（"O, what a noble mind is here o'erthrown! "）3.1

场景 11：宠辱偕忘（"Give me that man that is not passion's slave …"）3.2

场景 12：扪心自问（"O, what form of prayer can serve my turn? "）3.3

场景 13：人之为人（"What is a man if …"）4.4

场景 14：香消玉殒（"Your sister's drowned, Laertes."）4.7

场景 15：小丑骷髅（"Alas, poor Yorick."）5.1

场景 16：命中注定（"The readiness is all."）5.2

场景1：午夜显灵

（"Lo, where it comes again ... "）

> 寒夜里，城头站岗的卫兵看见了先王老哈姆莱特的亡灵，于是请来了哈姆莱特的挚友霍拉旭（Horatio）。霍拉旭博学多才，由此异象联想到凯撒遇刺，充满了不祥的预感。

Horatio A mote[1] it is to trouble the mind's eye.
In the most high and palmy[2] state of Rome
A little ere the mightiest Julius fell
The graves stood tenantless and the sheeted[3] dead
Did squeak and gibber[4] in the Roman streets;
At stars with trains of fire and dews of blood,
Disasters in the sun; and the moist star[5]
Upon whose influence Neptune's empire stands
Was sick almost to doomsday with eclipse.
And even the like precurse[6] of feared events,
As harbingers preceding still[7] the fates
And prologue to the omen coming on,
Have heaven and earth together demonstrated
Unto our climatures[8] and countrymen. [*Enter Ghost.*]
But soft[9], behold! Lo, where it comes again;
I'll cross[10] it though it blast[11] me. Stay, illusion.

---

[1] mote: piece of grit or dust.
[2] palmy: flourishing, worthy. The palm is a traditional symbol of triumph.
[3] sheeted: dressed in the winding sheets in which they had been buried.
[4] squeak and gibber: make inarticulate noises.
[5] the moist star: i.e. the moon, controller of the tides（"Neptune's empire"）.
[6] precurse: precursor(s), warning signs.
[7] still: always.
[8] climatures: climes, regions.
[9] soft: enough, be quiet.
[10] cross: cross its path, impede its progress; also suggests "make the sign of the cross", a traditional way of attempting to ward off the supernatural.
[11] blast: blight, destroy.

> If thou hast any sound or use of voice,
> Speak to me.
> If there be any good thing to be done
> That may to thee do ease and grace to me,
> Speak to me.
> If thou art privy[1] to thy country's fate
> Which happily foreknowing may avoid,
> O, speak!
> Or if thou hast uphoarded[2] in thy life
> Extorted treasure in the womb of earth —
> For which they say you spirits oft walk in death —
> Speak of it, stay and speak.

(*Hamlet* 1.1)

霍拉旭 那是扰乱我们心灵之眼的一点微尘。从前在富强繁盛的罗马，在那雄才大略的裘力斯·凯撒遇害以前不久，披着殓衾的死人都从坟墓里出来，在街道上啾啾鬼语，星辰拖着火尾，露水带血，太阳变色，支配潮汐的月亮被吞蚀得像一个没有起色的病人；这一类预报重大变故的朕兆，在我们国内的天上地下也已经屡次出现了。可是不要响！瞧！瞧！它又来了！（鬼魂重上）我要挡住它的去路，即使它会害我。不要走，鬼魂！要是你能出声，会开口，对我说话吧；要是我有可以为你效劳之处，使你的灵魂得到安息，那么对我说话吧；要是你预知祖国的命运，靠着你的指示，也许可以及时避免未来的灾祸，那么对我说话吧；或者你在生前曾经把你搜括得来的财宝埋藏在地下，我听见人家说，鬼魂往往在他们藏金的地方徘徊不散，要是有这样的事，你也对我说吧；不要走，说呀！

（朱生豪译《哈姆莱特》第1幕第1场）

评点

霍拉旭所描述的凯撒遇刺之前发生的种种不祥意象在莎士比亚历史剧《裘力斯·凯撒》的多个人物台词中均有描述，而这些素材又来源于古罗马时期的历史学家普鲁塔克（Plutarch）的《希腊罗马名人传》——莎士比亚悲剧与历史剧的一大取材来源。

---

[1] art privy to: have private knowledge of.
[2] uphoarded: hoarded up, accumulated.

场景 2：笼络人心

("'Tis sweet and commendable in your nature ...")

> 第1幕第1场阴郁而诡异，第1幕第2场则切换到新国王克劳狄斯（Claudius）的登基大典兼大婚仪式，众人拥戴，一片祥和。唯有王子哈姆莱特一袭黑衣，一脸阴云，还顶撞母后。于是，国王亲自训话。

Claudius 'Tis sweet and commendable in your nature, Hamlet,
To give these mourning duties to your father;
But you must know, your father lost a father;
That father lost, lost his, and the survivor bound
In filial obligation for some term
To do obsequious[1] sorrow; but to persever[2]
In obstinate condolement[3] is a course
Of impious stubbornness, 'tis unmanly grief,
It shows a will most incorrect to heaven,
A heart unfortified, a mind impatient,
An understanding simple and unschooled;
For what we know must be, and is as common
As any the most vulgar thing to sense —
Why should we in our peevish opposition
Take it to heart? Fie, 'tis a fault to heaven,
A fault against the dead, a fault to nature,
To reason most absurd, whose[4] common theme
Is death of fathers, and who still hath cried,
From the first corpse[5] till he that died to-day
'This must be so.' We pray you throw to earth
This unprevailing[6] woe, and think of us[7]

---

[1] obsequious: dutiful in regard to the dead.
[2] persever: persist, continue.
[3] condolement: grieving.
[4] whose: i.e. nature's.
[5] the first corpse: In Judaeo-Christian tradition, the first person to die was Abel, killed by his brother Cain.
[6] unprevailing: ineffective.
[7] us: The King uses the royal plural.

As of a father, for let the world take note
　　You are the most immediate to our throne,
　　And with no less nobility of love
　　Than that which dearest father bears his son
　　Do I impart toward you. For your intent
　　In going back to school in Wittenberg[1]
　　It is most retrograde[2] to our desire,
　　And we beseech you bend you to remain
　　Here in the cheer and comfort of our eye,
　　Our chiefest courtier, cousin, and our son.
(*Hamlet* 1.2)

国王　哈姆莱特，你这样孝思不匮，原是你天性中纯笃过人之处；可是你要知道，你的父亲也曾失去过一个父亲，那失去的父亲自己也失去过父亲；那后死的儿子为了尽他的孝道，必须有一个时期服丧守制，然而固执不变的哀伤，却是一种逆天悖理的愚行，不是堂堂男子所应有的举动；它表现出一个不肯安于天命的意志，一个经不起艰难痛苦的心，一个缺少忍耐的头脑和一个简单愚昧的理性。既然我们知道那是无可避免的事，无论谁都要遭遇到同样的经验，那么我们为什么要这样固执地把它介介于怀呢？嘿！那是对上天的罪戾，对死者的罪戾，也是违反人情的罪戾；在理智上它是完全荒谬的，因为从第一个死了的父亲起，直到今天死去的最后一个父亲为止，理智永远在呼喊，"这是无可避免的。"我请你抛弃了这种无益的悲伤，把我当作你的父亲；因为我要让全世界知道，你是王位的直接的继承者，我要给你的尊荣和恩宠，不亚于一个最慈爱的父亲之于他的儿子。至于你要回到威登堡去继续求学的意思，那是完全违反我们的愿望的；请你听从我的劝告，不要离开这里，在朝廷上领袖群臣，做我们最亲近的国亲和王子，使我们因为每天能看见你而感到欢欣。
（朱生豪译《哈姆莱特》第 1 幕第 2 场）

评点

　　对于哈姆莱特而言，克劳狄斯曾是他的叔父，如今是他的继父及国王。克劳狄斯并非等闲之辈，在上场伊始处理外交事务、笼络众臣方面表现得英明有为。对于桀骜不驯的哈姆莱特，他先软后硬、恩威并重、口若悬河，既教训了继子，又彰显了王者风范。

---

[1] Wittenberg: city in Germany, home of a university founded in 1502 and attended in reality by Martin Luther.
[2] retrograde: contrary.

场景3：脆弱之名

（"Frailty, thy name is Woman!"）

> 新国王的登基大典之后，众人退场，留下哈姆莱特一人在台上沉思，由此道出他的第一段独白（soliloquy）。即便母后与继父兼新国王对他释放了足够的善意，但他依然对亡父念念不忘，对母后的改嫁耿耿于怀，对叔父恨之入骨……

Hamlet But two months dead — nay not so much, not two —
So excellent a king, that was to this[1]
Hyperion[2] to a satyr[3], so loving to my mother
That he might not beteem[4] the winds of heaven
Visit her face too roughly. Heaven and earth,
Must I remember? Why, she would hang on him
As if increase of appetite had grown
By what it fed on. And yet within a month
(Let me not think on't — Frailty, thy name is Woman),
A little month, or e'er those shoes were old
With which she followed my poor father's body,
Like Niobe[5], all tears. Why, she —
O God, a beast that wants discourse of reason
Would have mourned longer — married with my uncle,
My father's brother (but no more like my father
Than I to Hercules[6]). Within a month,
Ere yet the salt of most unrighteous[7] tears

---

[1] to this: compared to this (this new king, his uncle Claudius).
[2] Hyperion: Greek god of the sun.
[3] satyr: half human and half goat in classical mythology.
[4] beteem: allow, permit.
[5] Niobe: Greek mythical figure who mourned for the deaths of her children until she was turned into a weeping stone statue.
[6] Hercules: Mythical hero famous for his twelve superhuman "labors" which included killing the many-headed Hydra and relieving atlas of his burden, the globe.
[7] unrighteous: false, wicked.

Had left the flushing[1] in her galled[2] eyes,
She married. O, most wicked speed, to post[3]
With such dexterity to incestuous[4] sheets,
It is not, nor it cannot come to good;
But break, my heart, for I must hold my tongue.

(*Hamlet* 1.2)

哈姆莱特 刚死了两个月！不，两个月还不满！这样好的一个国王，比起当前这个来，简直是天神和丑怪；这样爱我的母亲，甚至于不愿让天风吹痛了她的脸。天地呀！我必须记着吗？嘿，她会偎倚在他的身旁，好像吃了美味的食物，格外促进了食欲一般；可是，只有一个月的时间，我不能再想下去了！脆弱啊，你的名字就是女人！短短的一个月以前，她哭得像个泪人儿似的，送我那可怜的父亲下葬；她在送葬的时候所穿的那双鞋子还没有破旧，她就，她就——上帝啊！一头没有理性的畜生也要悲伤得长久一些——她就嫁给我的叔父，我的父亲的弟弟，可是他一点不像我的父亲，正像我一点不像赫剌克勒斯一样。只有一个月的时间，她那流着虚伪之泪的眼睛还没有消去红肿，她就嫁了人了。啊，罪恶的匆促，这样迫不及待地钻进了乱伦的衾被！那不是好事，也不会有好结果；可是碎了吧，我的心，因为我必须噤住我的嘴！

（朱生豪译《哈姆莱特》第 1 幕第 2 场）

评点

早在鬼魂出现之前，丹麦王子就已经忧郁了，满腔怒火直指叔父与母后二人。从这番独白可见，哈姆莱特对叔父的厌恶程度似乎远远不及他对母后迅速改嫁的介意程度。其中，"脆弱啊，你的名字就是女人"（Frailty, thy name is Woman）一句充分体现了哈姆莱特厌女态度。这种怨恨恰恰表现出他对女性的在乎程度——无论是心上人奥菲莉娅还是母亲乔特鲁德，都在哈姆莱特的生命中扮演重要角色。

---

[1] flushing: redness.
[2] galled: irritated, sore.
[3] post: move quickly, hurry.
[4] incestuous: Judaeo-Christian tradition forbade a man to marry his brother's wife (Leviticus, 18:16, 20:21).

场景 4：谆谆教诲

（"Do not believe his vows …"）

> 第 1 幕第 3 场聚焦于御前大臣波洛涅斯（Polonius）一家——父亲带着女儿奥菲利娅（Ophelia）在海边为儿子送行。父子二人都告诫奥菲利娅不要把哈姆莱特的甜言蜜语当真，甚至明令禁止她与哈姆莱特的来往。

Polonius　　Ay, springs[1] to catch woodcocks[2] — I do know
　　　　　　When the blood burns[3] how prodigal[4] the soul
　　　　　　Lends the tongue vows. These blazes[5], daughter,
　　　　　　Giving more light than heat, extinct in both
　　　　　　Even in their promise as it is a-making[6],
　　　　　　You must not take[7] for fire. From this time
　　　　　　Be something scanter[8] of your maiden presence;
　　　　　　Set your entreatments at a higher rate
　　　　　　Than a command to parley. For Lord Hamlet,
　　　　　　Believe so much in him, that he is young,
　　　　　　And with a larger tether[9] may he walk
　　　　　　Than may be given you. In few[10], Ophelia,
　　　　　　Do not believe his vows, for they are brokers[11]
　　　　　　Not of that dye[12] which their investments[13] show

---

[1] springes: snares, traps.
[2] woodcocks: These birds were proverbially thought to be easy to catch.
[3] When the blood burns: When sexual desire is aroused.
[4] prodigal: extravagant, recklessly generous.
[5] blazes: flashes of rhetoric, i.e. Hamlet's vows.
[6] as it is a-making: as it is being made.
[7] take: mistake.
[8] something scanter: somewhat more sparing (less generous).
[9] a larger tether: a longer rope for a tethered animal, thus a wider range to roam.
[10] in few: in brief.
[11] brokers: go-between, especially in financial and sexual matters.
[12] that dye: that colour.
[13] investments: ceremonial garments.

But mere implorators of unholy suits[1]
Breathing like sanctified and pious bonds,
The better to beguile. This is for all;
I would not in plain terms from this time forth
Have you so slander[2] any moment leisure
As to give words or talk with the Lord Hamlet.
Look to't[3], I charge you. Come your ways[4].

Ophelia　I shall obey, my lord.
(*Hamlet* 1.3)

波洛涅斯　嗯，这些都是捕捉愚蠢的山鹬的圈套。我知道在热情燃烧的时候，一个人无论什么盟誓都会说出口来；这些火焰，女儿，是光多于热的，刚刚说出口就会光销焰灭，你不能把它们当作真火看待。从现在起，你还是少露一些你的女儿家的脸；你应该抬高身价，不要让人家以为你是可以随意呼召的。对于哈姆莱特殿下，你应该这样想，他是个年轻的王子，他比你在行动上有更大的自由。总而言之，奥菲利娅，不要相信他的盟誓，它们不过是淫媒，内心的颜色和服装完全不一样，只晓得诱人干一些龌龊的勾当，正像道貌岸然大放厥词的鸨母，只求达到骗人的目的。我的言尽于此，简单一句话，从现在起，我不许你一有空闲就跟哈姆莱特殿下聊天。你留点儿神吧；进去。

奥菲利娅　我一定听从您的话，父亲。

（朱生豪译《哈姆莱特》第1幕第3场）

评点

御前大臣波洛涅斯与国王一家关系密切，性格温和，只是颇为唠叨。他十分关心他的一双儿女，总是千叮咛万嘱咐，每每长篇大论，有时不乏喜剧色彩却最终暴亡，成为悲剧人物之一。

对于奥菲利娅与哈姆莱特谈恋爱，父兄二人都生怕奥菲利娅吃亏，不乏经验之谈。对于涉世不深的名门闺秀而言，谨慎与矜持在婚恋问题上尤为重要。乖乖女奥菲利娅不同于《罗密欧与朱丽叶》里的朱丽叶，对父兄言听计从，哪怕有违于自己内心的意愿。

---

[1] unholy suits: immoral or wicked requests.
[2] slander: bring into disrepute.
[3] look to't: pay attention to this.
[4] come your ways: come away, i.e. let us go.

场景 5：发誓报仇

("… one may smile and smile and be a villain.")

> 在霍拉旭等人的带领下，哈姆莱特来到鬼魂出没之地。果然，半夜，鬼魂再次出现，带领哈姆莱特至僻静处，自称先王冤魂，要求哈姆莱特为其报仇。

Hamlet O all you host of heaven, O earth — what else? —
And shall I couple hell? O fie! Hold, hold, my heart,
And you, my sinews, grow not instant old,
But bear me swiftly up. Remember thee?
Ay, thou poor ghost, while memory holds a seat
In this distracted globe. Remember thee?
Yea, from the table of my memory
I'll wipe away all trivial fond[1] records[2],
All saws of books[3], all forms, all pressures past
That youth and observation copied there
And thy commandment all alone shall live
Within the book and volume of my brain
Unmixed with baser matter. Yes, by heaven,
O most pernicious woman,
O villain, villain, smiling damned villain,
My tables[4]! Meet[5] it is I set it down
That one may smile and smile and be a villain —
At least I am sure it may be so in Denmark.
So, uncle, there you are. Now to my word.
It is 'Adieu, adieu, remember me.'

---

[1] fond: foolish.
[2] records: recollections.
[3] saws of books: commonplaces or maxims copied form books.
[4] tables: writing tablets or notebooks.
[5] meet: fitting, appropriate.

I have sworn't.

(*Hamlet* 1.5)

哈姆莱特　天上的神明啊！地啊！再有什么呢？我还要向地狱呼喊吗？啊，呸！忍着吧，忍着吧，我的心！我的全身的筋骨，不要一下子就变成衰老，支持着我的身体呀！记着你！是的，我可怜的亡魂，当记忆不曾从我这混乱的头脑里消失的时候，我会记着你的。记着你！是的，我要从我的记忆的碑版上，拭去一切琐碎愚蠢的记录、一切书本上的格言、一切陈言套语、一切过去的印象、我的少年的阅历所留下的痕迹，只让你的命令留在我的脑筋的书卷里，不搀杂一些下贱的废料；是的，上天为我作证！啊，最恶毒的妇人！啊，奸贼，奸贼，脸上堆着笑的万恶的奸贼！我的记事簿呢？我必须把它记下来：一个人可以尽管满面都是笑，骨子里却是杀人的奸贼；至少我相信在丹麦是这样的。好，叔父，我把你写下来了。现在我要记下我的座右铭那是，"再会，再会！记着我。"我已经发过誓了。

（朱生豪译《哈姆莱特》第 1 幕第 5 场）

评点

鬼魂一直一言不发，直到与哈姆莱特单独相处。鬼魂向哈姆莱特表示自己是其亡父的灵魂（I am thy father's spirit），并且直言自己生前被兄弟所杀，由此被剥夺了生命、王位及王后。鬼魂多次强调凶手通奸、乱伦，进一步强化了哈姆莱特对母后的怨恨及对叔父的敌意。鬼魂在向哈姆莱特告别时的最后一句话就是"记着我"（remember me）。与鬼魂会面结束之后，哈姆莱特发誓报仇。

值得注意的是，他的怒火在针对叔父的同时，又表现出"厌女"倾向——"啊，最恶毒的妇人"（O most pernicious woman）。此时奥菲利娅尚未跟哈姆莱特提出分手，所以这显然不是针对奥菲利娅，而是针对他那改嫁的母后了。这为哈姆莱特在后续场景中对母后的咄咄逼人做好了铺垫。

场景 6：身陷囹圄

（"Denmark's a prison."）

> 哈姆莱特的两位同窗好友罗森格兰兹（Rosencrantz）和吉尔登斯吞（Guildenstern）突然造访，哈姆莱特预料来者不善，与二人交谈，虚虚实实，真假难辨，装疯卖傻，犹如玩文字游戏。

Hamlet ... Let me question more in particular. What have you, my good friends, deserved at the hands of Fortune that she sends you to prison hither?

Guildenstern Prison, my lord?

Hamlet Denmark's a prison.

Rosencrantz Then is the world one.

Hamlet A goodly one, in which there are many confines, wards, and dungeons[1] — Denmark being one o'th' worst.

Rosencrantz We think not so, my lord.

Hamlet Why, then 'tis none to you; for there is nothing either good or bad, but thinking makes it so. To me it is a prison.

Rosencrantz Why, then your ambition makes it one: 'tis too narrow for your mind.

Hamlet O God, I could be bounded in a nutshell and count myself a king of infinite space — were it not that I have bad dreams.

Guildenstern Which dreams, indeed, are ambition; for the very substance of the ambitious is merely the shadow of a dream.

Hamlet A dream itself is but a shadow.

Rosencrantz Truly, and I hold ambition of so airy and light a quality that it is but a shadow's shadow.

(*Hamlet* 2.2)

---

[1] confines, wards, and dungeons: various kinds of prisons.

哈姆莱特	……让我再仔细问问你们；我的好朋友们，你们在命运手里犯了什么案子，她把你们送到这儿牢狱里来了？
吉尔登斯吞	牢狱，殿下！
哈姆莱特	丹麦是一所牢狱。
罗森格兰兹	那么世界也是一所牢狱。
哈姆莱特	一所很大的牢狱，里面有许多监房、囚室、地牢；丹麦是其中最坏的一间。
罗森格兰兹	我们倒不这样想，殿下。
哈姆莱特	啊，那么对于你们它并不是牢狱；因为世上的事情本来没有善恶，都是各人的思想把它们分别出来的；对于我它是一所牢狱。
罗森格兰兹	啊，那是因为您的雄心太大，丹麦是个狭小的地方，不够给您发展，所以您把它看成一所牢狱啦。
哈姆莱特	上帝啊！倘不是因为我总做噩梦，那么即使把我关在一个果壳里，我也会把自己当作一个拥有着无限空间的君王的。
吉尔登斯吞	那种噩梦便是您的野心；因为野心家本身的存在，也不过是一个梦的影子。
哈姆莱特	一个梦的本身便是一个影子。
罗森格兰兹	不错，因为野心是那么空虚轻浮的东西，所以我认为它不过是影子的影子。

（朱生豪译《哈姆莱特》第 2 幕第 2 场）

> **评点**

  该选段只有对开本（Folio）《哈姆莱特》才有，而四开本（Quarto）《哈姆莱特》则没有，据说是因为当时英王詹姆士的王后安妮（Anne，丹麦人）的缘故，说"丹麦是一所牢狱"，肯定有所冒犯。

  文中，两位同学受国王与王后的嘱托，试图了解哈姆莱特的心病。哈姆莱特心知肚明，对其颇为戒备，虽不乏障眼法，但其言辞也不乏真诚，思维极为跳跃，充满了俏皮话。

  在哈姆莱特看来，丹麦如同监牢，世界如同监牢，正如我国古语所说："以我观物，故物皆著我之色彩。"这不仅是出于愤世嫉俗的感慨，而且也是从个人的具体困境上升到关乎人类社会、人性等方面的哲理思考。

场景 7：人生何为

（"What piece of work is a man!"）

> 哈姆莱特问两位突然来访的昔日同窗是否受人指使（"Were you not sent for?"），二人扭捏了一番才肯承认。哈姆莱特便主动告知自己性情大变的原因。

Hamlet I have of late, but wherefore I know not, lost all my mirth, forgone all custom of exercises[1] and, indeed, it goes so heavily with my disposition that this goodly frame the earth seems to me a sterile promontory[2], this most excellent canopy[3] the air, look you, this brave o'erhanging firmament, this majestical roof fretted[4] with golden fire, why it appeareth nothing to me but a foul and pestilent congregation of vapours. What piece of work is a man — how noble in reason; how infinite in faculty[5], in form and moving[6]; how express[7] and admirable in action; how like an angel in apprehension[8]; how like a god; the beauty of the world; the paragon[9] of animals. And yet to me what is this quintessence[10] of dust? Man delights not me — nor women neither, though by your smiling you seem to say so.

(*Hamlet* 2.2)

---

[1] custom of exercises: customary activities (such as the fencing and tennis mentioned in 2.1).
[2] sterile promontory: barren headland.
[3] canopy: sky.
[4] fretted: inlaid, decorated.
[5] faculties: capabilities.
[6] form and moving: shape and motion.
[7] express: well-framed or well-modelled.
[8] apprehension: understanding.
[9] paragon: supreme example.
[10] quintessence: concentration, extracted from earthly elements by a process of distillation.

哈姆莱特 我近来不知为了什么缘故,一点兴致都提不起来,什么游乐的事都懒得过问;在这一种抑郁的心境之下,仿佛负载万物的大地,这一座美好的框架,只是一个不毛的荒岬;这个覆盖众生的苍穹,这一顶壮丽的帐幕,这个金黄色的火球点缀着的庄严的屋宇,只是一大堆污浊的瘴气的集合。人类是一件多么了不得的杰作!多么高贵的理性!多么伟大的力量!多么优美的仪表!多么文雅的举动!在行为上多么像一个天使!在智慧上多么像一个天神!宇宙的精华!万物的灵长!可是在我看来,这一个泥土塑成的生命算得了什么?人类不能使我发生兴趣;不,女人也不能使我发生兴趣,虽然从你现在的微笑之中,我可以看到你在这样想。

(朱生豪译《哈姆莱特》第2幕第2场)

评点

哈姆莱特采用一连串排比修辞,描绘出一个象征他自己内心精神状态的荒凉宇宙。这番话虽然是对两个"探子"说的,具有一定表演性或迷惑性,但是"假作真时真亦假",此语并非全然言不由衷。毕竟,哈姆莱特在见到鬼魂之前的独白里就表达过这种悲观厌世之感——在第1幕第2场中,他声称"人世间的一切在我看来是多么可厌、陈腐、乏味而无聊"(How weary, stale, flat, and unprofitable / Seem to me all the uses of this world),而且这世界是"一个荒芜不治的花园,长满了恶毒的莠草"(an unweeded garden / That grows to seed; things rank and gross in nature / Possess it merely)。

关于人的自我认知,文艺复兴时期不乏讴歌人类的作品,后人甚至常常援引哈姆莱特台词中的"宇宙的精华、万物的灵长"作为证明。然而,哈姆莱特在表达这个观点时,不无讥讽。即便他曾深受人本主义理想的熏陶,在精神受打击之后,也更多地表现出保守传统的思想倾向。比如,哈姆莱特在此将人称为"泥土之精华"(this quintessence of dust),就是源于《圣经》上关于人"源于尘土,归于尘土"的说法,与文艺复兴时期积极乐观的人本主义思想截然不同。

场景 8：窥探人心

("I'll catch the conscience of the King.")

哈姆莱特的两位昔日同窗还顺路带来了一个巡演剧团，试图给哈姆莱特解闷。哈姆莱特虽然欢迎剧团的到来，但是心里念念不忘复仇之事。他甚至计划利用看戏的机会，试探国王的良心及鬼魂之言的真实性。

Hamlet   Hum, I have heard
That guilty creatures sitting at a play
Have by the very cunning of the scene
Been struck so to the soul that presently[1]
They have proclaimed their malefactions.
For murder, though it have no tongue, will speak
With most miraculous organ. I'll have these players
Play something like the murder of my father
Before mine uncle. I'll observe his looks,
I'll tent him to the quick[2]. If 'a[3] do blench[4]
I know my course. The spirit that I have seen
May be a de'il, and the de'il hath power
T'assume a pleasing shape. Yea, and perhaps
Out of my weakness and my melancholy,
As he is very potent with such spirits[5],
Abuses[6] me to damn me! I'll have grounds
More relative[7] than this. The play's the thing

---

[1] presently: immediately.
[2] tent him to the quick: probe him to his most sensitive point; the metaphor is from probing a wound.
[3] 'a: he.
[4] blench: flinch (=move away) and blanch (=turn pale).
[5] potent with such spirits: influential with people who are melancholy. It was believed that such people were particularly susceptible to demonic powers.
[6] abuses: deceives.
[7] relative: relevant, convincing or conclusive.

Wherein I'll catch the conscience of the King.
(*Hamlet* 2.2)

哈姆莱特　我听人家说，犯罪的人在看戏的时候，因为台上表演的巧妙，有时会激动天良，当场供认他们的罪恶；因为暗杀的事情无论干得怎样秘密，总会借着神奇的喉舌泄露出来。我要叫这班伶人在我的叔父面前表演一本跟我的父亲的惨死情节相仿的戏剧，我就在一旁窥察他的神色；我要探视到他的灵魂的深处，要是他稍露惊骇不安之态，我就知道我应该怎么办。我所看见的幽灵也许是魔鬼的化身，借着一个美好的形状出现，魔鬼是有这一种本领的；对于柔弱忧郁的灵魂，他最容易发挥他的力量；也许他看准了我的柔弱和忧郁，才来向我作祟，要把我引诱到沉沦的路上。我要先得到一些比这更切实的证据；凭着这一本戏，我可以发掘国王内心的隐秘。

（朱生豪译《哈姆莱特》第 2 幕第 2 场）

评点

哈姆莱特心思缜密，个性独立，除了霍拉旭之外，他不相信任何人，甚至一开始也不完全相信鬼魂——"我所见的可能是一个魔鬼"（The spirit that I have seen / May be a de'il）。为了真正伸张正义，他就必须找到足够证据，以证明叔父是弑君凶手、杀父仇人。

哈姆莱特对文艺的力量充满信心：戏剧不是现实，却是现实的一面镜子；演员对现实生活场景的模仿惟妙惟肖，能让罪人在身临其境的场景中深感不安。除了这一选段之外，在后续第 3 幕第 2 场 "戏中戏" 开演之前，哈姆莱特再次表达了他精心导演戏剧的试探目的："注视我的叔父，要是他在听到了那一段戏词以后，他的隐藏的罪恶还是不露出一丝痕迹来，那么我们所看见的那个鬼魂一定是个恶魔，我的幻想也就像铁匠的砧石那样黑漆一团了。"(Observe my uncle. If his occulted guilt / Do not itself unkennel in one speech, / It is a damned ghost that we have seen, / And my imaginations are as foul / As Vulcan's stithy.)

场景 9：两难抉择

("To be, or not to be ...")

> 在哈姆莱特琢磨如何试探国王的同时，国王也在试探他：先是通过哈姆莱特的两位老同学，而后是通过其恋人奥菲利娅。奥菲利娅的父亲深信哈姆莱特"发疯"是因为失恋。于是，他安排女儿与哈姆莱特"偶遇"，自己与国王、王后躲在幕后观察。此时，哈姆莱特伴随着他最著名的独白上场。

Hamlet　To be, or not to be — that is the question;
　　　　Whether 'tis nobler in the mind to suffer
　　　　The slings[1] and arrows of outrageous[2] fortune
　　　　Or to take arms against a sea of troubles
　　　　And by opposing end them; to die: to sleep —
　　　　No more, and by a sleep to say we end
　　　　The heartache and the thousand natural shocks
　　　　That flesh is heir to[3]: 'tis a consummation[4]
　　　　Devoutly to be wished — to die: to sleep —
　　　　To sleep, perchance to dream — ay, there's the rub[5],
　　　　For in that sleep of death what dreams may come
　　　　When we have shuffled off this mortal coil[6]
　　　　Must give us pause[7]: there's the respect[8]
　　　　That makes calamity of so long life[9].
　　　　For who would bear the whips and scorns of time,

---

[1] sling: a device which propels the missile (a hand-sling or catapult).
[2] outrageous: excessively or grossly offensive.
[3] That flesh is heir to: That are the normal heritage of humanity.
[4] consummation: completion, climax.
[5] rub: impediment, disincentive (from the game of bowls, where a rub is an obstacle of some kind which diverts the bowl from its proper course).
[6] this mortal coil: this moral flesh, this troublesome life.
[7] give us pause: cause us to hesitate.
[8] respect: consideration.
[9] That makes calamity of so long life: that allows calamitous experiences to last so long (long life itself can also be regarded as a calamity).

Th'oppressor's wrong, the proud man's contumely[1],
The pangs of despised love, the law's delay,
The insolence of office, and the spurns
That patient merit of th'unworthy takes,
When he himself might his quietus make[2]
With a bare[3] bodkin[4]. Who would these fardels[5] bear
To grunt and sweat under a weary life
But that the dread of something after death
(The undiscovered country from whose bourn[6]
No traveller returns) puzzles[7] the will
And makes us rather bear those ills we have
Than fly to others that we know not of.
Thus conscience does make cowards —
And thus the native hue[8] of resolution
Is sicklied o'er[9] with the pale cast of thought,
And enterprises of great pith[10] and moment[11]
With this regard their currents turn awry
And lose the name of action. Soft you[12] now,
The fair Ophelia! Nymph, in thy orisons[13]
Be all my sins remembered.

(*Hamlet* 3.1)

---

[1] contumely: insolence, insulting behaviour or treatment.
[2] his quietus make: pay his complete account, i.e. end his life; quietus est (Latin) was a phrase used to confirm that a bill or debt had been paid.
[3] bare: unsheathed, or perhaps puny.
[4] bodkin: stiletto or dagger.
[5] fardels: burdens.
[6] bourn: boundary.
[7] puzzles: bewilders, paralyses (a stronger sense than the modern one).
[8] native hue: natural colour. Hamlet personifies Resolution as a person whose normally healthy complexion is disguised by pallor.
[9] sicklied o'er: unhealthily covered.
[10] pitch: height, scope.
[11] moment: significance, importance.
[12] soft you: be quiet, wait a moment.
[13] orisons: prayers.

哈姆莱特 生存还是毁灭,这是一个值得考虑的问题;默然忍受命运的暴虐的毒箭,或是挺身反抗人世的无涯的苦难,通过斗争把它们扫清,这两种行为,哪一种更高贵?死了;睡着了;什么都完了;要是在这一种睡眠之中,我们心头的创痛,以及其他无数血肉之躯所不能避免的打击,都可以从此消失,那正是我们求之不得的结局。死了;睡着了;睡着了也许还会做梦;嗯,阻碍就在这儿:因为当我们摆脱了这一具朽腐的皮囊以后,在那死的睡眠里,究竟将要做些什么梦,那不能不使我们踌躇顾虑。人们甘心久困于患难之中,也就是为了这个缘故;谁愿意忍受人世的鞭挞和讥嘲、压迫者的凌辱、傲慢者的冷眼、被轻蔑的爱情的惨痛、法律的迁延、官吏的横暴和费尽辛勤所换来的小人的鄙视,要是他只要用一柄小小的刀子,就可以清算他自己的一生?谁愿意负着这样的重担,在烦劳的生命的压迫下呻吟流汗,倘不是因为惧怕不可知的死后,惧怕那从来不曾有一个旅人回来过的神秘之国,是它迷惑了我们的意志,使我们宁愿忍受目前的磨折,不敢向我们所不知道的痛苦飞去?这样,重重的顾虑使我们全变成了懦夫,决心的赤热的光彩,被审慎的思维盖上了一层灰色,伟大的事业在这一种考虑之下,也会逆流而退,失去了行动的意义。且慢!美丽的奥菲利娅!——女神,在你的祈祷之中,不要忘记替我忏悔我的罪孽。

(朱生豪译《哈姆莱特》第 3 幕第 1 场)

评点

这段著名独白是哈姆莱特忧郁个性的典型表现,即便不是剧情不可或缺的一部分,也淋漓尽致地体现了人物的微妙心理与复杂思想,同时也展现了剧作家的生花妙笔。

"To be, or not to be"这句名言广为人知,如何理解"to be",如何诠释"the question",却是谜一般的存在。各家解释不同,对"信、达、雅"的把握各异,各家翻译也就各有千秋。

梁实秋:"死后是存在,还是不存在,这是问题。"
田　汉:"还是活着好呢,还是不活的好呢?这是一个问题。"
卞之琳:"活下去还是不活:这是问题。"
孙大雨:"是存在还是消亡:问题底所在。"
方　平:"活着好,还是死了好,这是个难题。"

王佐良："生或死，这就是问题所在。"
何其莘："生存还是毁灭，这是一个问题。"
陈　嘉："'反抗还是不反抗'，或者简单一些'干还是不干'。"
黄兆杰："应活吗？应死吗？——问题还在。"
……

　　王子复仇，思绪万千，这段独白所涉及的话题并非局限于个人恩怨，而是站在悲天悯人的高度，思考人生、人性与人类社会，富于哲学思辨。选段中以"谁愿意忍受人世的鞭挞和讥嘲"（For who would bear the whips and scorns of time）开头的一句话占了七行，一长串的罗列排比，感叹人生多艰，抱怨社会不公，主题与莎士比亚第66首十四行诗相似，读者不妨比较二者的异同：

Sonnet 66

Tired with all these, for restful death I cry:
As[1] to behold desert[2] a beggar born,
And needy nothing trimmed in jollity[3],
And purest faith unhappily forsworn,
And gilded honour shamefully misplaced,
And maiden virtue rudely strumpeted[4],
And right perfection wrongfully disgraced,
And strength by limping sway disabled,
And art[5] made tongue-tied by authority,
And folly, doctor-like[6], controlling skill,
And simple truth miscalled simplicity[7],
And captive good attending captain ill:
　　Tired with all these, from these would I be gone,
　　Save that to die I leave my love alone.

---

[1] as: such as.
[2] desert: merit, a deserving person.
[3] needy nothing trimmed in jollity: a worthless nobody adorned with finery.
[4] strumpeted: prostituted.
[5] art: learning, science, literature.
[6] doctor-like: as if learned, posing as an expert.
[7] simplicity: stupidity.

场景 10：今非昔比

("O, what a noble mind is here o'erthrown!")

> 奥菲利娅遵从父命，将定情礼物当面归还给哈姆莱特，由此引发了哈姆莱特的震怒与辱骂，令奥菲利娅伤心欲绝。

Hamlet　If thou dost marry, I'll give thee this plague for thy dowry: be thou as chaste as ice, as pure as snow, thou shalt not escape calumny[1]. Get thee to a nunnery. Farewell. Or, if thou wilt needs marry, marry a fool, for wise men know well enough what monsters[2] you make of them. To a nunnery go, and quickly too. Farewell.

Ophelia　Heavenly powers restore him.

Hamlet　I have heard of your paintings well enough. God hath given you one face and you make yourselves another. You jig and amble and you lisp[3], you nickname God's creatures and make your wantonness your ignorance. Go to, I'll no more on't. It hath made me mad. I say we will have no more marriages. Those that are married already — all but one — shall live. The rest shall keep as they are. To a nunnery, go！　[*Exit.*]

Ophelia　O, what a noble mind is here o'erthrown! The courtier's, soldier's, scholar's eye, tongue, sword, Th'expectation and rose of the fair state, The glass of fashion[4] and the mould of form[5], Th'observed of all observers, quite, quite down[6]. And I, of ladies most deject and wretched, That sucked the honey of his musicked vows, Now see that noble and most sovereign reason[7] Like sweet bells jangled out of time and harsh — That unmatched form and stature of blown youth[8] Blasted with ecstasy[9]. O

---

[1] calumny: slander.
[2] monster: i.e. cuckolds (victims of marital infidelity) who were depicted as men with horns.
[3] lisp: speak in an affected way.
[4] glass of fashion: mirror or model of style.
[5] mould of form: pattern of behaviour.
[6] down: destroyed, ruined.
[7] most sovereign reason: Reason is seen as ruling the other faculties.
[8] stature of blown youth: image of youth in its full bloom.
[9] Blasted with ecstasy: devastated by madness.

woe is me T'have seen what I have seen, see what I see.
(*Hamlet* 3.1)

哈姆莱特	要是你一定要嫁人，我就把这一个咒诅送给你做嫁奁：尽管你像冰一样坚贞，像雪一样纯洁，你还是逃不过谗人的诽谤。进尼姑庵去吧，去；再会！或者要是你必须嫁人的话，就嫁给一个傻瓜吧；因为聪明人都明白你们会叫他们变成怎样的怪物。进尼姑庵去吧，去；越快越好。再会！
奥菲利娅	天上的神明啊，让他清醒过来吧！
哈姆莱特	我也知道你们会怎样涂脂抹粉；上帝给了你们一张脸，你们又替自己另外造了一张。你们烟视媚行，淫声浪气，替上帝造下的生物乱取名字，卖弄你们不懂事的风骚。算了吧，我再也不敢领教了；它已经使我发了狂。我说，我们以后再不要结什么婚了；已经结过婚的，除了一个人以外，都可以让他们活下去；没有结婚的不准再结婚，进尼姑庵去吧，去。（下）
奥菲利娅	啊，一颗多么高贵的心是这样殒落了！朝臣的眼睛、学者的辩舌、军人的利剑、国家所瞩望的一朵娇花；时流的明镜、人伦的雅范、举世注目的中心，这样无可挽回地殒落了！我是一切妇女中间最伤心而不幸的，我曾经从他音乐一般的盟誓中吮吸芬芳的甘蜜，现在却眼看着他的高贵无上的理智，像一串美妙的银铃失去了谐和的音调，无比的青春美貌，在疯狂中凋谢！啊！我好苦，谁料过去的繁华，变作今朝的泥土！

（朱生豪译《哈姆莱特》第 3 幕第 1 场）

> **评点**

　　也许失恋令哈姆莱特的狂躁心情雪上加霜，也许他感受到心上人背叛他的切肤之痛，也许他在指桑骂槐、借题发挥地骂偷听者，也许他有意装疯卖傻，哈姆莱特这番话不可谓不"厌女"，一连强调了五遍让奥菲利娅"进尼姑庵去"（Get thee to a nunnery），其指责却不着边际、毫无逻辑，甚至蛮不讲理。奥菲利娅面对如此变故，犹如五雷轰顶，回想心上人堪称完美的往日形象，而今却判若两人。她哀哭哈姆莱特的疯狂，也哭自己薄命。

　　对此，奥菲利娅的父亲依然深信这是失恋之后的绝望之举；而国王不这么认为，甚至还预感到哈姆莱特的"疯狂"可能造成极大危害——"大人物的疯狂是不能听其自然的"（Madness in great ones must not unwatched go），由此更加坚定了要送哈姆莱特去英格兰的决心。

场景 11：宠辱偕忘

（ "Give me that man that is not passion's slave ..." ）

> 剧中的哈姆莱特愤世嫉俗，似傻如狂，几乎对任何人都讥笑讽刺，对任何人都高度警惕，只有一人除外——霍拉旭。

Hamlet Horatio, thou art e'en[1] as just a man
 As e'er my conversation coped withal[2].

Horatio O my dear lord —

Hamlet   Nay, do not think I flatter,
 For what advancement may I hope from thee
 That no revenue hast but thy good spirits
 To feed and clothe thee? Why should the poor be flattered?
 No, let the candied[3] tongue lick absurd pomp
 And crook[4] the pregnant[5] hinges of the knee
 Where thrift may follow fawning. Dost thou hear?
 Since my dear soul was mistress of her choice
 And could of men distinguish her election
 Sh'ath sealed[6] thee for herself. For thou hast been
 As one in suffering all that suffers nothing —
 A man that Fortune's buffets[7] and rewards
 Hast ta'en with equal thanks. And blest are those
 Whose blood and judgment[8] are so well co-meddled[9]

---

[1] e'en: even, absolutely.
[2] withal: with this.
[3] candied: sugared.
[4] crook: bend.
[5] pregnant: prompt, readily inclined.
[6] Sh'ath sealed: She has selected of chosen as a sign of ownership.
[7] buffets: blows.
[8] blood and judgment: passion and reason.
[9] co-meddled: mixed together.

> That they are not a pipe for Fortune's finger
> To sound what stop she please. Give me that man
> That is not passion's slave, and I will wear him
> In my heart's core — ay, in my heart of heart —
> As I do thee.

(*Hamlet* 3.2)

哈姆莱特 霍拉旭,你是我所交接的人们中间最正直的一个人。
霍拉旭 啊,殿下!——
哈姆莱特 不,不要以为我在恭维你;你除了你的善良的精神以外,身无长物,我恭维了你又有什么好处呢?为什么要向穷人恭维?不,让蜜糖一样的嘴唇去吮舐愚妄的荣华,在有利可图的所在屈下他们生财有道的膝盖来吧。听着。自从我能够辨别是非、察择贤愚以后,你就是我灵魂里选中的一个人,因为你虽然经历一切的颠沛,却不曾受到一点伤害,命运的虐待和恩宠,你都是受之泰然;能够把感情和理智调整得那么适当,命运不能把他玩弄于指掌之间,那样的人是有福的。给我一个不为感情所奴役的人,我愿意把他珍藏在我的心坎,我的灵魂的深处,正像我对你一样。

(朱生豪译《哈姆莱特》第3幕第2场)

评点

哈姆莱特在秘密吩咐霍拉旭仔细观察国王看戏反应之前,对霍拉旭表达了由衷的信任与赞赏。这也许是为笼络人心,却也确实是王子的肺腑之言。剧中,霍拉旭对哈姆莱特一直忠心耿耿,是哈姆莱特能够放下戒备、敞开心扉说话的唯一人选。

哈姆莱特把霍拉旭描述为"不以物喜,不以己悲"的圣贤风范:"命运的虐待和恩宠,你都是受之泰然"(A man that Fortune's buffets and rewards / Hast ta'en with equal thanks);对于这样一个"不为感情所奴役的人"(not passion's slave),"命运不能把他玩弄于指掌之间"(not a pipe for Fortune's finger to sound what stop she please)。霍拉旭宠辱不惊、处变不惊、临危不惧,这种精神气质难能可贵,哈姆莱特即便身为王子也自愧不如。

场景 12：扪心自问

("O, what form of prayer can serve my turn?")

> 宫廷上下都来看戏，哈姆莱特却不断插科打诨、装疯卖傻。看戏过程中，国王克劳狄斯果然拂袖而去。哈姆莱特认为此举坐实了鬼魂之言，而旁人则认为哈姆莱特的举止冒犯了国王。国王退朝之后，一人独处，不得不面对良心和道义的谴责。

King   O, my offence is rank[1]: it smells to heaven;
        It hath the primal eldest curse[2] upon't —
        A brother's murder. Pray can I not:
        Though inclination be as sharp as will,
        My stronger guilt defeats my strong intent
        And like a man to double business bound[3]
        I stand in pause where I shall first begin
        And both neglect. What if this cursed hand
        Were thicker than itself with brother's blood?
        Is there not rain enough in the sweet heavens
        To wash it white as snow? Whereto serves mercy
        But to confront the visage of offence?
        And what's in prayer but this twofold force
        — To be forestalled[4] ere we come to fall
        Or pardoned, being down? Then I'll look up:
        My fault is past[5]. But O, what form of prayer
        Can serve my turn: 'Forgive me my foul murder'?

---

[1] rank: offensive, foul-smelling.
[2] primal eldest curse: The first murder in Judaeo-Christian tradition is Cain's killing of his brother Abel (see Genesis, 4.11–12).
[3] to double business bound: obliged to undertake two tasks at once.
[4] forestalled: prevented, kept from happening.
[5] past: already committed.

五、《哈姆莱特》　163

That cannot be, since I am still possessed
Of those effects[1] for which I did the murder,
My crown, mine own ambition and my queen.
May one be pardoned and retain th'offence[2]?
In the corrupted currents[3] of this world
Offence's gilded hand[4] may shove[5] by justice,
And oft 'tis seen the wicked prize itself
Buys out the law; but 'tis not so above:
There is no shuffling[6], there the action lies
In his[7] true nature, and we ourselves compelled
Even to the teeth and forehead[8] of our faults
To give in evidence. What then? What rests[9]?
Try what repentance can — what can[10] it not? —
Yet what can it, when one cannot repent?
O wretched state, O bosom black as death,
O limed[11] soul that struggling to be free
Art more engaged[12]. Help, angels! Make assay[13].
Bow, stubborn knees, and heart with strings of steel,
Be soft as sinews of the new-born babe.
All may be well.

(*Hamlet* 3.3)

---

[1] effects: advantages, benefits.
[2] retain th'offence: i.e. keep the profits of the crime.
[3] currents: i.e. procedures, ways of doing things.
[4] offence's gilded hand: the gold-bearing (and guilty) hand of an offender.
[5] shove: by thrust aside, evade.
[6] shuffling: trickery.
[7] his: its.
[8] teeth and forehead: Bared teeth and frowning brow are seen as expressing defiance or anger.
[9] rests: remains, is left (to say or do).
[10] can: i.e. can achieve.
[11] limed: trapped, as a bird with birdlime, a sticky substance spread on the branches of trees.
[12] engaged: involved, entangled.
[13] assay: effort.

国王 啊！我的罪恶的戾气已经上达于天；我的灵魂上负着一个元始以来最初的咒诅，杀害兄弟的暴行！我不能祈祷，虽然我的愿望像决心一样强烈；我的更坚强的罪恶击败了我的坚强的意愿。像一个人同时要做两件事情，我因为不知道应该先从什么地方下手而徘徊歧途，结果反弄得一事无成。要是这一只可咒诅的手上染满了一层比它本身还厚的兄弟的血，难道天上所有的甘霖，都不能把它洗涤得像雪一样洁白吗？慈悲的使命，不就是宽宥罪恶吗？祈祷的目的，不是一方面预防我们的堕落，一方面救拔我们于已堕落之后吗？那么我要仰望上天；我的过失已经犯下了。可是唉！哪一种祈祷才是我所适用的呢？"求上帝赦免我的杀人重罪"吗？那不能，因为我现在还占有着那些引起我的犯罪动机的目的物，我的王冠、我的野心和我的王后。非分攫取的利益还在手里，就可以幸邀宽恕吗？在这贪污的人世，罪恶的镀金的手也许可以把公道推开不顾，暴徒的赃物往往成为枉法的贿赂；可是天上却不是这样的，在那边一切都无可遁避，任何行动都要显现它的真相，我们必须当面为我们自己的罪恶作证。那么怎么办呢？还有什么法子好想呢？试一试忏悔的力量吧。什么事情是忏悔所不能做到的？可是对于一个不能忏悔的人，它又有什么用呢？啊，不幸的处境！啊，像死亡一样黑暗的心胸！啊，越是挣扎，越是不能脱身的胶住了的灵魂！救救我，天使们！试一试吧：屈下来，顽强的膝盖；钢丝一样的心弦，变得像新生之婴的筋肉一样柔嫩吧！但愿一切转祸为福！

（朱生豪译《哈姆莱特》第3幕第3场）

评点

《哈姆莱特》一剧不乏独白，通常出自哈姆莱特之口，而他的叔父国王则极少袒露内心。这一段恐怕是他在剧中的唯一独白。他扪心自问，备受良心谴责，暴露出内心的矛盾、纠结、自私与脆弱，与其平日的君王气派迥然不同。

显然，国王心中有愧，良心不安。尽管他频频使用 offence、guilt、fault 等表示冒犯、过错的词，似乎只是犯了一个小错，但是这也许是国王有意轻描淡写，逃避罪责。毕竟，这段独白还多次提及 brother's murder、brother's blood、my foul murder 等说法，不断影射该隐（Cain）杀害兄长亚伯（Abel）的圣经故事。即便他没有坦言其弑君之罪，也在很大程度上承认了自己难逃干系。关于作案动机，他明确点到了"我的王冠、我的野心和我的王后"。

在这段独白中,云山雾罩的事实与五味杂陈的情感交织成一张错综复杂的语言之网,即便是完全私密的自我告白,这位新国王也无法真正直面良心,不乏掩饰或逃避。因此,他无法祷告忏悔,在精神上无法解脱,在宗教上无法得到救赎。这种不乏良心的恶人形象在莎士比亚另一部悲剧《麦克白》中也得到了淋漓尽致的体现。人性的复杂、善恶的斗争、哲学与伦理上的追问……将人物形象塑造得入木三分,令观众产生共鸣。

国王孤身一人跪地祷告,正是刺杀良机。然而,哈姆莱特认为在人祈祷时杀人,就会送他上天堂,而非下地狱。于是,他把出鞘的剑又按回去了,随即去见母后。

场景 13：人之为人

("What is a man if ...")

> 哈姆莱特对母亲咄咄逼人，在争执之中误杀躲在幕后偷听的御前大臣波洛涅斯。因此，国王更有理由送他前往英国。在去海边乘船的路上，哈姆莱特看到挪威王子带领浩浩荡荡的军队奔赴战场，一时感慨万千。

Hamlet How all occasions[1] do inform against[2] me
　　　　And spur my dull revenge. What is a man
　　　　If his chief good and market[3] of his time
　　　　Be but[4] to sleep and feed? A beast — no more.
　　　　Sure he that made us with such large discourse[5],
　　　　Looking before and after, gave us not
　　　　That capability and godlike reason
　　　　To fust[6] in us unused. Now whether it be
　　　　Bestial oblivion[7] or some craven[8] scruple
　　　　Of[9] thinking too precisely on th'event[10]
　　　　(A thought which quartered hath but one part wisdom
　　　　And ever three parts coward) I do not know
　　　　Why yet I live to say this thing's to do,
　　　　Sith[11] I have cause and will and strength and means
　　　　To do't. Examples gross[12] as earth exhort[13] me —
　　　　Witness this army of such mass and charge[14],

---

[1] occasions: occurrences, circumstances.
[2] inform against: accuse, bring charges against.
[3] market: advantage, profit.
[4] but: only.
[5] large discourse: extensive powers of thought or reasoning.
[6] fust: grow musty, decay.
[7] bestial oblivion: the forgetfulness or heedlessness characteristic of animals.
[8] craven: cowardly.
[9] of: caused by.
[10] event: outcome.
[11] sith: since.
[12] gross: palpable, obvious.
[13] exhort: urge, persuade, compel, force.
[14] mass and charge: size and expense.

五、《哈姆莱特》　167

　　　　　Led by a delicate and tender prince,
　　　　　Whose spirit with divine ambition puffed
　　　　　Makes mouths at[1] the invisible event,
　　　　　Exposing what is mortal and unsure
　　　　　To all that fortune, death and danger dare
　　　　　Even for an egg-shell[2]. Rightly to be great
　　　　　Is not to stir without great argument
　　　　　But greatly to find quarrel in a straw
　　　　　When honour's at the stake.
(*Hamlet* 4.4)

哈姆莱特　我所见到、听到的一切，都好像在对我谴责，鞭策我赶快进行我的蹉跎未就的复仇大愿！一个人要是把生活的幸福和目的，只看作吃吃睡睡，他还算是个什么东西？简直不过是一头畜生！上帝造下我们来，使我们能够这样高谈阔论，瞻前顾后，当然要我们利用他所赋予我们的这一种能力和灵明的理智，不让它们白白废掉。现在我明明有理由、有决心、有力量、有方法，可以动手干我所要干的事，可是我还是在大言不惭地说："这件事需要做。"可是始终不曾在行动上表现出来；我不知道这是因为像鹿豕一般的健忘呢，还是因为三分懦怯一分智慧的过于审慎的顾虑。像大地一样显明的榜样都在鼓励我；瞧这一支勇猛的大军，领队的是一个娇养的少年王子，勃勃的雄心振起了他的精神，使他蔑视不可知的结果，为了区区弹丸大小的一块不毛之地，拼着血肉之躯，去向命运、死亡和危险挑战。真正的伟大不是轻举妄动，而是在荣誉遭遇危险的时候，即使为了一根稻秆之微，也要慷慨力争。

（朱生豪译《哈姆莱特》第4幕第4场）

评点

　　人应该如何度过此生？这是一个千古难题，不断有人试图回答这个问题，比如我们所熟知的："当他回首往事的时候，不会因虚度年华而悔恨，也不会因碌碌无为而羞愧。"（保尔·柯察金《钢铁是怎样炼成的》）

　　在哈姆莱特看来，人作为上帝的造物，具有神一般的理性（godlike reason），看重自身的荣誉（honour），他鄙视好吃懒做、毫无追求的人生。即便他迟迟没有采取复仇行动，他心里也绝没有"躺平"，而是一直伺机复仇。哈姆莱特目睹挪威王子的果敢行动，也决定不再犹豫。

---
[1] makes mouths at: makes faces at, laughs at.
[2] egg-shell: proverbially worthless.

场景 14：香消玉殒

("Your sister's drowned, Laertes.")

> 被哈姆莱特所误杀的老臣波洛涅斯有一儿一女，其女奥菲利娅发疯了，其子雷欧提斯（Laertes）气势汹汹地要为父报仇。正当国王与雷欧提斯密谋下毒除掉哈姆莱特时，王后带来一个噩耗：奥菲利娅已经落水而亡。

Gertrude　One woe doth tread upon another's heel,
　　　　　So fast they follow. Your sister's drowned, Laertes.
Laertes　　Drowned! O, where?
Gertrude　There is a willow[1] grows askant[2] the brook
　　　　　That shows[3] his hoary[4] leaves in the glassy stream.
　　　　　There with fantastic garlands did she make
　　　　　Of crowflowers, nettles, daisies, and long purples,
　　　　　That liberal shepherds give a grosser name
　　　　　But our cold[5] maids do dead men's fingers call them.
　　　　　There on the pendent[6] boughs her crownet weeds[7]
　　　　　Clambering to hang, an envious[8] sliver[9] broke,
　　　　　When down her weedy trophies and herself
　　　　　Fell in the weeping brook. Her clothes spread wide
　　　　　And mermaid-like[10] awhile they bore her up,
　　　　　Which time she chanted snatches of old lauds[11]

---

[1] willow: The willow was traditionally associated with unrequited love. Desdemona, the heroine killed by her husband in *Othello*, sings a song of willow before her death.
[2] askant: obliquely, i.e. across.
[3] shows: i.e. reflects.
[4] hoary: grey or white, usually associated with age or with cold.
[5] cold: i.e. chaste, the opposite of liberal.
[6] pendent: overhanging.
[7] crownet weeds: coronet of wild flowers.
[8] envious: malicious.
[9] silver: twig or splinter.
[10] mermaid-like: Mermaids are mythical creatures, half women and half fish.
[11] lauds: hymns.

As one incapable[1] of her own distress,
Or like a creature native and endued[2]
Unto that element. But long it could not be
Till that her garments, heavy with their drink,
Pulled the poor wretch[3] from her melodious lay[4]
To muddy death.

(*Hamlet* 4.7)

王后　　　一桩祸事刚刚到来，又有一桩接踵而至。雷欧提斯，你的妹妹掉在水里淹死了。

雷欧提斯　淹死了！啊！在哪儿？

王后　　　在小溪之旁，斜生着一株杨柳，它的毵毵的枝叶倒映在明镜一样的水流之中；她编了几个奇异的花环来到那里，用的是毛茛、荨麻、雏菊和长颈兰——正派的姑娘管这种花叫死人指头，说粗话的牧人却给它起了另一个不雅的名字——她爬上一根横垂的树枝，想要把她的花冠挂在上面；就在这时候，一根心怀恶意的树枝折断了，她就连人带花一起落下呜咽的溪水里。她的衣服四散展开，使她暂时像人鱼一样漂浮水上；她嘴里还断断续续唱着古老的谣曲，好像一点不感觉到她处境的险恶，又好像她本来就是生长在水中一般。可是不多一会儿，她的衣服给水浸得重起来了，这可怜的人歌儿还没有唱完，就已经沉到泥里去了。

（朱生豪译《哈姆莱特》第 4 幕第 7 场）

评点

关于奥菲利娅之死，王后描述得绘声绘色，呈现了一幅哀婉凄美的动人画面，后世画家常常以此为题作画。奥菲利娅作为美丽的花季少女，无论生前还是死时，在剧中都往往与花相伴，这一点在画作中也得到了明显体现。

王后与雷欧提斯的对话体现了二人的不同性格：前者措辞华丽，风范优雅，多用修辞手法与长句铺陈；后者则是人狠话不多，多用短句，他在得知至亲噩耗时的震惊、悲痛与愤怒跃然纸上。

---

[1] incapable: uncomprehending.
[2] endued: habituated, i.e. as if native.
[3] wretch: often used to indicate a mixture of pity and affection.
[4] melodious lay: sweet-sounding song.

场景 15：小丑骷髅

("Alas, poor Yorick.")

> 哈姆莱特在海上九死一生，捡了一条命回国，并且送两位毫不知情的老同学去英格兰送死。哈姆莱特秘密约霍拉旭在墓地会面，只见一位掘墓人一边唱歌一边干活，哈姆莱特手捧骷髅头感慨人生……

Hamlet Alas, poor Yorick. I knew him, Horatio. A fellow of infinite jest, of most excellent fancy. He hath bore me on his back a thousand times, and now how abhorred[1] in my imagination it is. My gorge[2] rises at it. Here hung those lips that I have kissed I know not how oft. Where be your jibes[3] now — your gambols[4], your songs, your flashes of merriment, that were wont to set the table on a roar? Not one now to mock your own grinning, quite chapfallen[5]. Now get you to my lady's table[6] and tell her, let her paint an inch thick, to this favour[7] she must come. Make her laugh at that. Prithee, Horatio, tell me one thing.

Horatio What's that, my lord?

Hamlet Dost thou think Alexander[8] looked o'this fashion i'th' earth?

Horatio E'en so.

Hamlet And smelt so? Pah!

Horatio E'en so, my lord.

Hamlet To what base uses we may return, Horatio! Why may not imagination trace

---

[1] abhorred: filled with horror.
[2] gorge: 1) stomach or throat; 2) contents of the stomach.
[3] jibes: taunts or scoffs.
[4] gambols: playful tricks.
[5] chapfallen: 1) lacking the cheeks or jaw; 2) crestfallen, dejected.
[6] table: presumably dressing-table.
[7] favour: facial appearance.
[8] Alexander: Alexander the Great.

the noble dust of Alexander till 'a find it stopping a bung-hole[1]? (*Hamlet* 5.1)

哈姆莱特	唉，可怜的郁利克！霍拉旭，我认识他；他是一个最会开玩笑、非常富于想象力的家伙。他曾经把我负在背上一千次；现在我一想起来，却忍不住胸头作呕。这儿本来有两片嘴唇，我不知吻过它们多少次。——现在你还会挖苦人吗？你还会蹦蹦跳跳，逗人发笑吗？你还会唱歌吗？你还会随口编造一些笑话，说得满座捧腹吗？你没有留下一个笑话，讥笑你自己吗？这样垂头丧气了吗？现在你给我到小姐的闺房里去，对她说，凭她脸上的脂粉搽得一寸厚，到后来总要变成这个样子的；你用这样的话告诉她，看她笑不笑吧。霍拉旭，请你告诉我一件事情。
霍拉旭	什么事情，殿下？
哈姆莱特	你想亚历山大在地下也是这副形状吗？
霍拉旭	也是这样。
哈姆莱特	也有同样的臭味吗？呸！（掷下骷髅）
霍拉旭	也有同样的臭味，殿下。
哈姆莱特	谁知道我们将来会变成一些什么下贱的东西，霍拉旭！要是我们用想象推测下去，谁知道亚历山大的高贵的尸体，不就是塞在酒桶口上的泥土？

（朱生豪译《哈姆莱特》第5幕第1场）

评点

《哈姆莱特》第5幕自始至终都完全被死亡所笼罩，这一幕开场以墓地为背景，思考人生意义与价值。在掘墓人刨出来的头骨中，有一个生前曾是哈姆莱特童年时代的宫廷弄臣，二人颇为亲近，如今却阴阳两隔，物是人非……人终有一死，无论是如今涂脂抹粉的妙龄女郎，还是威震天下的亚历山大大帝。

不同于《哈姆莱特》的其他场景大量使用素体诗（或称无韵诗），墓地一场的台词多为散文体。一方面是因为与掘墓人这样的"下里巴人"聊天，无须阳春白雪；另一方面，质朴自然的语言也更能配合思想主题上的返璞归真。

---

[1] bung-hole: A bung is the plug or stopper for a cask or barrel; a bung–hole the outlet or mouth the bung stops.

场景 16：命中注定

("The readiness is all.")

> 一心报仇的雷欧提斯，在国王的唆使与策划之下，向哈姆莱特提议比剑——名义上冠冕堂皇，实际上却暗藏杀机。霍拉旭预感凶多吉少，劝说哈姆莱特托词拒绝，而哈姆莱特不为所动，欣然接受了雷欧提斯的挑战。

Horatio You will lose, my lord.

Hamlet I do not think so. Since he went into France I have been in continual practice. I shall win at the odds. Thou wouldst not think how ill all's here about my heart — but it is no matter.

Horatio Nay, good my lord —

Hamlet It is but foolery, but it is such a kind of gaingiving[1] as would perhaps trouble a woman.

Horatio If your mind dislike anything, obey it. I will forestall their repair[2] hither and say you are not fit.

Hamlet Not a whit[3]. We defy augury[4]. There's a special providence in the fall of a sparrow. If it be, 'tis not to come. If it be not to come, it will be now. If it be not now, yet it will come. The readiness is all, since no man of aught he leaves knows what is't to leave betimes[5]. Let be[6].

(*Hamlet* 5.2)

---

[1] gaingiving: misgiving.
[2] repair: coming.
[3] not a whit: not at all.
[4] augury: the practice of learning secrets or predicting the future from the flight of birds.
[5] betimes: early.
[6] let be: leave it alone; say no more.

霍拉旭	殿下，您在这一回打赌中间，多半要失败的。
哈姆莱特	我想我不会失败。自从他到法国去以后，我练习得很勤；我一定可以把他打败。可是你不知道我的心里是多么不舒服；那也不用说了。
霍拉旭	啊，我的好殿下——
哈姆莱特	那不过是一种傻气的心理；可是一个女人也许会因为这种莫名其妙的疑虑而惶惑。
霍拉旭	要是您心里不愿意做一件事，那么就不要做吧。我可以去通知他们不用到这儿来，说您现在不能比赛。
哈姆莱特	不，我们不要害怕什么预兆；一只雀子的死生，都是命运预先注定的。注定在今天，就不会是明天，不是明天，就是今天；逃过了今天，明天还是逃不了，随时准备着就是了。一个人既然在离开世界的时候，只能一无所有，那么早早脱身而去，不是更好吗？随它去。

（朱生豪译《哈姆莱特》第 5 幕第 2 场）

评点

同样是为父报仇，雷欧提斯就不像哈姆莱特那样瞻前顾后、顾虑重重，他一旦认定哈姆莱特是仇人，就要不择手段地毁灭哈姆莱特，哪怕用阴谋与毒药。这种莽撞，也正好为国王所利用——国王得以借刀杀人，剪除心头之患。

哈姆莱特明知凶多吉少，却决定义无反顾地直面挑战，认为冥冥之中一切有定，个人在劫难逃。果然，在最后一幕中，这场宫廷比剑沦为屠杀现场，丹麦王子终于复仇成功，却代价惨重——不仅自己与仇人同归于尽，而且还连累了旁人，王后与雷欧提斯均沦为陪葬。

哈姆莱特台词中的麻雀之喻（There's a special providence in the fall of a sparrow）源于新约《马太福音》（Matthew 10:29-31）——"两个麻雀不是卖一分银子吗？若是你们的父不许，就一个也不能掉在地上。就是你们的头发，也都被数过了。所以，不要惧怕，你们比许多麻雀还贵重。"（Are not two sparrows sold for a farthing? And one of them shall not fall on the ground without your Father. But the very hairs of your head are all numbered. Fear ye not therefore, ye are of more value than many sparrows.）麻雀尚且如此，更何况人？哈姆莱特认为世间事务自有上天安排，世人无须过虑，也无法回避，"随时准备着就是了"（The readiness is all）。

William Shakespeare

六、《麦克白》

(*Macbeth*)

(1606)

"大洋里所有的水,能够洗净我手上的血迹吗?"

("Will all great Neptune's ocean wash this blood clean from my hand?")

麦克白将军立下了赫赫战功,获得国王邓肯的各种荣誉与封地的嘉奖。然而,麦克白的内心并不满足,他的妻子更是野心勃勃。为了夺取王位,夫妻俩合伙谋杀了前来做客的邓肯,又不惜一切代价,清除其他敌对势力,最后如愿以偿地坐上了王位。

然而,他们始终无法摆脱良心的煎熬;即便心狠手辣,他们内心的良知并没泯灭,自始至终都视自己为恶人、罪人,难以与自己和解或达成自洽,总是心神不宁,夜不能寐。麦克白在独处时会看到飘忽不定的带血匕首,在宴席上会受到索命亡灵的惊吓;麦克白夫人则常常在半夜梦游,总梦见手上血迹斑斑,却无论怎么洗也洗不掉……

尽管麦克白夫人在开场伊始就充当麦克白行凶的幕后指使者与坚定同路人,显得比麦克白更加心狠手辣,但是她后来精神崩溃,发疯而亡。麦克白最终也罪有应得。人性的复杂、善恶的交织、命运与意志的对抗在《麦克白》一剧中得到了淋漓尽致的展现。

诺贝尔文学奖获得者、美国现代主义小说家威廉·福克纳(William Faulkner, 1897—1962)的代表作《喧嚣与骚动》(*The Sound and the Fury*)的书名即出自《麦克白》一剧的麦克白独白。

《麦克白》（*Macbeth*）

场景 1： 善即是恶（"Fair is foul, and foul is fair."）1.1

场景 2： 恶念萌生（"The raven himself is hoarse ..."）1.5

场景 3： 笑里藏刀（"... look like th'innocent flower ..."）1.5

场景 4： 狼子野心（"I have ... vaulting ambition."）1.7

场景 5： 蛊惑人心（"When you durst do it, then you were a man."）1.7

场景 6： 血光之灾（"... art thou but a dagger of the mind ... ?"）2.1

场景 7： 夜不能寐（"Macbeth shall sleep no more!"）2.2

场景 8： 夜半敲门（"Whence is that knocking?"）2.2

场景 9： 覆水难收（"What's done is done."）3.2

场景 10： 金盆洗手（"Here's the smell of the blood still."）5.1

场景 11： 病入膏肓（"As she is troubled with thick-coming fancies ..."）5.3

场景 12： 万念俱灰（"Life's but a walking shadow ..."）5.5

场景 1: 善即是恶

("Fair is foul, and foul is fair.")

> 《麦克白》一剧与《哈姆莱特》同样以超自然的怪异现象开场，营造阴森诡异的氛围：荒郊野外，三女巫安排行动计划，即将去见麦克白。

First Witch　　When shall we three meet again?
　　　　　　　In thunder, lightning, or in rain?
Second Witch　When the hurlyburly's[1] done,
　　　　　　　When the battle's lost and won.
Third Witch　　That will be ere the set of sun.
First Witch　　Where the place?
Second Witch　Upon the heath.
Third Witch　　There to meet with Macbeth.
First Witch　　I come, Graymalkin[2]!
Second Witch　Paddock[3] calls.
Third Witch　　Anon.
All　　　　　　Fair is foul, and foul is fair.
　　　　　　　Hover through the fog and filthy air.

(*Macbeth* 1.1)

---

[1] hurlyburly: uproar, tumult, confusion.
[2] Graymalkin: a grey cat as a common witches' familiar.
[3] Paddock: a toad, another familiar of witches.

女巫甲　何时姊妹再相逢，
　　　　雷电轰轰雨蒙蒙？
女巫乙　且等烽烟静四陲，
　　　　败军高奏凯歌回。
女巫丙　半山夕照尚含辉。
女巫甲　何处相逢？
女巫乙　在荒原。
女巫丙　共同去见麦克白。
女巫甲　我来了，狸猫精。
女巫乙　癞蛤蟆叫我了。
女巫丙　来也。
三女巫　美即丑恶丑即美，翱翔毒雾妖云里。
（朱生豪译《麦克白》第1幕第1场）

评点

　　三女巫在《麦克白》一剧中出现多次，神秘莫测，善恶难辨。她们一步步地向麦克白预告其命运，也一次次地刺激麦克白的野心。她们是预言家，还是命运女神，抑或诱惑人心的鬼怪？

　　她们的开场预言阴森怪异，却不乏哲理，尤其是最后两行。其中的"fair"与"foul"这对反义词一方面截然对立，另一方面又相互转化。善恶美丑，似是而非；好坏福祸，模棱两可；世事复杂，人心难料。

　　这一对反义词同样出现在第1幕第3场麦克白登场的第一句台词里——"我从来没有见过这样阴郁而又光明的日子"（So foul and fair a day I have not seen），其中的"fair"与"foul"这两个词与三女巫的开场白遥相呼应。当时的麦克白刚刚凯旋，祸兮福兮？

　　相对于朱生豪的译文——"美即丑恶丑即美"，梁实秋译为"清白即是黑暗，黑暗即是清白"。两种译文差异不小，因为"fair"（美的、善的、清白的）与"foul"（丑的、恶的、龌龊的）这两个词的含义都颇为丰富，而两位译者各自选取了不同的释义。因此，这一句也不妨译为"善即是恶，恶即是善"。

场景 2：恶念萌生

（"The raven himself is hoarse …"）

麦克白夫妇二人志同道合、情感笃厚。麦克白从战场返回，尚未到家就迫不及待地给妻子写了一封长信。麦克白夫人得知三女巫的预言之后非常兴奋，一心要促成麦克白当上国王。正巧国王邓肯（Duncan）要来麦克白的府上做客，麦克白夫人顿时心生歹念。

Lady Macbeth   The raven himself is hoarse,

That croaks the fatal entrance of Duncan

Under my battlements. Come, you Spirits

That tend on mortal thoughts[1], unsex me here,

And fill me from the crown to the toe, top-full

Of direst cruelty! make thick my blood,

Stop up th'access and passage to remorse[2];

That no compunctious[3] visitings of Nature

Shake my fell purpose, nor keep peace between

Th'effect and it! Come to my woman's breasts,

And take my milk for gall[4], you murth'ring ministers[5],

Wherever in your sightless[6] substances

You wait on Nature's mischief! Come, thick Night,

And pall thee in the dunnest[7] smoke of Hell,

That my keen knife see not the wound it makes,

---

[1] mortal thoughts: murderous, deadly, or destructive designs.
[2] remorse: compassion, tenderness.
[3] compunctious: pricking the conscience.
[4] gall: bile（胆汁）.
[5] ministers: attendant spirits.
[6] sightless: invisible.
[7] dun: dark, swarthy.

> Nor Heaven peep through the blanket of the dark,
> To cry, 'Hold, hold!'

(*Macbeth* 1.5)

麦克白夫人 报告邓肯走进我这堡门来送死的乌鸦,它的叫声是嘶哑的。来,注视着人类恶念的魔鬼们!解除我的女性的柔弱,用最凶恶的残忍自顶至踵贯注在我的全身;凝结我的血液,不要让怜悯钻进我的心头,不要让天性中的恻隐摇动我的狠毒的决意!来,你们这些杀人的助手,你们无形的躯体散满在空间,到处找寻为非作恶的机会,进入我的妇人的胸中,把我的乳水当作胆汁吧!来,阴沉的黑夜,用最昏暗的地狱中的浓烟罩住你自己,让我的锐利的刀瞧不见它自己切开的伤口,让青天不能从黑暗的重衾里探出头来,高喊:"住手,住手!"

(朱生豪译《麦克白》第1幕第5场)

评点

这是麦克白夫人的一段著名独白。麦克白夫人有意作恶,但她并不全是一个毫无是非观念、善恶不分的人,只不过她偏偏要呼唤地狱,藐视天堂。她为了追求世俗权力而不惜一切代价,刻意抹杀自己的女性气质、同情心、良心与人性,转而变为一个杀人不眨眼的女魔头,与"乌鸦"(raven)、"魔鬼"(Spirits)、"胆汁"(gall)、"黑夜"(thick Night)、"地狱"(Hell)等一切黑暗事物为伍。

麦克白夫人在极力促成麦克白上位的同时,也是在为自己实现王后梦。此时的麦克白夫人尚未料到她要为此付出她无法承受的代价。正如《红楼梦》中的王熙凤,麦克白夫人也是"机关算尽太聪明,反误了卿卿性命",到头来,一场空,甚至还搭上了身家性命。

场景 3：笑里藏刀

("… look like th'innocent flower …")

> 麦克白一回家就重申国王当晚要来做客，麦克白夫人便坦言自己的弑君计划，而此时的麦克白尚未做好为非作歹的心理准备。

Macbeth	My dearest love, Duncan comes here to-night.
Lady Macbeth	And when goes hence?
Macbeth	To-morrow, as he purposes.
Lady Macbeth	O! never Shall sun that morrow see! Your face, my Thane, is as a book, where men May read strange matters. To beguile the time[1], Look like the time; bear welcome in your eye, Your hand, your tongue: look like th'innocent flower, But be the serpent under't. He that's coming Must be provided for; and you shall put This night's great business into my dispatch; Which shall to all our nights and days to come Give solely sovereign sway and masterdom.
Macbeth	We will speak further.
Lady Macbeth	Only look up clear; To alter favour ever is to fear: Leave all the rest to me.

(*Macbeth* 1.5)

---

[1] beguile the time: deceive the world, delude all observers.

麦克白　　　我的最亲爱的亲人，邓肯今晚要到这儿来。

麦克白夫人　什么时候回去呢？

麦克白　　　他预备明天回去。

麦克白夫人　啊！太阳永远不会见到那样一个明天。您的脸，我的爵爷，正像一本书，人们可以从那上面读到奇怪的事情。您要欺骗世人，必须装出和世人同样的神气；让您的眼睛里、您的手上、您的舌尖，随处流露着欢迎；让人家瞧您像一朵纯洁的花朵，可是在花瓣底下却有一条毒蛇潜伏。我们必须准备款待这位将要来到的贵宾；您可以把今晚的大事交给我去办；凭此一举，我们今后就可以日日夜夜永远掌握君临万民的无上权威。

麦克白　　　我们还要商量商量。

麦克白夫人　泰然自若地抬起您的头来；脸上变色最易引起猜疑。其他一切都包在我身上。

（朱生豪译《麦克白》第 1 幕第 5 场）

评点

麦克白夫人密谋刺杀国王，叮嘱麦克白在外人面前要不露声色、笑里藏刀，要装作"一朵纯洁的花朵，可是在花瓣底下却有一条毒蛇潜伏"。

麦克白的兴亡成败，与麦克白夫人在背后的怂恿教唆休戚相关。虽然二人都野心勃勃，但是麦克白一开始只有贼心而无贼胆，麦克白夫人则不但自己心狠手辣，而且还摇旗呐喊、添油加醋，一举将麦克白推上为非作歹的不归路。

当然，麦克白本人也不是无辜的。他自己不乏想当国王的野心；面对刺杀国王、夺取王位的诱惑，他也没有断然拒绝，只是一时没有下定决心而已。

场景 4：狼子野心

("I have ... vaulting ambition.")

国王一行大驾光临麦克白府上，麦克白夫妇设宴款待，表面上热情好客，却心怀鬼胎。在迟疑不决的过程中，麦克白无比纠结。

Macbeth　If it were done when 'tis done, then 'twere well
It were done quickly: if the assassination
Could trammel up[1] the consequence, and catch
With his surcease[2] success; that but this blow
Might be the be-all and the end-all — here,
But here, upon this bank and shoal[3] of time,
We'd jump[4] the life to come[5]. — But in these cases,
We still have judgment here; that we but teach
Bloody instructions, which, being taught, return
To plague th'inventor: this even-handed[6] Justice
Commends[7] th'ingredience of our poison'd chalice[8]
To our own lips. He's here in double trust:
First, as I am his kinsman and his subject,
Strong both against the deed; then, as his host,
Who should against his murderer shut the door,
Not bear the knife myself. Besides, this Duncan
Hath borne his faculties[9] so meek, hath been
So clear[10] in his great office, that his virtues
Will plead like angels, trumpet-tongu'd, against
The deep damnation of his taking-off;

---

[1] trammel up: entangle as in a net. A trammel was a net for partridges or for catching fish.
[2] surcease: (a legal term) the stop or stay of proceedings. Here it is a euphemism for death.
[3] shoal: a stretch of shallow water.
[4] jump: risk.
[5] life to come: i.e. the future life.
[6] even-handed: impartial.
[7] commends: offers.
[8] poison'd chalice: 金杯毒酒。
[9] faculties: powers, prerogatives of the crown.
[10] clear: free from guilt or stain.

>   And Pity, like a naked new-born babe,
>   Striding the blast, or heaven's Cherubins, hors'd
>   Upon the sightless couriers[1] of the air,
>   Shall blow the horrid deed in every eye,
>   That tears shall drown the wind. — I have no spur
>   To prick the sides of my intent, but only
>   Vaulting ambition, which o'erleaps itself
>   And falls on th'other —
>
> (*Macbeth* 1.7)

麦克白 要是干了以后就完了，那么还是快一点干；要是凭着暗杀的手段，可以攫取美满的结果，又可以排除了一切后患；要是这一刀砍下去，就可以完成一切、终结一切、解决一切——在这人世上，仅仅在这人世上，在时间这大海的浅滩上；那么来生我也就顾不到了。可是在这种事情上，我们往往逃不过现世的裁判；我们树立下血的榜样，教会别人杀人，结果反而自己被人所杀；把毒药投入酒杯里的人，结果也会自己饮鸩而死，这就是一丝不爽的报应。他到这儿来本有两重的信任：第一，我是他的亲戚，又是他的臣子，按照名分绝对不能干这样的事；第二，我是他的主人，应当保障他身体的安全，怎么可以自己持刀行刺？而且，这个邓肯秉性仁慈，处理国政，从来没有过失，要是把他杀死了，他的生前的美德，将要像天使一般发出喇叭一样清澈的声音，向世人昭告我的弑君重罪；"怜悯"像一个赤身裸体在狂风中飘游的婴儿，又像一个御气而行的天婴，将要把这可憎的行为揭露在每一个人的眼中，使眼泪淹没叹息。没有一种力量可以鞭策我实现自己的意图，可是我的跃跃欲试的野心，却不顾一切地驱着我去冒颠踬的危险——

（朱生豪译《麦克白》第1幕第7场）

评点

　　麦克白与哈姆莱特一样，拥有丰富的内心世界与多角度多层面的哲思维度，因而瞻前顾后，迟迟难以下定决心。这段独白生动地展现了麦克白的内心纠结与矛盾——要不要暗杀国王，一如哈姆莱特"生存还是毁灭"的艰难抉择。只是麦克白不是像哈姆莱特那样出于为父报仇、扭转乾坤的目的，他只是为了满足自己和麦克白夫人的勃勃野心。

　　麦克白很清楚：没有任何正当理由能够支持弑君行动，而且种种理由都在论证不应杀邓肯；而且，这种暴力行动没法做到一劳永逸、一了百了；如此勃勃野心，必有报应与恶果。于是，理性思考令他一时退缩，有心叫停刺杀计划。

---

[1] sightless couriers: invisible runners, i.e. the winds.

场景 5：蛊惑人心

("When you durst do it, then you were a man.")

> 麦克白夫妇款待国王及其他贵宾，毫无破绽。麦克白试图叫停刺杀计划。然而，他无法抵御麦克白夫人软硬兼施的劝导与撺掇，最终还是决定按照原计划进行下去。

Macbeth We will proceed no further in this business:
He hath honour'd me of late; and I have bought
Golden opinions from all sorts of people,
Which would be worn now in their newest gloss[1],
Not cast aside so soon.

Lady Macbeth   Was the hope drunk,
Wherein you dress'd yourself? hath it slept since?
And wakes it now, to look so green and pale
At what it did so freely? From this time
Such I account thy love. Art thou afeard[2]
To be the same in thine own act and valour,
As thou art in desire? Would'st thou have that
Which thou esteem'st the ornament of life[3],
And live a coward in thine own esteem,
Letting 'I dare not' wait upon 'I would,'
Like the poor cat i'th'adage[4]?

Macbeth   Pr'ythee, peace.
I dare do all that may become a man;
Who dares do more, is none.

---

[1] gloss: lustre of the surface, specious appearance.
[2] afeard: afraid, being in fear.
[3] ornament of life: i.e. the crown.
[4] adage: saying. The phrase "cat i'th'adage" refers to the cat that would eat fish but would not get its feet wet.

Lady Macbeth	What beast was't then,
	That made you break this enterprise to me?
	When you durst do it, then you were a man;
	And, to be more than what you were, you would
	Be so much more the man. Nor time nor place
	Did then adhere, and yet you would make both:
	They have made themselves, and that their fitness now
	Does unmake you. I have given suck, and know
	How tender 'tis to love the babe that milks me:
	I would, while it was smiling in my face,
	Have pluck'd my nipple from his boneless gums[1],
	And dash'd the brains out, had I so sworn
	As you have done to this.
Macbeth	If we should fail?
Lady Macbeth	We fail? But[2] screw your courage to the sticking-place,
	And we'll not fail. When Duncan is asleep
	(Whereto the rather shall his day's hard journey
	Soundly invite him), his two chamberlains[3]
	Will I with wine and wassail so convince[4],
	That memory, the warder of the brain,
	Shall be a fume, and the receipt of reason
	A limbeck[5] only: when in swinish sleep
	Their drenched[6] natures lie, as in a death,
	What cannot you and I perform upon
	Th'unguarded Duncan? what not put upon
	His spongy[7] officers, who shall bear the guilt
	Of our great quell[8]?

---

[1] gums: 牙龈，牙床。
[2] but: only.
[3] chamberlains: gentlemen-of-the-bedchamber.
[4] convince: overpower.
[5] limbeck: a vessel in which the liquids to be distilled are heated（蒸馏器）.
[6] drenched: drowned.
[7] spongy: drunken.
[8] quell: kill, murder.

Macbeth	Bring forth men-children only;

For thy undaunted mettle[1] should compose
Nothing but males. Will it not be receiv'd,
When we have mark'd with blood those sleepy two
Of his own chamber, and us'd their very daggers,
That they have done't?

Lady Macbeth　　　　　　　　Who dares receive it other[2],
As we shall make our griefs and clamour roar
Upon his death?

Macbeth　　　　　　　I am settled, and bend up
Each corporal agent to this terrible feat.
Away, and mock the time[3] with fairest show:
False face must hide what the false heart doth know.

(*Macbeth* 1.7)

麦克白　我们还是不要进行这一件事情吧。他最近给我极大的尊荣；我也好容易从各种人的嘴里博到了无上的美誉，我的名声现在正在发射最灿烂的光彩，不能这么快就把它丢弃了。

麦克白夫人　难道你把自己沉浸在里面的那种希望，只是醉后的妄想吗？它现在从一场睡梦中醒来，因为追悔自己的孟浪，而吓得脸色这样苍白吗？从这一刻起，我要把你的爱情看作同样靠不住的东西。你不敢让你在行为和勇气上跟你的欲望一致吗？你宁愿像一头畏首畏尾的猫儿，顾全你所认为生命的装饰品的名誉，不惜让你在自己眼中成为一个懦夫，让"我不敢"永远跟随在"我想要"的后面吗？

麦克白　请你不要说了。只要是男子汉做的事，我都敢做；没有人比我有更大的胆量。

麦克白夫人　那么当初是什么畜生使你把这一种企图告诉我的呢？是男子汉就应当敢作敢为；要是你敢做一个比你更伟大的人物，那才更是一个男子汉。那时候，无论时间和地点都不曾给你下手的方便，可

---

[1] mettle: material, spirit.
[2] other: otherwise.
[3] mock the time: i.e. delude all observers.

	是你却居然决意要实现你的愿望；现在你有了大好的机会，你又失去勇气了。我曾经哺乳过婴孩，知道一个母亲是怎样怜爱那吮吸她乳汁的子女；可是我会在它看着我的脸微笑的时候，从它的柔软的嫩嘴里摘下我的乳头，把它的脑袋砸碎，要是我也像你一样，曾经发誓下这样毒手的话。
麦克白	假如我们失败了——
麦克白夫人	我们失败！只要你集中你的全副勇气，我们决不会失败。邓肯赶了这一天辛苦的路程，一定睡得很熟；我再去陪他那两个侍卫饮酒作乐，灌得他们头脑昏沉、记忆化成一阵烟雾；等他们烂醉如泥、像死猪一样睡去以后，我们不就可以把那毫无防卫的邓肯随意摆布了吗？我们不是可以把这一件重大的谋杀罪案，推在他的酒醉的侍卫身上吗？
麦克白	愿你所生育的全是男孩子，因为你的无畏的精神，只应该铸造一些刚强的男性。要是我们在那睡在他寝室里的两个人身上涂抹一些血迹，而且就用他们的刀子，人家会不会相信真是他们干下的事？
麦克白夫人	等他的死讯传出以后，我们就假意装出号啕痛哭的样子，这样还有谁敢不相信？
麦克白	我的决心已定，我要用全身的力量，去干这件惊人的举动。去，用最美妙的外表把人们的耳目欺骗；奸诈的心必须罩上虚伪的笑脸。

评点

麦克白不乏道德与良知，几番踌躇。当他表示洗手不干了时，麦克白夫人便用激将法，迫使他坚持对理想（野心）的追求，哪怕不择手段。麦克白最终经不起妻子的怂恿，由此走上了一条不归路……

麦克白在这一场的最后一句台词——"去，用最美妙的外表把人们的耳目欺骗；奸诈的心必须罩上虚伪的笑脸"（Away, and mock the time with fairest show: / False face must hide what the false heart doth know），正呼应麦克白夫人此前叮嘱他装作"一朵纯洁的花朵，可是在花瓣底下却有一条毒蛇潜伏"的说法。夫妇两人一唱一和，同心同德。

场景 6：血光之灾

（ "… art thou but a dagger of the mind … ?" ）

> 宴会当晚，国王下榻麦克白府上，夜深人静之时，麦克白一段独白。

Macbeth Is this a dagger, which I see before me,
The handle toward my hand? Come, let me clutch thee: —
I have thee not, and yet I see thee still.
Art thou not, fatal vision, sensible[1]
To feeling, as to sight? or art thou but
A dagger of the mind, a false creation,
Proceeding from the heat-oppressed[2] brain?
I see thee yet, in form as palpable
As this which now I draw.
Thou marshall'st me the way that I was going;
And such an instrument I was to use. —
Mine eyes are made the fools o'th'other senses,
Or else worth all the rest: I see thee still;
And on thy blade, and dudgeon, gouts of blood,
Which was not so before. — There's no such thing.
It is the bloody business which informs
Thus to mine eyes. — Now o'er the one half-world
Nature seems dead, and wicked dreams abuse
The curtain'd sleep: Witchcraft celebrates
Pale Hecate's off'rings; and wither'd Murther,
Alarum'd by his sentinel, the wolf,
Whose howl's his watch, thus with his stealthy pace,
With Tarquin's ravishing strides, towards his design
Moves like a ghost. — Thou sure and firm-set earth,
Hear not my steps, which way they walk, for fear

---

[1] sensible: capable of being perceived by the senses, perceptible.
[2] heat-oppressed: fevered.

Thy very stones prate[1] of my where-about[2],
And take the present horror from the time,
Which now suits with it. — Whiles I threat, he lives:
Words to the heat of deeds too cold breath gives. [*A bell rings.*]
I go, and it is done: the bell invites me.
Hear it not, Duncan; for it is a knell[3]
That summons thee to Heaven, or to Hell.

(*Macbeth* 2.1)

麦克白　在我面前摇晃着、它的柄对着我的手的，不是一把刀子吗？来，让我抓住你。我抓不到你，可是仍旧看见你。不祥的幻象，你只是一件可视不可触的东西吗？或者你不过是一把想象中的刀子，从狂热的脑筋里发出来的虚妄的意匠？我仍旧看见你，你的形状正像我现在拔出的这一把刀子一样明显。你指示着我所要去的方向，告诉我应当用什么利器。我的眼睛倘不是上了当，受其他知觉的嘲弄，就是兼领了一切感官的机能。我仍旧看见你；你的刃上和柄上还流着一滴一滴刚才所没有的血。没有这样的事；杀人的恶念使我看见这种异象。现在在半个世界上，一切生命仿佛已经死去，罪恶的梦景扰乱着平和的睡眠，作法的女巫在向惨白的赫卡忒献祭；形容枯瘦的杀人犯，听到了替他巡哨、报更的豺狼的嗥声，仿佛淫乱的塔昆蹑着脚步像一个鬼似的向他的目的地走去。坚固结实的大地啊，不要听见我的脚步声音是向什么地方去的，我怕路上的砖石会泄漏了我的行踪，把黑夜中一派阴森可怕的气氛破坏了。我正在这儿威胁他的生命，他却在那儿活得好好的；在紧张的行动中间，言语不过是一口冷气。（钟声）我去，就这么干；钟声在招引我。不要听它，邓肯，这是召唤你上天堂或者下地狱的丧钟。

（朱生豪译《麦克白》第 2 幕第 1 场）

评点

　　这番独白通过大量修辞意象，营造出令人心惊胆寒的氛围，人物内心的纠结与痛苦暴露无遗。这个人物虽然邪恶，但是不乏人性，再加上细腻的情感、丰富的想象、活跃的思维、生动的描述……独白颇具艺术感染力。

---

[1] prate: tattle, talk idly, particularly in a bragging manner.
[2] where-about: i.e. whereabouts.
[3] knell: the sound of a bell rung at a funeral.

场景 7：夜不能寐

（"Macbeth shall sleep no more!"）

完成刺杀之后，麦克白随即向麦克白夫人汇报。这位昔日在战场上出生入死的勇士此时惊慌失措，手里一把血迹斑斑的匕首，麦克白夫人则安抚宽慰……

Lady Macbeth　　　　　　　These deeds must not be thought
　　　　　　　After these ways: so, it will make us mad.
Macbeth　Methought[1] I heard a voice cry, 'Sleep no more!
　　　　Macbeth does murther[2] Sleep,' — the innocent Sleep;
　　　　Sleep, that knits up the ravell'd sleeve of care,
　　　　The death of each day's life, sore labour's bath,
　　　　Balm of hurt minds, great Nature's second course,
　　　　Chief nourisher in life's feast; —
Lady Macbeth　　　　　　　　　　　What do you mean?
Macbeth　Still it cried 'Sleep no more!' to all the house:
　　　　'Glamis hath murder'd sleep, and therefore
　　　　Cawdor shall sleep no more, Macbeth shall sleep no more!'
Lady Macbeth　Who was it that thus cried? Why, worthy Thane,
　　　　You do unbend[3] your noble strength, to think
　　　　So brainsickly of things. Go, get some water,
　　　　And wash this filthy witness[4] from your hand.

(*Macbeth* 2.2)

---

[1] Methought: It seemed to me.
[2] murther: i.e. murder.
[3] unbend: free from flexure (as a bow); remit from a strain, relax.
[4] witness: evidence.

麦克白夫人	我们干这种事，不能尽往这方面想下去；这样想是会使我们发疯的。
麦克白	我仿佛听见一个声音喊着："不要再睡了！麦克白已经杀害了睡眠，"那清白的睡眠，把忧虑的乱丝编织起来的睡眠，那日常的死亡，疲劳者的沐浴，受伤的心灵的油膏，大自然的最丰盛的菜肴，生命的盛筵上主要的营养——
麦克白夫人	你这种话是什么意思？
麦克白	那声音继续向全屋子喊着："不要再睡了！葛莱密斯已经杀害了睡眠，所以考特将再也得不到睡眠，麦克白将再也得不到睡眠！"
麦克白夫人	谁喊着这样的话？唉，我的爵爷，您这样胡思乱想，是会妨害您的健康的。去拿些水来，把您手上的血迹洗净。

（朱生豪译《麦克白》第2幕第2场）

评点

麦克白刺杀了熟睡中的国王邓肯，因而魂不守舍。他所听到的喊声也许来自自己的良心，产生某种精神失常状态下的幻觉，也许来自某种超自然力量的干预。麦克白反复强调自己杀死了"睡眠"（sleep），表现出心中的无限悔恨。

哪怕麦克白夫人劝解宽慰，麦克白内心的阴影也依然挥之不去……麦克白夫人此时尚未受到良心的谴责，还劝麦克白不要多想，但是从后续剧情可知，无论是麦克白还是麦克白夫人都承担着沉重的精神压力，麦克白夫人反而比麦克白更早精神崩溃。

场景 8：夜半敲门

("Whence is that knocking?")

> "为人不做亏心事，半夜不怕鬼敲门"，麦克白在夜深人静之时行凶完毕，正心神不宁、做贼心虚，偏偏此时传来了敲门声，更令其心惊肉跳……

Macbeth　　　　　　　　Whence is that knocking? —
　　　　　　How is't with me, when every noise appals me?
　　　　　　What hands are here? Ha! they pluck out mine eyes.
　　　　　　Will all great Neptune's[1] ocean wash this blood
　　　　　　Clean from my hand? No, this my hand will rather
　　　　　　The multitudinous seas[2] incarnadine[3],
　　　　　　Making the green one red[4].

Lady Macbeth　My hands are of your colour; but I shame
　　　　　　To wear a heart so white. [*Knock.*] I hear a knocking
　　　　　　At the south entry: — retire we to our chamber.
　　　　　　A little water clears us of this deed:
　　　　　　How easy is it, then! Your constancy
　　　　　　Hath left you unattended. — [*Knock.*] Hark! more knocking.
　　　　　　Get on your night-gown, lest occasion call us,
　　　　　　And show us to be watchers. — Be not lost
　　　　　　So poorly in your thoughts.

Macbeth　　　To know my deed, 'twere best not know myself. [*Knock.*]
　　　　　　Wake Duncan with thy knocking: I would thou couldst!

(*Macbeth* 2.2)

---

[1] Neptune: (Roman mythology) god of the sea; counterpart of Greek Poseidon.
[2] multitudinous seas: countless masses of waters on the surface of the globe.
[3] incarnadine: a verb here meaning "turn red".
[4] making the green one red: i.e. changing the green sea into total red.

麦克白　　　那打门的声音是从什么地方来的？究竟是怎么一回事，一点点的声音都会吓得我心惊肉跳？这是什么手！嘿！它们要挖出我的眼睛。大洋里所有的水，能够洗净我手上的血迹吗？不，恐怕我这一手的血，倒要把一碧无垠的海水染成一片殷红呢。

麦克白夫人　我的两手也跟你的同样颜色了，可是我的心却羞于像你那样变成惨白。（内敲门声）我听见有人打着南面的门；让我们回到自己房间里去；一点点的水就可以替我们泯除痕迹；不是很容易的事吗？你的魄力不知道到哪儿去了。（内敲门声）听！又在那儿打门了。披上你的睡衣，也许人家会来找我们，不要让他们看见我们还没有睡觉。别这样傻头傻脑地呆想了。

麦克白　　　要想到我所干的事，最好还是忘掉我自己。（内敲门声）用你打门的声音把邓肯惊醒了吧！我希望你能够惊醒他！

（朱生豪译《麦克白》第 2 幕第 2 场）

评点

麦克白夫人几番催促麦克白洗手，似乎只要洗手，累累血债就能一笔勾销。后续剧情则不然：麦克白夫妇此后总是受血污幻象的困扰，不仅麦克白哀叹手上的血污永远也洗不掉了——"大洋里所有的水，能够洗净我手上的血迹吗"，而且麦克白夫人也同样如此。在第 5 幕里的梦游中，她说自己的手上还是有血腥味，她不断洗手却无论如何也洗不干净。

夜深人静之时的敲门声令凶手毛骨悚然，门外是人还是鬼？暗杀是否败露？19 世纪的英国散文家托马斯·德·昆西（Thomas De Quincey）就此写了一篇著名的文学评论《论〈麦克白〉中的敲门声》（"On the Knocking at the Gate in *Macbeth*"），详细分析这只闻其声、不见其人的敲门声及其对当事人产生的心理影响。

场景 9：覆水难收

("What's done is done.")

> 在成功刺杀国王之后，麦克白夫妇清除异己，如愿以偿地成为国王与王后，但是麦克白依然顾虑重重，忧心忡忡，几乎羡慕死去的国王邓肯……

Lady Macbeth　　How now, my lord? why do you keep alone,
　　　　　　　　Of sorriest fancies your companions making,
　　　　　　　　Using[1] those thoughts, which should indeed have died
　　　　　　　　With them they think on? Things without all remedy[2]
　　　　　　　　Should be without regard: what's done is done.

Macbeth　　We have scorch'd the snake, not kill'd it:
　　　　　　She'll close, and be herself; whilst our poor malice
　　　　　　Remains in danger of her former tooth.
　　　　　　But let the frame of things[3] disjoint, both the worlds suffer,
　　　　　　Ere we will eat our meal in fear, and sleep
　　　　　　In the affliction of these terrible dreams,
　　　　　　That shake us nightly. Better be with the dead,
　　　　　　Whom we, to gain our peace, have sent to peace[4],
　　　　　　Than on the torture of the mind to lie
　　　　　　In restless ecstasy. Duncan is in his grave;
　　　　　　After life's fitful fever he sleeps well;
　　　　　　Treason has done his worst: nor steel, nor poison,
　　　　　　Malice domestic, foreign levy, nothing
　　　　　　Can touch him further!

Lady Macbeth　　　　　　　　　　　　　　Come on:

---

[1] using: keeping company with, entertaining as companions.
[2] without all remedy: i.e. beyond all remedy.
[3] frame of things: i.e. the universe, both the worlds, celestial and terrestrial.
[4] to gain our peace, have sent to peace: i.e. to gain the peace of satisfied ambition, have sent to the peace of the grave.

> Gentle my Lord, sleek o'er your rugged looks;
> Be bright and jovial among your guests to-night.

(*Macbeth* 3.2)

麦克白夫人　啊！我的主！您为什么一个人孤零零的，让最悲哀的幻想做您的伴侣，把您的思想念念不忘地集中在一个已死者的身上？无法挽回的事，只好听其自然；事情干了就算了。

麦克白　我们不过刺伤了蛇身，却没有把它杀死，它的伤口会慢慢平复过来，再用它的原来的毒牙向我们的暴行复仇。可是让一切秩序完全解体，让活人、死人都去受罪吧，为什么我们要在忧虑中进餐，在每夜使我们惊恐的噩梦的谑弄中睡眠呢？我们为了希求自身的平安，把别人送下坟墓里去享受永久的平安，可是我们的心灵却把我们磨折得没有一刻平静的安息，使我们觉得还是跟已死的人在一起，倒要幸福得多了。邓肯现在睡在他的坟墓里；经过了一场人生的热病，他现在睡得好好的，叛逆已经对他施过最狠毒的伤害，再没有刀剑、毒药、内乱、外患，可以加害于他了。

麦克白夫人　算了算了，我的好丈夫，把您的烦恼的面孔收起；今天晚上您必须和颜悦色地招待您的客人。

（朱生豪译《麦克白》第3幕第2场）

评点

　　麦克白深知自己罪孽深重，内心极度煎熬，即便夺取王位，也没有换来幸福快乐的生活，反而丧失了内心的平静与满足。各种疑神疑鬼，使他最终毁灭。

　　此时，麦克白夫人劝慰麦克白，让他不要心思过重，好好举办登基庆典的群英晚宴。她所说的"事情干了就算了"（What's done is done）一句可以更精确地译为"做了的事情就已成定局"——不要为过去的事而纠结，既来之，则安之。麦克白夫人不止一次表达这一观点，她在第5幕中的梦话里也说"已经做了的事情没法重来"（What's done cannot be undone），字面意思相似，而情感口吻则有所变化。

　　覆水难收，过去发生的一切都对现在、对将来形成持久影响。麦克白在当天的晚宴上产生了可怕的幻觉，看到了别人都看不到的索命鬼魂，顿时导致言语异常，颜面尽失。

场景 10：金盆洗手

("Here's the smell of the blood still.")

> 即便当上了国王与王后，麦克白夫妇却也寝食难安，因为他们为了篡位，欠了太多血债。麦克白夫人梦游，说梦话，其冷酷外表下的脆弱内心暴露无遗……医生与侍女则在一旁观察。

Lady Macbeth　　Yet here's a spot.

……

Lady Macbeth　　Out, damned spot! out, I say!—One; two[1]: why, then 'tis time to do't.—Hell is murky[2].—Fie, my lord, fie! a soldier, and afeard?—What need we fear who knows it, when none can call our power to accompt[3]?—Yet who would have thought the old man to have had so much blood in him?

……

Lady Macbeth　　The thane of Fife had a wife: where is she now?—What, will these hands ne'er be clean?—No more o' that, my Lord, no more o' that: you mar all with this starting.

……

Lady Macbeth　　Here's the smell of the blood still: all the perfumes of Arabia will not sweeten this little hand. Oh! oh! oh!

……

Lady Macbeth　　Wash your hands, put on your night-gown; look not so pale.—I tell you yet again, Banquo's buried: he cannot come out on's grave.

……

Lady Macbeth　　To bed, to bed: there's knocking at the gate. Come, come, come, come, give me your hand. What's done cannot be undone. To bed, to bed, to bed.

(*Macbeth* 5.1)

---

[1] One; two: Lady Macbeth thinks she hears the clock strike.
[2] murkey: dark, gloomy.
[3] accompt: account, reckoning.

麦克白夫人	可是这儿还有一点血迹。

....

麦克白夫人	去，该死的血迹！去吧！一点、两点，啊，那么现在可以动手了。地狱里是这样幽暗！呸，我的爷，呸！你是一个军人，也会害怕吗？既然谁也不能奈何我们，为什么我们要怕被人知道？可是谁想得到这老头儿会有这么多血？

....

麦克白夫人	费辅爵士从前有一个妻子；现在她在哪儿？什么！这两只手再也不会干净了吗？算了，我的爷，算了；你这样大惊小怪，把事情都弄糟了。

....

麦克白夫人	这儿还是有一股血腥气；所有阿拉伯的香料都不能叫这只小手变得香一点。啊！啊！啊！

....

麦克白夫人	洗净你的手，披上你的睡衣；不要这样面无人色。我再告诉你一遍，班柯已经下葬了；他不会从坟墓里出来的。

....

麦克白夫人	睡去，睡去；有人在打门哩。来，来，来，来，让我搀着你。事情已经干了就算了。睡去，睡去，睡去。

（朱生豪译《麦克白》第5幕第1场）

评点

俗话说："日有所思，夜有所梦。"麦克白夫人的这番梦话重现了此前的多个场景片段：手上的血迹，半夜的敲门声，劝慰麦克白，暗杀班柯（Banquo），灭门麦克德夫（Macduff）一家……尽管麦克白夫人表面上强悍冷酷，但是她的良心折磨与日俱增，在睡梦中不由自主地暴露出来。

麦克白夫人称"所有阿拉伯的香料都不能叫这只小手变得香一点"（all the perfumes of Arabia will not sweeten this little hand），呼应着麦克白此前暗杀国王之后的痛心："大洋里所有的水，能够洗净我手上的血迹吗？"（Will all great Neptune's ocean wash this blood / Clean from my hand？）

类似的愧疚之词也出现在《哈姆莱特》里的篡位者口中，表达如出一辙——"难道天上所有的甘霖，都不能把它洗涤得像雪一样洁白吗？"（Is there not rain enough in the sweet heavens / To wash it white as snow？）上述三位犯下弑君之罪的野心家、阴谋家都试图通过洗手来摆脱罪责，却都无济于事。

场景 11：病入膏肓

（"As she is troubled with thick-coming fancies …"）

> 叛军兴起，麦克白积极备战，鼓舞士气，但其内心充满悔恨与空虚，深知自己罪孽深重。无论这场战役胜负如何，他都已失去了太多；更何况，此时的麦克白夫人精神崩溃，却无药可医……

Macbeth　I have liv'd long enough: my way of life[1]
　　　　　Is fall'n into the sere[2], the yellow leaf;
　　　　　And that which should accompany old age,
　　　　　As[3] honour, love, obedience, troops of friends,
　　　　　I must not look to have; but, in their stead,
　　　　　Curses, not loud, but deep, mouth-honour, breath,
　　　　　Which the poor heart would fain deny, and dare not.

……

Macbeth　How does your patient, doctor?
Doctor　Not so sick, my lord,
　　　　　As she is troubled with thick-coming fancies,
　　　　　That keep her from her rest.
Macbeth　Cure her of that:
　　　　　Canst thou not minister to a mind diseas'd,
　　　　　Pluck from the memory a rooted sorrow,
　　　　　Raze out the written troubles of the brain,
　　　　　And with some sweet oblivious[4] antidote
　　　　　Cleanse the stuff'd bosom of that perilous stuff
　　　　　Which weighs upon the heart?
Doctor　Therein the patient

---

[1] way of life: course of life.
[2] sere: the withered state.
[3] as: i.e. namely.
[4] oblivious: causing forgetfulness.

               Must minister to himself.
Macbeth   Throw physic to the dogs; I'll none of it.
(*Macbeth* 5.3)

麦克白   我已经活得够长久了；我的生命已经日就枯萎，像一片凋谢的黄叶；凡是老年人所应该享有的尊荣、敬爱、服从和一大群的朋友，我是没有希望再得到的了；代替这一切的，只有低声而深刻的诅咒，口头上的恭维和一些违心的假话。

…………

麦克白   大夫，你的病人今天怎样？
医生   回陛下，她并没有什么病，只是因为思虑太过，继续不断的幻想扰乱了她的神经，使她不得安息。
麦克白   替她医好这一种病。你难道不能诊治那种病态的心理，从记忆中拔去一桩根深蒂固的忧郁，拭掉那写在脑筋上的烦恼，用一种使人忘却一切的甘美的药剂，把那堆满在胸间、重压在心头的积毒扫除干净吗？
医生   那还是要仗病人自己设法的。
麦克白   那么把医药丢给狗子吧；我不要仰仗它。

（朱生豪译《麦克白》第5幕第3场）

评点

麦克白一边准备披挂上阵，一边向医生询问麦克白夫人的病情。一听说此病无药可治，麦克白难以掩饰其巨大失望。麦克白不仅是在为麦克白夫人求医问药，而且也是在为自己同样饱受折磨的内心寻找良方。

然而，这种心病无可救药，医生说"要仗病人自己设法"，不无道理。人一旦走上了犯罪道路，就无法回头。过去发生的一切都将终身伴随，一切欠债都要偿还。

场景 12：万念俱灰

("Life's but a walking shadow ...")

> 麦克白的政敌前来讨伐，内战当前，麦克白积极应对，不失开场之时的大将风范……然而，一阵女子的凄厉哭声又把他的思绪拉回充满阴谋与杀戮的过去。

Macbeth　… What is that noise? [*A cry*[1] *within, of women.*]
Seyton　It is the cry of women, my good lord. [*Exit.*]
Macbeth　I have almost forgot the taste of fears.
　　　　The time has been, my senses would have cool'd
　　　　To hear a night-shriek; and my fell of hair[2]
　　　　Would at a dismal treatise[3] rouse, and stir,
　　　　As life were in't. I have supp'd full with horrors:
　　　　Direness[4], familiar to my slaughterous thoughts,
　　　　Cannot once start me. [*Re-enter Seyton.*]
　　　　Wherefore was that cry?
Seyton　The Queen, my Lord, is dead.
Macbeth　She should have died hereafter:
　　　　There would have been a time for such a word. —
　　　　To-morrow, and to-morrow, and to-morrow,
　　　　Creeps in this petty pace from day to day,
　　　　To the last syllable of recorded time;
　　　　And all our yesterdays have lighted fools
　　　　The way to dusty death. Out, out, brief candle!
　　　　Life's but a walking shadow; a poor player,
　　　　That struts and frets his hour upon the stage,

---

[1] cry: Lady Macbeth has not died a natural death.
[2] fell of hair: skin with the hair on.
[3] treatise: story, recital.
[4] direness: horror.

And then is heard no more: it is a tale
Told by an idiot, full of sound and fury,
Signifying nothing.

(*Macbeth* 5.5)

麦克白　……那是什么声音？（内妇女哭声）

西登　是妇女们的哭声，陛下。（下）

麦克白　我简直已经忘记了恐惧的滋味。从前一声晚间的哀叫，可以把我吓出一身冷汗，听着一段可怕的故事，我的头发会像有了生命似的竖起来。现在我已经饱尝无数的恐怖；我的习惯于杀戮的思想，再也没有什么悲惨的事情可以使它惊悚了。（西登重上）那哭声是为了什么事？

西登　陛下，王后死了。

麦克白　她反正要死的，迟早总会有听到这个消息的一天。明天，明天，再一个明天，一天接着一天地蹑步前进，直到最后一秒钟的时间；我们所有的昨天，不过替傻子们照亮了到死亡的土壤中去的路。熄灭了吧，熄灭了吧，短促的烛光！人生不过是一个行走的影子，一个在舞台上指手划脚的拙劣的伶人，登场片刻，就在无声无臭中悄然退下；它是一个愚人所讲的故事，充满着喧哗和骚动，却找不到一点意义。

（朱生豪译《麦克白》第 5 幕第 5 场）

评点

面对爱妻的死讯，麦克白表现淡定，内心却是长期痛彻心扉之后的一种豁然与麻木。以"明天"开头的这番独白极为出名，寥寥数行，没有哭天抢地，没有挽歌悼词，而是在形而上的层面上反思人生。一连串生动而多样的修辞意象（人生如旅、人生如烛、人生如戏、人生如荒诞故事……）描绘了一个饱经沧桑、看破红尘的心灵。

在最后一幕中，麦克白困境重重，大势已去，然而，他绝不会屈服于命运的安排，他那强大的意志力一直支持他负隅顽抗到生命终结的最后一刻。麦克白最终被麦克德夫所杀，麦克德夫由此为自己的妻儿报了血仇。

William Shakespeare

七、莎士比亚十四行诗
(*Shakespearean Sonnets*)

"如果音乐与甜美的诗歌相合……"
(If music and sweet poetry agree …)

尽管莎士比亚如今以剧作闻名于世,但是让他在文坛上崭露头角的其实是诗歌——不仅是十四行诗,而且还有两部长诗《维纳斯与阿杜尼斯》(*Venus and Adonis*)与《鲁克丽丝受辱记》(*The Rape of Lucrece*)。此外,莎士比亚还有若干诗集传世。坊间有这样一种说法,即便莎士比亚一生一部剧也不写,仅凭诗作他也能在英国文学史上占有一席之地。

十四行诗(sonnet)起源于13世纪的意大利——大诗人彼得拉克(Petrarch)即为杰出代表,在16世纪传入英国。与莎士比亚同时代的西德尼(Philip Sidney)、斯宾塞(Edmund Spenser)等英国诗人都留下了不少传世之作。

各家十四行诗虽然长度都是十四行,但是格律不尽相同,主要分为三种:彼得拉克十四行诗(Petrarchan sonnet)、莎士比亚十四行诗(Shakespearean sonnet)、斯宾塞十四行诗(Spenserian sonnet)。

莎士比亚的十四行诗大多是情诗,通常采用第一人称"我"的口吻,对"你"表达爱慕。十四行诗也可用于叙事,例如本章选录的第五首。

莎士比亚十四行诗（Shakespearean Sonnets）

1. Sonnet 18

    "Shall I compare thee to a summer's day?"（卿如夏日）

2. Sonnet 29

    "When in disgrace with fortune and men's eyes"（不离不弃）

3. Sonnet 60

    "Like as the waves make towards the pebbled shore"（与世长存）

4. Sonnet 71

    "No longer mourn for me when I am dead"（至死不渝）

5. Prologue to *Romeo and Juliet*

    "Two households, both alike in dignity"（不共戴天）

1. Sonnet 18

> 如何形容你的心上人？花朵？月亮？……如何比喻得贴切而不落俗套？

Shall I compare thee[1] to a summer's day?
Thou[2] art[3] more lovely and more temperate[4]:
Rough winds do shake the darling buds of May,
And summer's lease[5] hath all too short a date[6]:
Sometime[7] too hot the eye of heaven shines,
And often is his gold complexion dimmed;
And every fair[8] from fair[9] sometime declines[10],
By chance[11], or nature's changing course, untrimmed[12]:
But thy[13] eternal summer shall not fade,
Nor lose possession of that fair thou ow'st[14],
Nor shall death brag thou wander'st in his shade
When in eternal[15] lines[16] to time thou grow'st
　　So long as men can breathe or eyes can see,
　　So long lives this, and this gives life to thee.

---

[1] thee: you（第二人称，单数，宾格）.
[2] Thou: you（第二人称，单数，主格）.
[3] art = are.
[4] temperate: gentle, mild, moderate.
[5] lease:（土地、房产）租赁期限。
[6] date: duration, a limited period of time.
[7] sometime: sometimes, from time to time.
[8] every fair: every beautiful thing or person.
[9] fair: fairness, beauty.
[10] decline: fade.
[11] chance: (bad) luck.
[12] untrimmed: stripped of beauty.
[13] thy: your.
[14] ow'st = own. 其中，"-st"为第二人称变位。以下 wander'st、grow'st 同理。这三个词都带有一个省音符，用于保证每一行的音节数一致。
[15] eternal: everlasting, forever.
[16] lines: 双关，既指"诗行"，又指"绳、线"。

评点

诗人把心上人比作初夏（五月）——英国最宜人的时节。这个比喻可谓不俗，诗人势必绞尽脑汁；即便如此，他还不敢冒犯，只是小心翼翼地问："我能否……？"随后，不等对方回答，诗人自己先否定了，认为心上人比夏日更加美好，并罗列了一连串理由。最后且最重要的一个理由是夏日终将逝去，而心上人永生——永生在诗行中。这种机智俏皮的说法巧妙地从爱情主题转向歌颂文学永恒。

对于莎士比亚的这首脍炙人口的十四行诗，美国20世纪诗人霍华德·莫斯（Howard Moss，1922—1987）写过如下这篇戏仿之作（parody）。试比较古今两首诗在思想主题、节奏韵律、语言风格、修辞意象等方面有什么区别与联系。

Shall I Compare Thee to a Summer's Day?

Howard Moss

Who says you're like one of the dog days?
You're nicer. And better.
Even in May, the weather can be gray,
And a summer sublet doesn't last forever.
Sometimes the sun's too hot;
Sometimes it is not.
Who can stay young forever?
People break their necks or just drop dead!
But you? Never!
If there's just one condensed reader left
Who can figure out the abridged alphabet,
    After you're dead and gone,
    In this poem you'll live on!

2. Sonnet 29

> 诗人感叹自己时运不济、一无所有,在旁人的夺目光芒中,自己灰头土脸……如此铺陈渲染,诗人的着眼点与意图何在?

When in disgrace[1] with fortune[2] and men's eyes
I all alone beweep[3] my outcast state[4],
And trouble deaf heav'n with my bootless[5] cries,
And look upon myself, and curse my fate,
Wishing me like to[6] one[7] more rich in hope,
Featured like him, like him with friends possessed,
Desiring this man's art[8] and that man's scope,
With what I most enjoy contented least;
Yet in these thoughts myself almost despising,
Haply[9] I think on thee[10], and then my state[11],
Like to the lark at break of day arising,
From sullen[12] earth sings hymns at heaven's gate;
  For thy sweet love remembered such wealth brings
  That then I scorn to change my state[13] with kings.

---

[1] in disgrace: out of favor.
[2] fortune: luck.
[3] beweep: weep over, lament.
[4] state: condition, 处境。
[5] bootless: useless, hopeless, futile, in vain.
[6] like to = like.
[7] one: someone.
[8] art: learning.
[9] haply: by chance, fortunately.
[10] think on thee: think of you.
[11] state: state of mind, 心境。
[12] sullen: dull, somber.
[13] state: 双关,一方面可以指 condition,另一方面也可以指 kingdom。

评点

全诗十四行，前面8行都在自怨自艾，描述自己的潦倒落魄。其中，第3行能令中国读者想起"叫天天不应，叫地地不灵"的说法。在一长串铺陈排比之后，突然笔锋一转（Yet）："我一想起你"（Haply I think on thee），无论什么阴霾都顿时云开雾散，足以可见"你"在"我"心目中的重要地位。

这首诗还有同主题、同结构的姊妹篇（见下文）：同样是先极力渲染自己灾难深重，与第29首相比，有过之而无不及——长达12行，直到末尾两行才反转（But）；同样是只要"我想起你"（I think on thee），之前的一切困苦都无足挂齿。之前越是描述自己的不幸，之后转悲为喜的戏剧生变化就越能突显"我"对"你"的珍重。

Sonnet 30

When to the sessions of sweet silent thought
I summon up remembrance of things past,
I sigh[1] the lack of many a thing I sought,
And with old woes new[2] wail my dear time's waste;
Then can I drown an eye (unused to flow)
For precious friends hid in death's dateless[3] night,
And weep afresh love's long since cancelled woe,
And moan th'expense of many a vanished sight.
Then can I grieve at grievances foregone[4],
And heavily[5] from woe to woe tell o'er[6]
The sad account[7] of fore-bemoaned[8] moan,
Which I new pay, as if not paid before;
　　But if the while[9] I think on thee, dear friend,
　　All losses are restored, and sorrows end.

---

[1] sigh: sigh for, lament.
[2] new: newly.
[3] dateless: having no determined time of expiry, hence endless.
[4] foregone: in the past, over and done with.
[5] heavily: sadly, laboriously.
[6] tell o'er: sum up, recount.
[7] account: bill, financial reckoning; narrative.
[8] fore-bemoaned: already lamented. 与第9行的 grievances foregone 同义。
[9] the while: meanwhile.

3. Sonnet 60

> 人生短暂而诗歌永恒的主题在莎士比亚十四行诗中频频出现，且花样各异、推陈出新。除了上述第18首十四行诗之外，第60首也是一例典型。

Like as the waves make[1] towards the pebbled shore,
So do our minutes hasten to their end,
Each changing place with that which goes before,
In sequent toil[2] all forwards do contend[3].
Nativity[4], once in the main of light[5],
Crawls to maturity; wherewith[6] being crowned[7]
Crooked[8] eclipses[9] 'gainst[10] his glory fight,
And time, that gave, doth now his gift confound[11].
Time doth transfix[12] the flourish set on youth,
And delves[13] the parallels in beauty's brow;
Feeds on the rarities of nature's truth[14],
And nothing stands but for his scythe to mow.
  And yet to times in hope[15] my verse shall stand[16],
  Praising thy worth, despite his cruel hand.

---

[1] make: move.
[2] sequent toil: successive effort.
[3] contend: struggle, strive.
[4] nativity: 不仅指人的出生，同时还指圣婴降生。
[5] the main of light: full sun, broad daylight.
[6] wherewith: with which.
[7] being crowned: maturity.
[8] crooked: ominous, malignant.
[9] eclipse: 日食，月食。
[10] 'gainst = against.
[11] confound: destroy.
[12] transfix: pierce, run through.
[13] delve: dig.
[14] nature's truth: nature's essential integrity; an integrity which is natural.
[15] to times in hope: until hoped-for (future) times.
[16] stand: endure.

评点

人生如海潮，前赴后继、步履匆匆。从出生到成熟，最终到死亡，各有天时。时间，作为自然界的客观力量，无人能敌，但在诗人看来，唯有文学艺术能与时间抗衡，在有限的人生中活出永恒的精彩，在无情的世上留下温情。同时，诗人有足够的自信，相信自己的诗作流芳百世。最后一行突然点出这首诗是为赞颂"你"而作，因而"你"将随此诗而长存。

莎士比亚的这首十四行诗令人想起英国文艺复兴时期的另一位大诗人斯宾塞（Edmund Spenser）的第75首十四行诗（如下）。同样以海边为背景，同样认为诗歌能够对抗时间的无情，同样希望自己所爱之人在自己的诗作中得到永生。

Sonnet 75 from Amoretti

Edmund Spenser

One day I wrote her name upon the strand,
But came the waves and washed it a way:
Agayne I wrote it with a second hand,
But came the tyde, and made my paynes his pray.
"Vayne man," sayd she, "that doest in vaine assay,
A mortall thing so to immortalize,
For I my selve shall lyke to this decay,
And eek my name bee wyped out lykewize.
"Not so," quod I, "let baser things devize,
To dy in dust, but you shall live by fame:
My verse your vertues rare shall eternize,
And in the heavens wryte your glorious name.
    Where whenas death shall all the world subdew,
    Our love shall live, and later life renew."

4. Sonnet 71

> 感人至深的爱情不仅体现在艰难困苦之中，而且也能体现在生死考验之时。至死不渝的忠贞爱情在文学史上经久不衰，以下这首十四行诗即为一例。

No longer mourn for me when I am dead
Than you shall hear the surly[1] sullen[2] bell
Give warning to the world that I am fled
From this vile world, with vilest worms to dwell:
Nay, if you read this line, remember not
The hand that writ it, for I love you so[3]
That I in your sweet thoughts would be forgot,
If thinking on me then should make you woe[4].
O if (I say) you look upon this verse,
When I, perhaps, compounded[5] am with clay,
Do not so much as my poor name rehearse[6],
But let your love even with my life decay[7];
  Lest the wise world should look into your moan[8],
  And mock you with me after I am gone.

评点

  全诗以一个将死之人"我"的口吻，对"你"说话，丝毫没有对死亡的恐惧，而是充满了对"你"的依恋与不舍。表面上反复强调"不要为我悲伤""不必记得我"，字里行间却都是在表达"我"心中纠结，割舍不下。
  19世纪中叶的英国女诗人克里斯蒂娜·罗塞蒂（Christina Rossetti）也特

---

[1] surly: stern.
[2] sullen: gloomy.
[3] so: so much; in such a manner.
[4] make you woe: cause you to be sorrowful.
[5] compounded: combined with.
[6] rehearse: repeat.
[7] decay: fall away, die.
[8] look into your moan: investigate the cause of your sorrow.

别热衷于写爱情与死亡。比如，以下这首罗塞蒂的诗也以临死之人的口吻，对爱人千叮咛万嘱咐：

When I am dead, my dearest,
Sing no sad songs for me;
Plant thou no roses at my head,
Nor shady cypress tree:
Be the green grass above me
With showers and dewdrops wet;
And if thou wilt, remember,
And if thou wilt, forget.

I shall not see the shadows,
I shall not feel the rain;
I shall not hear the nightingale
Sing on, as if in pain:
And dreaming through the twilight
That doth not rise nor set,
Haply I may remember,
And haply may forget.

诗人在乎的是情感与精神，而无关功利或物质。对比莎士比亚上述十四行诗让"你"忘记"我"，罗塞蒂还有一首要求"你"记住"我"的小诗：

Remember me when I am gone away,
Gone far away into the silent land;
When you can no more hold me by the hand,
Nor I half turn to go yet turning stay.
Remember me when no more day by day
You tell me of our future that you plann'd:
Only remember me; you understand
It will be late to counsel then or pray.
Yet if you should forget me for a while
And afterwards remember, do not grieve:
For if the darkness and corruption leave
A vestige of the thoughts that once I had,
Better by far you should forget and smile
Than that you should remember and be sad.

这三首诗都在"你"与"我"之间展开，"铭记"（remember）与"遗忘"（forget）是一对充满张力的关键词。为何要求"铭记"？又为何要求"遗忘"？二者之间是否存在矛盾？

5. Prologue to *Romeo and Juliet*

> 序言（prologue）在古希腊戏剧中十分普遍，却并不常见于莎士比亚戏剧——莎士比亚四大悲剧都没有序言。不过，《罗密欧与朱丽叶》一剧却有开场序言，从形式上看就是一首标准的十四行诗。

Chorus　Two households, both alike in dignity[1],

In fair Verona, where we lay our scene,

From ancient grudge[2] break to new mutiny,

Where civil blood[3] makes civil hands unclean.

From forth the fatal loins of these two foes

A pair of star-crossed[4] lovers take their life;

Whose misadventured[5] piteous overthrows

Doth with their death bury their parents' strife.

The fearful passage[6] of their death-marked[7] love,

And the continuance of their parents' rage,

Which but their children's end naught could remove,

Is now the two hours' traffic[8] of our stage;

The which, if you with patient ears attend,

What here shall miss[9], our toil shall strive to mend[10].

---

[1] dignity: honorable social status.
[2] ancient grudge: old feud.
[3] civil blood: the blood of citizens.
[4] star-crossed: thwarted by the influence of malign stars.
[5] misadventured: unlucky, unfortunate, hapless.
[6] passage: trajectory.
[7] death-marked: doomed.
[8] traffic: business.
[9] miss: prove inadequate or deficient in the performance.
[10] mend: improve (in the future).

评点

序言站在全知叙述者的视角，借"歌队"（Chorus）之口道出，向观众预告剧情梗概：在"美丽的维罗纳"（fair Verona）——意大利北部的一座繁荣的城市，有两个高贵而富有的家族。两家旗鼓相当（both alike in dignity），却因为新仇（new mutiny）与旧恨（ancient grudge）而势不两立。偏偏造化弄人、阴差阳错，两家的独生子女一见钟情，最终双双自杀（A pair of star-crossed lovers take their life）。

《罗密欧与朱丽叶》的剧本里不止开头的这一首十四行诗。歌队在第1幕之后、第2幕之前再次上场，又吟诵了一首夹叙夹议、承上启下的十四行诗，总结并点评了剧中两仇家子女的一见钟情：

> Now old desire[1] doth in his deathbed lie,
> And young affection gapes[2] to be his heir;
> That fair[3] for which love groaned for and would die,
> With tender Juliet matched[4] is now not fair.
> Now Romeo is beloved and loves again[5],
> Alike betwitched by the charm of looks,
> But to his foe supposed he must complain[6],
> And she steal love's sweet bait from fearful hooks.
> Being held a foe, he may not have access
> To breathe such vows as lovers use to swear,
> And she as much in love, her means much less
> To meet her new beloved anywhere.
> But passion lends them power, time means, to meet,
> Tempering extremities with extreme sweet.

此外，罗密欧与朱丽叶在初次见面时的对白也以十四行诗的形式呈现，浪漫之至。参见本书第二章《罗密欧与朱丽叶》的场景5"以吻涤罪"。

---

[1] old desire: i.e. Romeo's love for Rosaline.
[2] gape: long, yearn.
[3] that fair: that beauty, the fair Rosaline.
[4] matched: compared.
[5] again: in return. Juliet reciprocates her love.
[6] complain: make lamentation.

后 记
Afterword

Sometimes people are surprised when I tell them I teach Shakespeare to Chinese students. "How can these students understand a form of the language that even native speakers find difficult?" they ask. "Wouldn't it be better for them to study newspaper articles, for example, or American short stories?" Despite these obvious objections, my experience has been that Chinese students are moved by the beauty of Shakespeare's language, develop confidence by speaking his lines and performing his scenes, and expand their cultural understanding by study of his presentations of character and situation.

My first experience of teaching Shakespeare in China was at Xiamen University in 1984/85. Since the city was just opening up as a Special Economic Zone, the Dean of Foreign Languages thought that a knowledge of western cultural traditions would help Xiada students understand "why Americans are so irrational". I had a small class of hard-working MA students, and they seemed eager to learn about western ideas of personal identity and social organization—for example, how the courtly love tradition explains the bizarre custom by which a European gentleman holds a door open for a lady. A memorable moment of the class was the showing of Zeffirelli's film of *Romeo and Juliet*, which contains a shot of the hero's bare buttocks in the scene of the lovers' awakening after their wedding night. Even though the average age of the students was 30, they were speechless with shock.

In 1990/91 I again had a chance to teach Shakespeare to a small class of five fourth-year undergrads at the University of Macau. In the second term of a year-long class, we decided to try a production of the casket scenes from *Merchant of Venice* and called it *The Lucky Draw*. It was performed in the university Senate Room for a small but appreciative audience. Returning to UM in 2000 I taught Shakespeare for four years. Class sizes of five were gone for good, of course, which made doing productions more difficult. Every year I had a few sleepless nights worrying whether the students in the various groups would be able to pull everything together by the performance date, but every year I was pleasantly surprised. Of course, doing a play like *King Lear* with a nearly all-female cast can be a challenge. But just as Elizabethan audiences had to accept the convention of female parts being played by men and boys, so UM audiences became accustomed to male parts, even old men, being played by young women. Finally, in the spring of 2021, a leave of absence by the Shakespeare specialist in the PKU English Department gave me the chance to teach a few of the plays to "the best students on the planet", and they lived up to their reputation, despite an eye problem at the end of term that prevented me from clearly seeing their rehearsals. "You should be smiling when you say those lines." "She is smiling!"

Chinese students can gain benefits beyond language skills from reading and performing Shakespeare's plays. Vocabulary and grammar are not sufficient for a fully working knowledge of English—cultural/social/historical knowledge is also essential, and a study of Shakespeare can provide a deep insight into western ideas of both personal and social relations. The plays deal with perennial themes—love and hatred, good and evil, war and peace. Shakespeare's understanding of human character and his ability to portray its complexities are unparalleled in western literature.

Most relevant, perhaps, for our own increasingly divided world is Shakespeare's tolerance. What Zhiyanzhai wrote of the author of *Honglou Meng* could also be said of Shakespeare: "With the heart of a Bodhisattva and a pen as sharp as a knife or ax, he wrote his book." There are few characters in the plays that are so evil that the audience cannot in part identify with them—Macbeth, Othello, Lear, Shylock, and others awaken the audience's sympathy despite their faults. As well, there are few good characters who are not somewhat flawed. Because of Shakespeare's comprehensive generosity of spirit, contemporary Ben Jonson wrote that The Bard was "Not of an age, but for all time." And in my experience, Shakespeare is not only for all time, but also for all places, including China.

Thomas Rendall[1]

Visiting Research Professor

Department of English

Peking University

---

[1] Thomas Rendall（托马斯·伦德尔）教授毕业于斯坦福大学英文系，主攻中世纪与文艺复兴时期欧洲文学，精通古英语、中古英语、意大利语、拉丁语、德语、法语等，在北大英语系任教多年。

William Shakespeare